AF476882

30127 05538923 8

THE SHADOW
OF MY HAND

Also by Alun Chalfont

The Sword and the Spirit (1963)
The Great Commanders (1973)
Montgomery of Alamein (1976)
Waterloo: Battle of Three Armies (ed.) (1979)
Star Wars: Suicide or Survival (1985)
Defence of the Realm (1987)
By God's Will: A Portrait of the Sultan of Brunei (1989)

THE SHADOW OF MY HAND

Alun Chalfont

Weidenfeld & Nicolson
LONDON

First published in Great Britain in 2000
by Weidenfeld & Nicolson

© 2000 Alun Chalfont

A CIP catalogue record for this book is
available from the British Library.

ISBN 0 297 813323

Typeset by Selwood Systems, Midsomer Norton

Set in Monotype Sabon

Printed in Great Britain by
Butler & Tanner Ltd, Frome and London

Weidenfeld & Nicolson

The Orion Publishing Group Ltd
Orion House
5 Upper Saint Martin's Lane
London, WC2H 9EA

For Mona
Who has shared most of these days with me.

Contents

Acknowledgements

I would like to thank Robert Hannigan for his invaluable help in compiling these memoirs. Robert has been a trusted collaborator since he catalogued my library while he was still at school and subsequently undertook most of the groundwork for my biography of the Sultan of Brunei. He has, once again, been conscientious and indefatigable in his researches.

Gail Caskie, my personal assistant, has not only typed numerous versions of this book, but has also been meticulous in the organisation of documents and research notes.

The Librarian and his staff at the House of Lords have been unfailingly helpful and Ion Trewin, the Managing Director of Weidenfeld & Nicolson, has been a patient and sympathetic publisher. His colleague, Rachel Leyshon, has provided valuable guidance and advice.

Finally, I owe a great debt of gratitude to my wife, Mona, to whom this book is dedicated. She has not only given me encouragement when it was most needed, but has also corrected typescripts with a copy editor's eye for solecisms and infelicities of style.

Illustrations

With the Prince and Princess of Wales at the International Eisteddfod 1985
On *Britannia* with the Queen and the Duke of Edinburgh as minister-in-attendance, 1968
Mona and I on our way to a Royal garden party, c.1985
The Chadlington children
'The liberty of the individual'

Unless otherwise attributed all photographs are from the author's collection.

The title of these memoirs may be a little obscure – especially to those who are not Welsh. It is taken from a
poem by the great Anglo-Welsh poet Dylan Thomas, who
was growing up in South Wales at the same time as I was.
'Fern Hill' is a tender evocation of carefree childhood, and
especially of its capacity to remain untouched by thoughts
of age and death. This is reflected in a couplet of magical
beauty near the end of the poem:

Nothing I cared, in the lamb white days, that time would take me
Up to the swallow-thronged loft by the shadow of my hand.

Prologue

I begin this story, not when I was born in South Wales at the end of the First World War, but forty-five years later in London on Friday 23rd October 1964. It was a hard, grey winter's day, the pavements of London covered in that familiar urban powdering of frost and dirt; a cold wind was blowing across Hyde Park. The Labour Party had just won the general election with a majority of four in the House of Commons, and the Prime Minister, Harold Wilson, was in the final stages of forming his ministry. The ritual transfer of the machinery of government was proceeding with customary absence of incident or fuss. As Robert Graves once wrote in a different context, 'it was all very tidy.'

Much the same could have been said of my own life at that time. I was the defence correspondent of *The Times*, an appointment which I had held for three enjoyable years under the civilised and enlightened editorship of Sir William Haley. We were still living in the days when the serious newspapers, and especially *The Times*, had a real influence on the making of national policy. A leading article or a 'turnover' (the 1500-word article which used to appear in the two right-hand columns of the leader page of *The Times*) was regarded by most politicians as a constructive contribution to public debate. As defence correspondent, I was writing leaders and turnovers as well as reporting on developments in military strategy, tactics, organisation and equipment.

I was, also, the first correspondent of the newspaper to break, with the Editor's encouragement, the convention of anonymity. In those days *The Times* had no personal bylines, no gossip columnists and no 'star' journalists. Articles and reports came from 'Our Diplomatic Correspondent', 'Our Defence Correspondent' or 'Our Washington Correspondent' and were often composed according to the archaic but elegant convention that they were personal letters to the Editor from one of a number of correspondents thoughtfully disposed around the country and the world.

In the early 1960s the BBC had invited me to take part in, and subsequently to present, a number of programmes on defence and other political issues. As I was identified as the defence correspondent of *The Times* in these television appearances, it became impossible to preserve the fiction of anonymity and for the first time one of the newspaper's army of correspondents emerged as a recognisable figure. By October 1964 I had, therefore, established a modest reputation in the world of journalism and broadcasting and was looking forward to building on it in whatever political climate Mr Wilson and his new government had in store for the country.

It was in this somewhat self-satisfied mood that I entered the United Hunts Club, just off Park Lane, at about eleven o'clock in the morning. At *The Times*, as in most daily newspapers, journalists took either Friday or Sunday as their day of rest, and on this particular Friday I had the fixed intention of starting my day with a glass of champagne. This was not because there was anything to celebrate, but rather because I shared a fairly widely held belief that nothing would ever be quite the same again. I remembered especially a day earlier that year when Julian Amery, a notably convivial member of the outgoing Conservative administration, had invited me to meet him at eleven o'clock in his club in St James's where his public spirited mission was to correct some ill-informed comments which had appeared in one of my recent articles. On my arrival he handed me a glass of Dom Perignon with the classic one-upman's comment, 'I always take a little at this time in the morning.' As I sat now in the bar of the United Hunts, I reflected sadly that those days had almost certainly gone. I did not know that in a few moments something would happen which proved how right I was.

The United Hunts in those days was a pleasant little private club with, apart from its name, no obvious association with blood sports. The barman, who subsequently migrated to the less tranquil atmosphere of Annabel's, told me discreetly as he served my champagne that he had just taken a message asking me to telephone *The Times*, where I had left details of my whereabouts. When I did so, the Editor's secretary told me that my presence was required at 10 Downing Street as soon as possible. This did not immediately strike me as being of any unusual significance, as I had had several conversations about defence policy with Harold Wilson and his close adviser George Wigg during Wilson's campaign for the leadership of the Labour Party and later in the weeks leading up to the general election.

Indeed, my contacts with political leaders were to give rise later to some confusion in the minds of a few commentators. In the course of my brief career at *The Times*, all three political parties had from time to time sought my views on defence issues, a circumstance which I regarded as fairly straightforward. As a professional soldier for over twenty years I had no party political affiliation of any kind and I was able to give the same advice, based on my articles in *The Times*, to anyone who was kind enough to ask for it. As it later became clear, some of the recipients of this advice evidently regarded my readiness to be consulted as a sign of adherence to their own party, and reacted badly when this turned out not to be the case.

At this stage I simply assumed that someone at Downing Street might want to discuss something I had written – possibly an article which had recently appeared on the new government's proposals for the control of nuclear weapons, a contentious piece which might have gone down rather badly with the corn-flakes. However, when I arrived at No. 10, I was, much to my surprise, conducted straight to the Cabinet room, where Harold Wilson sat, his pipe drawing very nicely, at the Cabinet table. Without much in the way of preamble, he told me that he would like me to be his 'Minister for Disarmament', a somewhat emotive title used to describe an appointment as Minister of State at the Foreign Office with special responsibility for matters of arms control and disarmament. He said, almost in parenthesis, that I would, of course, have a seat in the House of Lords and membership of the Privy Council. All this, he observed, would require the approval of the Queen and, as Her Majesty was leaving for Balmoral that evening, he would like my answer within the hour.

A telephone was placed at my disposal and I spoke to my wife who concealed any misgivings she may have felt and told me that she would be happy to go along with whatever decision I might make. After a further brief period of contemplation, I went back to the Cabinet Office to tell the Prime Minister that I would be honoured to accept his offer, provided that the Editor of *The Times* would release me from my contract. I also asked for an assurance that my responsibilities would be in the foreign affairs and defence field only, and that I would not be expected to become a committed advocate of every aspect of Labour Party policy, especially in domestic affairs. Wilson replied, in characteristically sardonic style, that such ideological commitment, if conscientiously pursued, would mark me as unique in his administration.

From Downing Street I went straight to *The Times* to report to the Editor on this remarkable encounter and to seek his blessing. After I had finished my account, Sir William Haley regarded me for a moment in silence and then delivered his lapidary judgement. 'Well, Mr Gwynne Jones, this is a challenge which you cannot, of course, fail to take up. But you should know that when you leave Printing House Square and move into Whitehall, you will miss two things. One will be your freedom of action; the other will be your influence on government policy.' He was, I suppose, not too wide of the mark.

That evening, my wife and I went to Covent Garden for a splendid performance of *Giselle*, and when we arrived back home in Chelsea, late at night, it was to find our house under siege by a bombilating swarm of reporters and photographers. The announcement of my appointment had been made during the evening. As I had vaguely discerned on my way through Hyde Park that morning, nothing would ever be quite the same again.

I

The Lamb White Days

My journey to 10 Downing Street and the House of Lords began in December 1919, when the world was still returning to sanity after the trauma of the Great War. I was born, to use the formal language of autobiography, in modest circumstances. My mother was a schoolteacher, my father worked for the local electricity supply company. Nancy Mitford once wrote to her sister, the Duchess of Devonshire, 'If one writes an autobiography, it's not enough, as so many people seem to suppose, to tell how many housemaids one's father employed – one must unmask oneself.' My father employed no housemaids; and as for the unmasking, well, we shall see.

We lived in the village of Llantarnam in the eastern valley of Monmouthshire. I was the eldest of four brothers, with a sister who still lives in Wales and another who died as a baby when I was nine. One of my earliest memories is of her last hours, when all hope had gone, and my mother turned to me and said very quietly, 'Come on, boy, she doesn't need us anymore'; together we left the weeping aunts and grandmothers and went out into the little garden behind the house and stood hand in hand by a lilac bush looking up at the stars. For the first time, but by no means the last, I wondered what it all meant.

Otherwise my childhood was, quite simply, happy and uncomplicated. Our house was a place of much love and a lot of laughter. When the Second World War eventually broke up our family, my sister became an officer in the ATS and my two brothers joined the RAF; and about that time my mother, somewhat belatedly, produced another son to complete the family. There were occasional crises brought about by what I

7

now understand to have been sibling rivalry, but most of the time we enjoyed each others' company and the security of sensible, thoughtful and affectionate parents. My mother encouraged a love of literature and a lasting fascination with the use of words. By contrast, my father used few words himself but communicated a strong moral sense.

Discipline was firm, but not draconian, except on one occasion following a village cricket match in which, although still at school, I had been invited to play. We won the match and I was unwise enough to accompany the other players to the local inn, Y Ty Gwyrdd, The Green House, where much celebratory cider was consumed from pint mugs. When I eventually arrived home I was not totally in command of my faculties, a state of affairs which my father, although somewhat puritanical by nature, was disposed to regard with mild amusement until, in the execution of some expansive gesture, I swept one of my mother's china ornaments from the chimneypiece. My father contemplated the shattered remains for a brief moment and then restored me to total sobriety with a blow which even now, when I remember it, starts a ringing in my ears.

Although I know how easy it is to invest one's childhood with the golden glow of eternal sunshine and innocent delights – the *Cider with Rosie* syndrome – these were indeed, in Dylan Thomas's magic phrase, 'lamb white days'. Behind our house meadows full of wild flowers led up to the slopes of the Mynydd Maen, a gentle ridge which runs north and south from Pontypool to Risca. At its southern end is a great tumulus, Twyn Barllwm, usually known locally as Twm Barlum. There is a good deal of academic chatter about its origin. Some revisionist pedants claim that it was built as a fortress by the Normans, who naively believed that it would enable them to dominate the valleys of Gwent. The more realistic belief in Wales is that it is the grave of a prehistoric British chieftain and, as far as I am concerned, that is what it is.

This was the skyline which dominated the landscape of our childhood. It has been vividly described by Fred Hando, the great chronicler of the 'most beloved land of Gwent': 'Stark and forbidding on a March morning; green and inviting in June; an upland paradise of blazing glory, its bracken flesh-pink beneath an October sun; or white in its winter cloak.' It is not surprising that, as we climbed the hill with our sandwiches and lemonade (or 'pop') we were, as Dylan says, 'green and carefree, famous among the barns'; and I still firmly believe that I once heard the legendary Mountain Organ, strange chords of music which sound over the slopes of Twyn Barllwm when the wind blows from the south.

The place names in the valleys still have a powerfully evocative effect on the memory. Just as for Marcel Proust the name Florence or Venice 'would awaken the desire for sunshine, for lilies, for the Palace of the Doges and for Santa Maria del Fiore', so, for me, at a more mundane level, Llanfrechfa, Henllys, Croesyceiliog and Caerleon bring back instant images of the woodlands full of bluebells, the meadows, rivers and valleys of Gwent. There are echoes and glimpses, too, of lost voices and faces, especially of one little girl called Rachel, known to me and her other friends as Rae. In memory she seems as beautiful as Olwen of the *Mabinogion*, but she died when we were all still children and I remember even now the feeling of desolation as we walked with her small coffin to the village churchyard.

My first school was the village school at St Dial's in Cwmbran, where all the teachers were women and 'Please, Miss' was a part of everyone's early vocabulary. Here I was able to build upon my mother's lessons in reading and writing, although I was not then, and have never been since, able to make much of arithmetic. From here I won a scholarship to Jones's West Monmouth School, a Haberdashers' foundation built on a hill outside the town of Pontypool. It was then a solid, old-fashioned grammar school, although it is now, in more demotic times, no longer so. Indeed, I was able to impose a small symmetrical flourish on the pattern of its life and mine when, in 1981, almost fifty years after I first went there as a very small and very apprehensive second former, I was invited to be the guest speaker at the last prize day before it 'went comprehensive'.

West Monmouth was a new world for a small boy from a

small village. In a genuflection to the public school ethos, the boys were divided into houses – not, of course, residential houses, as we were for the most part day boys – but depending on the part of the valley in which we lived. Each house had its own distinguishing colour and its own team for cricket and rugby, a system designed to encourage the development of team spirit. We had a school tie which incorporated the colours of all the houses in a dazzling rainbow pattern and a school badge with a motto which, although I did not know it at the time, was to have a lasting resonance in my own life – 'Serve and Obey'.

As I told the boys on that valedictory prize day a half a century later, the pursuit of excellence was at the centre of the school culture. The masters were, in retrospect, a remarkable and dedicated group of men. The headmaster, Mr R. Ivor Jones, lives in my memory as a man of daunting presence and of gently patrician aspect, except when he was wielding a cane which he did with great force and concentration. Of the other masters, one who remains most clearly in my mind is my sixth form French master, Ifor Davies, or 'Spike' as he was known to both his colleagues and his pupils. He had a great talent for opening young minds and the study of the French language under his imaginative guidance became an absorbing exploration rather than a chore. I still remember to this day his exegesis of Victor Hugo's great poem 'A Villequier' in which he drew fresh meaning and revelation out of the lines:

> Le monde est sombre, ô Dieu! l'immuable harmonie
> Se compose des pleurs aussi bien que des chants;
> L'homme n'est qu'un atome en cette ombre infinie,
> Nuit où montent les bons, où tombent les méchants.

With the help of a little imagination, I can still hear him declaim those lines in his light tenor voice. French with a North Wales accent – there's poetry for you!

The school also gave me the opportunity to treat sport with all the seriousness it demanded in Wales, or rather, that the

Welsh demanded of it. I had first handled a rugby ball when I was five (by Welsh standards a deplorably late start) and I knew almost at once what it was that had given the game a near religious significance amongst my countrymen. Already the names of F. E. Hancock and A. J. Gould shone like beacons in the sombre valleys, and before long I had prevailed upon my father to take me to Rodney Parade to watch Newport play against Cardiff – an occasion generating more passion than the Indians must have felt towards Custer.

Later I was to play alongside some of the Newport giants – W. H. Travers, Bill Jones and Ernie Coleman – but then, to a small boy on the terraces, those incredible gladiators in their blue-and-black and black-and-amber jerseys seemed like beings from another world. At school (the school which produced K. J. Jones, for my money the greatest wing threequarter of his generation and, indeed, one of the best ever), I began to play the game seriously. The school sportsground was not far from Pontypool Park, the home ground of one of the leading Welsh clubs and later of a certain T. J. Cobner, who played for Wales in the 'golden years' of the 1970s.

I spent more time at school with a rugby ball in my hands than a Latin grammar, and I have to confess that, with hindsight, it was the wise choice. The division of Gaul into three parts was undoubtedly a matter of profound significance, but not to be compared with the historic experience of watching Llanelli beat the All Blacks (or 'Seland Newydd', as they were identified on the scoreboard at Stradey Park on that memorable day).

By the time I reached the sixth form I had made a tolerably respectable reputation for myself at the school. I had been awarded my colours for rugby, cricket and athletics and was editor of the school magazine, to which I contributed poems under the pretentious and totally inappropriate pen name of *Y Delyn Aur* (The Golden Harp). I had performed creditably in what was then known as School Certificate (now GCSEs) and in Higher Certificate (A levels). I was awarded a Distinction in French, perhaps not surprisingly in the light of Ifor Davies' special influence on my intellectual aspirations.

When I returned to speak at the school's final prizegiving I was presented with a set of school magazines from my own time. Looking through them was a chastening, if nostalgic, experience. Those who have endured my speeches in the House of Lords may or may not be surprised by a report of the school's debating society for 1937 describing A. G. Jones as 'a suave man of affairs whose private life seemed to form the background of the majority of his speeches. It is to be hoped that his example will not blind the junior members to the real purpose of the Society, which is to encourage budding Ciceros, not juvenile lotharios.' The author was a little kinder about my speech defending patriotism, a subject now imbued with immediate relevance and urgency by developments in Europe.

There was an event at this time which had a lasting impact on my mind and which might fairly be said to have marked the faint beginnings of a social and political awareness. It was the visit to South Wales of King Edward VIII. In the grim winter of 1936 he spent two days travelling through the mining villages of the Rhondda and Monmouth valleys – Penygraig, Merthyr Tydfil, Penrhiwceiber and Mountain Ash. As the King later wrote in his memoirs as Duke of Windsor, 'the once rich coal mines upon which the wealth and power of Britain so largely depended had become a monument to the transitoriness of human institutions.'

South Wales was in the grip of demoralising depression and I still recall the mood of the crowds in which I stood to watch him arrive at the railway station in Cwmbran to be greeted by the Lord Lieutenant of Monmouthshire. There was a warm welcome for this slight, somewhat insubstantial figure who had once been our Prince of Wales and was even at that moment about to take the awful decision to renounce the throne in order to marry Mrs Simpson; at the same time there was a vague, inarticulate hope that somehow he might do something to alleviate the suffering which the depression had brought to the people of the valleys.

At one moment in his contemplation of the tragic scenes of ruined industry and impoverished families, he commented, not unnaturally, 'Something must be done.' This restrained humanitarian reaction aroused animosity in government circles, where it was regarded as an implication that the government had not already done everything in its power. This led the King to reflect later, in a sentiment which still has resonance today, that it was no longer possible for the King, 'to move unhindered among his subjects, and speak what is in his mind'.

After the King's visit, in the general mood of 'something must be done', I began to think in a more focused way of life after school.

University seemed the next obvious step, and at morning prayers in the Assembly Hall at school I would study the gold-lettered names on the Honours Board of those who had won State Scholarships to Oxford. However, it was by now 1938, and a combination of gathering clouds on the international scene and financial pressures at home put all this out of the reckoning, and I left school to join the Health Department of the Monmouthshire County Council. After a brief and entirely forgettable interlude as a minor local government official, my life, like that of the whole of my generation, was changed irrevocably.

By now it was clear that war with Germany was inevitable and, together with a number of my friends – mostly Newport rugby players – I joined the 1st (Rifle) Battalion, the Monmouthshire Regiment, a Territorial unit which was part of the Corps of the South Wales Borderers. When I joined up, in the tradition of rifle regiments, we wore black buttons on our tunics and marched at 140 paces to the minute – considerably faster than a normal infantry unit. This enhanced mobility, however, was not an essential accomplishment at the time, as the battalion had been converted into a Searchlight Regiment, with the task of illuminating the skies above Monmouthshire in the event of night-time air raids. When war was declared in September 1939, we were mobilised (or 'embodied' to use the somewhat arcane language of the day) and despatched to await the arrival of the Luftwaffe. There followed the long days and nights of the phoney war, leading to a change of direction for me when the

Commanding Officer decided that my burgeoning talents were not being fully exploited, and I was sent to an Officer Training Unit in Scotland, where, after being shouted at for several months by a succession of savage and incomprehensible sergeants in kilts, I emerged as a second lieutenant in the South Wales Borderers and was posted to the newly raised 6th Battalion, then on coastal defence duties in Swansea in South Wales.

In contemporary jargon, this might be described as 'a defining moment' in my life. Although the battalion which I joined was not a regular battalion, but a cadre of regular and Territorial officers and NCOs in charge of 800 conscripts, it had inherited much of the tradition and all the proud spirit of the South Wales Borderers, the 24th Foot. Raised in 1689 by King William, this regiment soon came under the influence of the greatest soldier this country has ever produced, the Duke of Marlborough, who became the colonel of the regiment. The colonelcy of the regiment in those days bore no resemblance to the largely honorary post of today. Marlborough was the commanding officer of the regiment in the field, and under his command they took part in all his great battles during the War of the Spanish Succession – Blenheim, Ramillies, Oudenarde, Malplaquet – when he soundly defeated the French armies which until then had dominated Europe.

The Marlborough years created the remarkable family spirit which has always been an outstanding characteristic of the South Wales Borderers. Most of the officers serving at the outbreak of World War Two had fathers or grandfathers who had served in the regiment, some in the historic battle of Rorke's Drift, with which the name of the South Wales Borderers is almost synonymous, and in which nine officers and men of the 24th Regiment won Victoria Crosses in twenty-four hours, a record unsurpassed to this day by any other regiment.

In the heart of South Africa the Buffalo River meanders southwards between Natal and Zululand and joins the great Tugela River which flows eastwards to the sea; and one of the many crossing places along the Buffalo is a small 'drift', or fording-place, called Rorke's Drift. In the late nineteenth century, at the time of the Zulu War, it was the site of a small hospital and a commissary, an insignificant huddle of buildings and stone kraals lying on the west bank of the river, one of many isolated British outposts in the region. It was there, on 22nd January 1879, that an officer and a handful of men of the 24th Foot, later known as the South Wales Borderers, wrote the words Rorke's Drift for ever into the history of their regiment of the British Army.

On that day, a small detachment was busy improving the defences of the little garrison. 'B' Company, 2nd Battalion, the 24th Regiment, had been left to protect the hospital and the commissariat, in all about eighty men under the command of a subaltern, Lieutenant Bromhead. With them were a few men of the Royal Artillery and the Royal Engineers and thirty-six NCOs and men lying sick in the hospital. For them, the morning of 22nd January passed uneventfully and there was nothing to suggest that the night was to bring the savage and bloody battle of Rorke's Drift.

Eleven miles away to the east, at the hill of Isandhlwana, one of the most terrible battles in the history of the regiment was already taking place. In a bitter fight to the death with over 3000 Zulus, the 24th lost over twenty officers and 500 men in that single morning. As hordes of spear-throwing Zulus swamped the men of the 24th by the sheer weight of their numbers, Lieutenant Colonel Pulleine, the Commanding Officer of the 1st Battalion, ordered one of his officers, Lieutenant Melvill, to save the Queen's Colour. In the days of the Zulu War, the Colours, which are silken flags embroidered with the regiment's battle honours, were still carried into battle as a rallying point for the men; and it fell to Lieutenant Melvill to prevent the Queen's Colour from falling into the hands of the enemy. He rode off with it towards the Buffalo River, to be joined by another survivor of the battle, Lieutenant Coghill. Together the two rode through continuous enemy fire to the river, forty yards wide, and running in flood between high, steep banks. Together they plunged into the river, but the fierce current was too much for them. Melvill lost his hold on the

Colour and when they reached the far bank they were too utterly exhausted to escape. Two weeks later a special patrol of the 24th found their bodies, covered in spear-wounds, and in the river nearby the Colour for which they had given their lives. It was eventually brought back to England, where Queen Victoria bestowed a unique honour on the regiment by personally placing on the pole of the Colour a wreath of immortelles (everlasting flowers), desiring that facsimile wreaths should always be borne on the Queen's Colour of the South Wales Borderers.

It is not always easy for me to say exactly when I first became aware of the South Wales Borderers. There was not always a clear division between family, village and regiment. I remember a soldier of the South Wales Borderers who came home to our village on leave when I was a boy. His arrival was always a great occasion and he would make the most of it by parading in full uniform, a figure of unimaginable glamour to us as children. And I had stood in the churchyard of Llantarnam as a very small child and watched the soldiers of the regiment salute the grave of Private John Williams with a volley of rifle fire, a lone bugler sounding the last post. Later, I heard the story of Rorke's Drift and was told that Williams was the last of the VCs from that little African village, the jewel in the crown of the regiment's battle honours.

It would not be an exaggeration to see the regiment as an extended family. Indeed, that culture was deliberately fostered, for good reason, as I was later to discover. The phrase 'brother officers' was an accurate indication of the depth of the bond, which is not broken by departure from army life. One can leave the battalion but membership of the regiment seems to have no time limit. Even today I return to the dining club of the regular officers and to the annual reunion of the 6th Battalion, a group which shrinks in size as the years go by.

I dwell on the regiment because, although I could not have foreseen it at the time, its culture and ideals have had an impact on my life far beyond the years of active military service. I believe it was Herder who reflected on the effect of communal military activity in shaping a man. The sense of shared history and the importance of symbol, ritual and tradition in binding a group together with a common purpose and identity, have remained with me.

Even today in the House of Lords I am reluctant to see tradition abandoned unthinkingly: ceremony and ritual have a power far beyond the decorative or quaint. This does not mean that all traditions should be maintained merely for their own sake, or that new traditions cannot be developed to suit a changed society and greater cultural diversity. But we should at least pause to reflect before jettisoning pieces of shared history. At a time when we are constantly debating the source of our society's values and coherence, we may find that tradition and history are two ingredients in the glue that holds us together at the beginning of the twenty-first century.

I was not, of course, troubled by any such reflection as I began army life. It was into this fiercely proud and exclusive corps of officers and men that I entered, somewhat apprehensively, on a bleak winter evening in 1940. The welcome was warm and reassuring, and after I had overcome a tendency to address the regimental sergeant major as 'sir', I began to fit fairly quickly into the scheme of things. I was introduced to my first command as an infantry officer – a platoon of about thirty men, none of whom had any previous military experience, and a regular army sergeant who referred to the men affectionately as a 'bloody shower'. He suggested to me on my first day that we might have to revive the ancient military device of tying bundles of hay and straw to their boots so that when marching they could be kept in step not with the customary 'Left, right' commands which they might be too slow-witted to understand, but with the more bucolic exhortation of 'Hayfoot, strawfoot'.

This was, of course, a piece of ponderous, NCO-type humour. The men were, with one or two inevitable exceptions, bright, quick and adaptable, some of them slightly more so than the platoon sergeant. The bond between them and their new second lieutenant was quickly forged and soon strengthened immeasurably by a German air raid on Swansea which we watched together from our stand-to positions on the coast of Swansea Bay. A few stray incendiary bombs landed on the sand dunes around us, and in the distance the centre of the town was on fire. It was a shared experience which is still talked about quietly when those of us who survive meet at regimental reunions.

For the next few months we were engaged in the absorbing process of transforming ourselves from a random collection of civilians in uniform, bank clerks, steelworkers, miners, schoolteachers and hill farmers – 'a bloody shower' – into a disciplined military unit. The cadre of regular officers and NCOs were tireless and dedicated and the almost daily change in the appearance and demeanour of the men was dramatic. From time to time we were called out at night to repel German parachute troops who had been clearly seen and positively identified by a Home Guard sentry, but who never actually materialised. It was during this time that I celebrated my twenty-first birthday and the first Christmas of the war, both of which events traumatised the staff of the Swansea hotel in which we were billeted.

At the beginning of 1941 we moved to Boston in Lincolnshire in convoys of bakers' vans, tradesmen's lorries and commandeered saloon cars. Here we began serious infantry training, a process which lost some of its urgency when we were told that we were about to be converted into a tank unit. The first step in this metamorphosis took the form of a visit to the unit by a team of psychiatrists, an event accepted with good humour by the men of the battalion, who took the realistic view that anyone who went to war in a steel box needed to have his head examined anyway.

Actually, the task of these monitors of our collective subconscious was allegedly to weed out anyone who was not sufficiently intelligent or mechanically minded to cope with life in an armoured regiment (a concept which seemed to discount the fact that many existing armoured regiments had begun life as cavalry units). Most of the men had little trouble with the intelligence tests and were, indeed, able to give some assistance to the officers. After some of the interviews, however, a certain amount of doubt was expressed by the soldiers on such matters as whether Private Watkins's relationship with his mother had anything to do with his ability to drive a tank.

The next stage consisted of six months of special training. I was sent to Bovington in Dorset on a gunnery course. I never discovered whether this choice of further education had any Freudian symbolism, but it was an experience which remains in my mind even today, not only because of the appalling noise made in the turret of a tank by the firing of a 75-millimetre gun, but also because of the memory of eating fresh crab at the Picnic Inn in the little village of Osmington, a few miles from Bovington Camp. This was an experience to which I was introduced by a brother officer of Rabelaisian tendencies, whose tastes had been developed and refined in the demanding school of the City of London. Tom Orpin, who in the post-war years became Commercial Director of British Airways, was then the senior subaltern of the battalion, and a formidable drinking companion. Many years later, when I was a Minister in the Foreign Office, we met again during negotiations about aircraft landing rights, and he has remained a close friend to this day.

In the summer of 1940, the battalion moved once again, this time to Southend, where we changed our title to 158 Regiment, Royal Armoured Corps (The South Wales Borderers). We exchanged our khaki head-dress for the black beret of the RAC and, after a great deal of correspondence, some of it of a somewhat exasperated nature, we were allowed to retain our own regimental cap badges instead of adopting the art deco badge of the Royal Armoured Corps. As the cap badge of the South Wales Borderers incorporated a silver replica of Queen Victoria's wreath of immortelles, the importance of this apparently trivial piece of military protocol, and its impact on the morale of the regiment, can scarcely be overestimated.

The battalion (or regiment as it was now more correctly described since the RAC did not have battalions) was judged to be ready for overseas service and, after a train journey across England which had all the hallmarks of a serious nightmare, we arrived at Liverpool Docks and, in pouring rain, embarked in the liner *Athlone Castle*, now converted into a troopship. On the morning of 29th October 1942 we headed out into the Atlantic, on our way to India.

2

The Jungle is *not* Neutral

The voyage was for the most part like any other move of troops by sea in wartime – in other words, fairly disagreeable. Although the officers shared reasonably comfortable cabins, the troops lived below decks, sleeping in hammocks in overcrowded conditions with bad ventilation and inadequate sanitary arrangements. It is a reflection on their spirit and character that they remained indomitably cheerful and most of the time uncomplaining. Some of this was due to the efforts of a young officer who was, I suppose, one of the most unlikely characters ever to put on the uniform of an infantry officer.

Second Lieutenant Alun Lewis was already emerging as a significant voice in Anglo-Welsh poetry. He was a young man of brooding and saturnine aspect, non-conformist and iconoclastic by instinct. His appearance in uniform was, to say the least, unconventional. He had a remarkable ability to make everything he wore look as though it had been made for someone else, either much smaller or much bigger than he was. If a piece of equipment could be worn backwards or upside down, that is how he was inclined to wear it. He was, as he frequently declared, much more at home with the soldiers or other ranks than with the officers. His nature was almost unnaturally gentle, his smile disarmingly sweet and his voice, with marked Welsh inflections, soft and insinuating.

He had been appointed ship's entertainments officer, whether because of his 'artistic' background or his affinity with the troops is uncertain. As well as organising endless quizzes, concerts and boxing matches, he formed a regimental choir, generally making life on board a great deal less oppressive than it might otherwise have been. We had a running battle over our respective programmes of recorded music on the ship's radio, his mainly Tchaikovsky and Beethoven, mine Benny Goodman and John Kirby, whose recordings he resolutely declined to regard as music. In spite of our obvious incompatibility of temperament, character and taste, we became good friends and he will re-emerge to play a significant part in the unfolding of this story.

Our days were not entirely without incident. The convoy in which we were sailing stopped once to pick up survivors from a Norwegian ship which had been torpedoed the previous day; and one night a French merchant ship disappeared completely from the convoy. Then, about a week into the voyage, the ship's captain received a message warning him of the possibility of a submarine attack and the *Athlone Castle* was ordered to take evading action by crossing the Atlantic to South America instead of taking the direct route around the Cape. We therefore made for the Brazilian port of Salvador de Bahia, one of the oldest cities in Brazil and its original capital.

The city, which is divided into two separate sections, the lower city around the port (*ciudade baixa*) and the upper residential area (*ciudade alta*), is especially famous for its great number of baroque colonial churches and it was the sight of these, in their almost endless variety of pastel colours, which greeted us in the sparkling sunshine when we sailed into the Bay of All Saints on the morning of 15th November, after two weeks of grey Atlantic tedium.

Any thought of a brief interlude of rest and recreation was dispelled by the news that battalion headquarters had decided to take advantage of our short stay in Bahia by organising a route march through the upper city. As the temperature was in the high seventies, it was decided to use the occasion to try out the tropical uniforms which had been issued before we left England. There had, however, been no opportunity for any individual fittings, with the result that when the battalion, attired in their new uniforms, paraded on deck for inspection, the spectacle was uniquely hilarious. In some cases, the dome-shaped pith helmets not only covered the head of the wearer but almost rested on his shoulders totally obscuring his view; in others, the helmet rested precariously on top of the head like a teacup on a haystack. Similarly, 'shorts' either enveloped the knees or exposed the upper thighs (not a pretty sight in some cases) and shirtsleeves were often several inches longer than the wearer's arms. The older regular officers and soldiers, who had their own tropical uniforms from previous service and looked reasonably normal, spent most of the parade convulsed and weak with laughter.

After a measure of sanity had been restored by the battalion tailor, we went ashore for the march through the town. This had been intended partly to give the men a change from the cramped conditions on board and partly as a show of good will to the people of Brazil. Unfortunately, the people had not been apprised of our benevolent motives and, seeing a contingent of foreign troops being disembarked on their soil, they came to the conclusion that they were about to be occupied. This provoked the local population into some distinctly unfriendly behaviour, which mainly consisted of uncomplimentary verbal reflections on the appearance, demeanour and parentage of the troops, but which occasionally led to physical jostling, causing march discipline to suffer in the ranks, at least one NCO being heard to reprimand his soldiers with the sharp reminder that this was 'a parade, not a bleeding conga'.

However, everything changed when the troops marched past the Provincial Governor, who delivered a friendly speech of welcome. As his message quickly spread among the crowds, the atmosphere was at once transformed and the march back to the ship was an occasion for cheering crowds and much blowing of kisses. As we sailed from the harbour there were friendly waves and bouquets of flowers; and as I leaned on the rail for what I thought was my last glimpse of the church of the convent of St Francis, I could not possibly have imagined that a quarter of a century later I would be back among the cheering crowds of the *ciudade alta*, but in a very different ship and on a very different mission.

Our next stop was back across the Atlantic in Durban. Here the South Wales Borderers were not as unfamiliar as they had been to the people of Brazil. Rorke's Drift and Isandhlwana had made a lasting reputation for the regiment in South Africa and this, together with the legendary hospitality of the South African people, guaranteed a warm welcome in Durban. We were allowed ashore without the need to engage in route marches or other organised manifestations of that kind and, as we reached the bottom of the gangway, officers and men were greeted with invitations to dinner, sightseeing tours and that very special South African custom, the *brai* or barbecue.

The lavish hospitality was too much for some of the less hardened members of the battalion and, as I wrote later, 'many who went down the gangway vertically returned horizontally.' My friend Tom Orpin, noted for his belligerent demeanour when modestly stimulated by alcohol, had to be rescued from a Durban night club where he insisted on 'requesting' the dance band to play 'Sospan Fach', a tune much favoured by crowds at rugby matches in Wales. What is familiar in Llanelli, however, does not necessarily have any deep significance for the people of Natal, especially those who make a living playing the trumpet in a night club. The bandleader politely declined the request, whereupon Tom, overcome by emotion, offered to fight the entire band, the offer being accompanied by disobliging remarks about their appearance and racial background. He was quickly escorted back to the troopship and instructed not to leave it again during our stay in Durban.

This was not as long as we hoped it would be. The following day the *Athlone Castle* and the *Stirling Castle* were ordered to detach themselves from the convoy and sail unescorted to India. We reached Bombay a week before Christmas and moved immediately to Nira, a small village in Maharashtra, not far from the legendary garrison town of Poona. I had by now been appointed intelligence officer, an occupation which later became a recurrent theme in my military career; but on arrival in Nira, I was promoted to the rank of captain and appointed adjutant, the principal administrative officer and assistant to the Commanding Officer. Alun Lewis replaced me as intelligence officer, a move which was soon to have significant consequences.

No sooner had we begun to master some of the essentials of armoured warfare than the inevitable happened. Our tanks were removed and we were reconverted into an infantry battalion. We handed in our dashing black berets and were obliged to wear what must be the most bizarre headgear ever designed for troops in combat – the Australian bush hat, with its brim turned up on one side and a chinstrap, presumably to hold it in place in high winds, which were, as one might expect, rare in the jungle. The battalion now joined the 36th Division, which was training as an amphibious assault group in the Bombay area. The Divisional Commander was a very large and very eccentric officer, General 'Frankie' Festing, whose disconcerting custom it was to materialise suddenly in the middle of a training exercise, equipped with a walking stick like a large shepherd's crook, and to assume the theoretically dangerous role of leading scout in a company attack. The 6th Battalion, the South Wales Borderers, as we were now once again called, became part of 72 Infantry Brigade, one of the two brigades of the division.

We settled down to some intensive training in amphibious warfare, first on a lake at Kharakvasla near Poona and then on the beaches in the Bombay area, culminating in a full-scale practice assault landing at the idyllic bay of Ratnagiri, about 150 miles south of Bombay. It was a reasonably successful exercise, enlivened by the spectacle of an entire platoon of assault troops leaping from their landing craft with suitably menacing gestures and noises, only to disappear entirely in about ten feet of water as a result of a minor navigational error by the naval officer in charge. The lasting memory of Ratnagiri, however, is not so much of warlike manoeuvres, as of a brief rest period after the landing, when we removed our clothes and equipment at midnight and swam naked in the warm waters of the Arabian Sea, watching long trails of phosphorescence sparkling from our fingers and toes, not to mention other extremities.

In intervals during this period of training we did not neglect more important matters, such as rugby football. As well as being adjutant, I was captain of the rugby XV, regarded in a Welsh unit as being a marginally more important responsibility. We won the divisional cup, which is still on display in the Officers' Mess at Brecon, in doing so beating the Royal Welch Fusiliers in the final. We went on to the final of the Bombay Gymkhana Tournament but were beaten in the final of the competition by the Welch Regiment. I think there were some English regiments also involved in some of these competitions but they were not, as rugby teams, regarded very seriously.

Eventually we were judged to be ready for amphibious operations and in February 1944 we moved to Calcutta where the division was preparing for Operation PORPOISE, designed to recover from the Japanese the Burmese port of Akyab on the Bay of Bengal by a landing from the sea. The journey to Calcutta by rail was appallingly slow and uncomfortable, even by the standards of wartime travel on Indian Railways; but the officers and men of the battalion, approaching their next task with a mixture of excitement and apprehension, were able to bear it with a degree of resignation. However, we were now informed of a change of plan of the kind which makes the conduct of war so interesting. Operation PORPOISE had been cancelled and we were to go instead to Arakan, in eastern Burma, to take part in jungle operations against the Japanese Army. So all our leaping out of boats and charging up beaches had been about as much use to us as the tank ranges at Bovington.

From Calcutta we went on to Chittagong and then by coastal steamer to Cox's Bazaar, a small Indian fishing port close to the Burmese frontier. From here we marched south across the border along a 'road' which was about twelve inches deep in finely powdered dust. On this nightmarish journey there was one episode in which one of our senior officers displayed all the laconic stoicism of the true professional. As we passed a small group of British soldiers resting by the roadside, he waved a greeting and one of them waved back and called out to him by name. However, we did not stop, and a little further on I commented on this and asked if he knew the man concerned. 'Oh yes,' he said, 'it was my brother. I haven't seen him for over four years.'

Eventually we arrived at the small Burmese village of Bawli Bazaar, where we took up defensive positions at the foot of the Mayu hills, part of a jungle-covered range which is the dominant feature of Arakan. Our task here was to patrol the jungle to try to establish the exact whereabouts of the Japanese. I set up battalion headquarters in the village, occupying a Burmese hut, or *basha*, with Alun Lewis and his intelligence section under a banyan tree nearby.

We had been in position for a few days when Lewis came to me and asked permission to visit one of the companies on the hill just above our headquarters, with the quite reasonable purpose of reconnoitring the situation for himself instead of just basing his intelligence assessments entirely on periodic reports from the outlying companies. I was a little uneasy about this request, as he had seemed depressed and distracted for some time and was obviously in some kind of emotional turmoil – not an ideal frame of mind for someone proposing to go on a jungle reconnaissance. However, I eventually gave in to his pressing arguments and agreed that he could go and spend a few days on the hill, on the strict condition that he attached himself to the troops already there and did not go thrashing about the jungle on his own.

He had only been gone a day or so when I received a radio message from the officer commanding the company on the hill that there had been 'an accident' and that they were bringing Lieutenant Lewis back to battalion headquarters. Sensing that something really serious had happened, I quickly assembled a small patrol and set off up the hill. About halfway up, I met a stretcher party carrying the body of Lewis, who had an obvious gunshot wound in his head. Everyone subsequently involved in the enquiries into the circumstances of his death was anxious to avoid any more distress than was necessary to his wife and family and the official version was that his death was the result of an accident, although those on the spot at the time were convinced that he had taken his own life.

The incident had a dispiriting effect on the troops, especially at battalion headquarters where, as intelligence officer, he had become a familiar and popular figure. I experienced especially acute feelings of depression and guilt. As adjutant and therefore his immediate superior, I felt that I should have probed more into the emotional problems which had clearly been preying on his mind in the days before his death; and, of course, I blamed myself for letting him leave battalion headquarters and go up the hill where he was exposed, not only to possible attack from the enemy, but more dangerously to whatever devils were at work in the depths of his own mind. Perhaps I should have read more carefully the poem which he wrote for me and gave to me on our first Christmas in India in 1942 and of which I still have the stained and crumpled manuscript. It ended:

> The nearness that lies waiting in my bed
> The gradual self-effacement of the dead.

I am sure that such an event always prompts profound questioning in the minds and consciences of those left behind. This was true for me professionally, as the officer responsible for Alun Lewis's safety, but also personally. Despite an incompatibility which might have been glaring in civilian life, war had forged a remarkable closeness. We were the only men in the battalion with literary pretensions – his far more credible than mine – and we shared a love of Anglo-Welsh poetry. Moreover, because of our respective duties, we had spent an enormous amount of time together, so that his sudden and violent death left a gaping hole. I will never be sure of what pushed him to take such a terrible step, but I suspect that he was deeply afraid – not of dying, but of the knowledge that he might soon have to kill.

Alun Lewis's life and death had one personal postscript for me. By some process not entirely susceptible to rational explanation, after his death I became known as Alun and have been so ever since, although it was not my name when I was christened. Indeed, my name has passed through a number of mutations over the years. I was named at birth after my father, Arthur

Gwynne, and known as Arthur when I was a small boy. At school I had a number of nicknames, some more disobliging than others. When I joined my regiment I was known as Gwynne, and many of my older army friends still know me by that name. Then came the change to Alun, which has, so far, survived; but when one adds to all that my assumption of the title Chalfont on my elevation to the House of Lords (after the village in which I was living at the time) the possibilities for confusion become almost endless. However, most of this was not especially relevant to the problems of jungle warfare.

Patrolling the slopes of the Mayu range was a severe test for the young soldiers of the battalion. The jungles of north Burma had the reputation of being one of the most disease-ridden regions of the world. They were infested by leeches and other unpleasant wildlife; malaria, dengue fever, dysentery and typhus were endemic and among the less life-threatening afflictions were suppurating jungle sores which quickly festered all over the body, especially in places from which a blood-gorged leech had been carelessly removed. During the monsoon season, everything and everybody became soaked for days and weeks on end and the jungle floor turned into a swamp. In these awful conditions each man had to carry his rifle or sub-machine gun and ammunition and, on his back, three days' rations, grenades and spare clothing; at the start of a patrol this could amount to 90–100 lbs of equipment. This had to be carried through dense scrub and bamboo thickets, up and down peaks which rose to 1500 feet, often in tropical rain storms; and somewhere in the jungle were highly professional Japanese infantry, fanatically brave and trained in the techniques of jungle warfare.

A month of intensive patrol activity, however, brought no contact with the enemy and on 18th March we received orders which were to result in our first battle with the Japanese and our first casualties from enemy action. A little way to the south the road linking the strategic port of Maungdaw to the inland town of Buthidaung passed through two tunnels, each about 200 yards long, dug under the Mayu range. Intelligence reports suggested that the first, or western tunnel, contained a Japanese gun emplacement, together with stocks of ammunition and other supplies. Its entrance was covered by Japanese machine guns and mortars. The Royal West Kent Regiment had been trying for some time, without success, to clear the area. The South Wales Borderers now moved to the tunnels area to relieve the Royal West Kents and to press home the attack.

For three days we took cover every day while the Japanese positions were shelled by artillery and dive-bombed from the air. The attack, which went in on 26th March, led to a savage battle which lasted all day. It ended with the Japanese still in occupation of the tunnels and on the following day we brought a Sherman tank up to the tunnel entrance. It fired one high-explosive shell into the western tunnel, with spectacular results. There was a huge and prolonged explosion and Japanese bodies, together with all kinds of debris, shot out of the far end. Ammunition in the tunnel burned for hours.

Next day the enemy, suitably impressed by the pyrotechnics, had gone. The battle had cost the battalion the lives of one officer and ten soldiers, with three officers and twenty-six soldiers wounded. There were several decorations for bravery and today the battle honour 'Mayu Tunnels' is borne on the regimental colours of the Royal Regiment of Wales, which was formed when the South Wales Borderers and the Welch Regiment were amalgamated in 1969.

This had been an unforgettable experience. We had fought our first battle against a determined, well trained and well armed enemy. There was an almost tangible new spirit in the air as officers and men experienced the exhilaration of comradeship forged in common danger. As I reflect now on the battle for the Mayu Tunnels, I am surprised that we took the sheer bloodiness of the conflict, fought in appalling conditions, almost in our stride. It is extraordinary that young men, some barely out of school, should have had the psychological strength to survive the trauma of such an experience.

The truth is that, as a disparate group of individuals, no doubt we should not have survived. But the mixture of pride in the spirit and tradition of the regiment, combined with what amounted to the support of a family unit, was a powerful prop. This pressure worked both ways, of course: for a young officer with anything from twenty to 120 men under his command, there was a tremendous obligation not to let others down. This did not prevent private reflections on the madness taking place all around. For me, Tolstoy's pre-eminence as the chronicler of men at war comes not from his ability to marshal disparate detail across a vast canvas; it is rather the sense of chaos which he conveys at the heart of warfare. He comes closer than most in portraying the reality of the experience of war, but the sheer arbitrariness of death and destruction remains stranger than fiction.

I remember, even now, walking down a jungle track with a brother officer in a relaxed manner, since we knew that we had scouts patrolling ahead of us. In an instant a bullet from a Japanese sniper shot him through the heart. I am constantly aware that for him – as for so many of my comrades – his biography finished at an early chapter. As I write this, the eightieth anniversary of the First World War armistice is approaching and the field of remembrance around St Margaret's, Westminster, is already beginning to fill with poppies; the ever dwindling number of survivors has actually increased my sense of gratitude as the years go by.

Even if those events have not left mental scars, they have certainly conditioned my thinking on war and peace ever since. From the ugliness and bloodiness of war came my conviction that it is a grotesque and indefensible way of conducting relations between states. The connection between this and my thoughts on nuclear deterrence is not as tenuous as it might seem. I came to feel that a nuclear capability could actually prevent others from going through the same experience.

Indeed, one of the most painful features of my long debates with the unilateralists of the CND during the 1980s was the tendency of my opponents to speak of 'conventional warfare', as if that was obviously preferable to nuclear conflict. I know from experience that there is no such thing as 'conventional' warfare, and for those friends who never returned from Burma, the difference is self-evidently academic.

For the same reason I have generally been less enthusiastic than some politicians and journalists about the concept of armed intervention in the conflicts of other states. Again, I know only too well, as any soldier does, who will have to pay the price for these decisions, however well-intentioned they may be. In short, the experience of warfare has conditioned me to view the use of military power as an effective weapon in foreign policy precisely because, if it is used judiciously and appropriately as a threat, it can actually help us to avoid war. It is, of course, an uncomfortable paradox that this can only be achieved from a position of military strength.

Needless to say, these abstract reflections were not uppermost in our minds during the Burma campaign itself – exhaustion and activity kept thought to a merciful minimum.

We remained in the tunnels area for two more weeks, engaged once more in intensive patrolling; and on 13th May we crossed the Mayu range through the Ngakedauk Pass and by that afternoon we were resting in a transit camp. After a night of blessed sleep, we set off for Shillong, in northern Assam, to rest, reorganise and refit.

But nothing in life – especially in the army – is quite as simple as that. Although Shillong is only about 300 miles north of Arakan, the journey took us eight days. First we took a river steamer to a transit stop at Dohazar, just south of Chittagong. Here we spent four days, during which we were entertained by a concert party from the Indian equivalent of ENSA, the organisation responsible for entertaining British troops on active service. It was an experience only marginally less confusing than the Battle of the Tunnels. We then boarded a train in Chittagong bound for Sylhet, the nearest station to Shillong; but our troubles were not quite over.

As we headed north through Comilla, some observant members of the regiment (possibly the intelligence section) had noticed bits flying off the wheels of the train and, judging this to be an emergency, pulled the communication cord. However, when the train had been assembled in Chittagong, someone had overlooked an important aspect of the operation, with the result that the communication cord did not, in fact, communicate with anyone. Eventually the wheels came off one of the carriages, derailing five others which crashed down a steep embankment. Although railway maintenance was one of the few things the battalion had *not* been trained for, we eventually succeeded in extricating those who had been trapped in the wrecked coaches. Miraculously there were no serious injuries, and we were able to complete our rest and recreation journey with no further excitement, arriving in Shillong on 22nd May, shortly before the D-day landings in Normandy.

3

The End of the War

Shillong in those days was a typical Indian hill station, a delightful and colourful little town, 2000 feet up in the Khasi and Jaintin hills of Assam. In contrast to the unbroken jungle vegetation of Arakan, there were fir trees, green fields and tea plantations. The climate was almost perfect, the only problem being the rain, which was frequent and torrential – not surprisingly, as we were only thirty miles from Cherrapungi and Mawsinram, which have the highest recorded annual rainfall in the world. However, warm tropical rain does not have the same dispiriting effect as a chill northern downpour, and we soon learned to behave like the local population who seemed positively to enjoy getting wet.

The Naga people of the region were open and friendly, their rudimentary English entirely comprehensible as, much to our surprise, they spoke with a strong Welsh accent, the result of being educated by successive generations of Welsh missionaries. There was also a British community, for the most part tea planters and their families, whose hospitality seemed endless. For a young officer lately liberated from the heat of the Burmese jungle and its oppressive dangers and discomforts it was an especially peaceful experience to sit on the verandah of a planter's house with a gin and tonic and then go in to dinner in a pleasant dining room with a coal fire.

However, Shillong was not all rest and recreation; there was some retraining and reorganisation as well. In accordance with the well-established military principle which dictates that as soon as someone has learned to do something reasonably well he should be required to go and do something else, I handed over the responsibilities of adjutant and went to be second-in-command of one of the rifle companies. At about this time the 14th Army Commander, General 'Bill' Slim, visited the battalion and addressed the assembled officers with an inspiring speech which left me with the impression, later reinforced by events, that he was one of the really great military leaders of World War Two.

After just over a month in Shillong we were on the move again, this time to join the American-Chinese forces led by the almost legendary General Stilwell – 'Vinegar Joe'. This was not a prospect to be contemplated with unalloyed pleasure, as General Stilwell, as well as having a reputation as an abrasive disciplinarian, was generally believed to regard all non-Americans, with the possible exception of the Chinese, as inferior beings. We moved by rail to Ledo, a railhead near the India-Burma border, and then by air to a landing strip recently captured from the Japanese near Myitkina. It was still under enemy artillery fire when we landed, and the sense of menace was reinforced by the brooding presence of General Stilwell, the monsoon rain pouring from his scoutmaster-style hat and waterproof cape, watching with unconcealed disenchantment the arrival of these miserable limeys.

Our task was, together with the other British units, to clear the railway corridor which runs through the middle of northern Burma from Myitkina to Mandalay, and our first objective was a minor river called Sahmaw Chaung where the Japanese held strong defensive positions. The move towards the Chaung – the 'advance to contact' to use the military terminology – took us along the railway line in torrential rain. On either side the foetid swamps were pock-marked with shell craters, filled with water and often with decomposing Japanese bodies, the smell of which was even stronger than that of the rotting vegetation. After a week of this misery, we reached the approaches to Sahmaw Chaung, and in the early hours of 5th August we began to move towards the Japanese positions.

My company soon came under heavy machine gun fire from a Japanese bunker and the company commander, Major E. J.

(Jenkin) Jones, summoned the officers and began to give orders for the assault on the position, and at that moment he was killed by a single shot from a sniper. It was my first experience of something which I often encountered again in various military operations – the sheer banality which often characterises death in battle. At one moment Jenkin, a big, rough, tough character, was confidently issuing orders; suddenly, without a sound, he was lying in the mud with only a small black hole over the breast pocket of his jungle green shirt to tell us what had happened.

I reported his death to battalion headquarters on the radio, took over the command of the company and completed the orders for the assault, which eventually destroyed the Japanese position after a bayonet charge led by a young officer, Lieutenant Ian Tibbs, who was subsequently awarded the Military Cross. I now realise that for me this was what in today's language would be called a defining moment. It was the moment in which I think I really grew up – the lamb white days were over. Commanding a company of infantry at the age of twenty-four in an attack on a heavily defended Japanese machine gun position can be very character-forming.

Meanwhile other units had been attacking other Japanese defences; by dawn the objective had been secured and we moved forward for the next phase of the advance. It was at this time that my own part in the proceedings came to an end. I was suddenly disabled by a raging fever and had to be left on a stretcher in a jungle clearing, from where I was eventually 'air-evacuated', in other words, strapped to the undercarriage of a light aircraft and flown to a field hospital where the doctors established that I was suffering from what one of them called 'a full house'. In addition to the malaria which had struck me down, I had contracted typhus and a particularly unpleasant tropical disease called ankylostomiasis. The prognosis was that I would not be fit for jungle operations for some considerable time, and I was flown to the Indian Base General Hospital in Poona.

Here I slowly recovered, thanks entirely to the constant care and dedication of the doctors of the Royal Army Medical Service and the remarkable QAs, the nurses of Queen Alexandra's Imperial Military Nursing Service. On my discharge from hospital I completed my service in India as the station staff officer, Poona, an administrative appointment of no great *réclame*. However, it involved me in the social life of Poona, which still retained vestiges of the affectations of the Raj – cocktails at the Gymkhana, dinner dances at the Poona Club and visits to the Chinese and Indian restaurants of the town for egg fuyong and spring rolls or curries of blistering heat. I also had an opportunity to play some cricket, including a match against an Australian service XI in which I had my off stump uprooted by a fast bowler who subsequently became one of the great figures of Test cricket.

Meanwhile, the 6th Battalion had continued its advance down the railway corridor, fighting its last battle in Burma at the end of April. When VJ day came, after the bombing of Hiroshima and Nagasaki, the battalion was sent to Sumatra, where thousands of Japanese troops had to be disarmed and sent home. In March 1946, orders came for the disbandment of the battalion and by the end of April it had ceased to exist. During its six years' service, the 6th Battalion had fought through more than 500 miles of Burmese jungle; eight officers and eighty-one soldiers had been killed in action, eighteen officers and 251 soldiers wounded. Although I was not with them at the end, my service with them was a turning point in my life. The bravery, dedication and loyalty of these officers and men set values and standards which I have ever since tried, perhaps not always entirely successfully, to live by.

It is a paradox that the great misfortune of being caught up in a war brought with it remarkable benefits. Even now it is difficult – and sometimes a sensitive matter – to distinguish the positive from the destructive. I have already discussed the all-consuming horror of war, but I know too that it had a strangely cleansing effect on me and, I am sure, on many of my generation. By this I do not simply mean that it united us in a common purpose, although that was important enough. I think rather that it purged us of a degree of selfishness as individuals. The conduct of war was such that we were forced to subordinate our own wishes to the common good, in fact we were often unable even to think of our own good as individuals – 'the platoon' or 'the battalion' became everything. This is not to say that war produced a utopia of perfect individuals but it was, as I say, in some sense a cleansing experience.

It was also momentous: in the midst of the daily grind we knew that we were involved in a decisive struggle in human history, the outcome of which would be critical for the future direction of much of the world's population. That this struggle was primarily a moral one, a fight in defence of values, made the sacrifice of self-interest and the support of institutions to which we felt a common allegiance, all the more obviously necessary.

As the Second World War fades from the nation's memory, these musings actually seem to take on a new urgency and relevance. At the turn of the old century, we find ourselves conscious of a lack of communal values, a growth of individualism, a rootlessness and an inability to belong, a distrust of all established institutions and, perhaps, a lack of idealism. We debate and agonise over the effects of these developments on everything from family life to the welfare state. We are aware that our society offers as its highest ambition the acquisition of personal wealth and the horizon of personal happiness and fulfilment, these latter to be acquired through the shifting sands of self-actualisation. As a society it seems that the nearest we can offer to a titanic struggle is a successful bout of currency speculation, the greatest issue a debate about the euro.

There are no easy answers because there are no great external enemies; indeed, as I have persistently argued, we must do everything in our power to avoid replacing our Cold War adversaries with the chimera of an 'Islamic threat'. Nor could any sane person suggest that every generation needs another war: if we are tempted by the voice which argues that 'humanity has grown great in eternal struggle and only in eternal peace has it grown weak', we should remember that the voice was Hitler's.

But we do not need to abandon the quest for something which can change society as radically as conflict. Maintaining confidence in the ability of a democratic society to develop in a healthy direction during peacetime should be our starting point. I still believe, as I argued in the 1970s, that some form of national communal service would be beneficial: something to raise the horizons of young people above concern for their own fulfilment, something which could encourage their best instincts of service to others. Ironically, the self-interest imposed on politicians makes it very difficult for them to suggest any such thing.

This period of two or three years might for the odd bellicose Welshman even involve military service, if that was preferred. A significant section of the armed forces is resolutely opposed to this, no doubt because they do not wish to be landed with the job of nannying, still less improving, hordes of languid youth. But this attitude does not serve the forces well. One of the principal benefits of national service was to place the armed forces at the heart of the country, making them part of the lives of every citizen, rather than a small 'special interest' group. This was unquestionably to the advantage of the forces and led almost inevitably to a greater cohesion which a basic common shared experience gives to a group of individuals. There are even some senior officers who will admit privately that, for all their irritations, national service men also helped to keep the armed forces in closer touch with the reality outside the closed cultural world of the services.

My own war service completed, I returned to England in 1945 and relinquished the temporary rank of major which I had briefly held in India. I was posted to the Headquarters of Mid West District in Shrewsbury as a staff captain. This was an appointment of numbing tedium, consisting principally of maintaining files and minutes on a succession of trivial administrative problems. However, Shrewsbury was a pleasant market town and there was plenty of time for sport and other extra-mural pursuits. I played cricket for the Gentlemen of Shropshire, provoking various predictable comments from my brother officers to the effect that I was not qualified on either count.

On the rugby football scene, which was flourishing with a number of first-class players still serving in the army, I was involved in a bizarre incident. I was captain of one of the teams in a representative Army match at Shrewsbury and one of the local generals, an officer of rather limited horizons, was sitting amongst the spectators. At the end of the game, in which my side had performed reasonably well, I received a message saying that the General would like to see me at his seat in the grandstand before I went off to change. Assuming that I was about to receive a word or two of congratulation, I climbed the steps and presented myself to the great man. Not being in uniform I was not, of course, able to salute, but I managed to stand to attention, not an entirely easy matter in football boots. Looking up at me balefully, the General uttered four words which apparently summed up his appreciation of the situation – 'Get your hair cut.'

My tonsorial shortcomings were apparently not a matter of widespread concern in the army, as it was about this time that I was asked if I would like to be considered for a regular commission – in effect, to make the army my career. It did not take me long to decide. I had already become much attached to the structured, organised certainties of military life; I enjoyed the comradeship and the close family spirit; the opportunities for sport and the predominantly outdoor life were added attractions; and I contemplated the alternative of civilian life without any great degree of enthusiasm. I was interviewed at some length and in due course, on 24th August 1946, I received King George VI's commission 'to be an Officer in Our Land Forces' (my Regiment to be the South Wales Borderers) with the rank of lieutenant, but containing the encouraging words 'or such other rank as we may from time to time hereafter be pleased to promote or appoint you...'

It is even more important to record that it was at Mid West District Headquarters in Shrewsbury that I met my wife, Mona. I had been married before, in a wartime marriage which did not survive the war, and which was dissolved immediately after its end. Mona, a Scot, was at this time an officer in the Royal Army Medical Corps, one of the doctors responsible for the health and fitness of the staff of the Headquarters. We were married in London in 1948, when I left Shrewsbury and was engaged on a Russian language course at London University. We have had a happy marriage, sometimes enlivened by the inevitable clash of two strong personalities, and occasionally beset by crises, largely, it must be said, of my making, not hers. When she left the army she went into general practice and later specialised in paediatrics. She now restricts her medical activities to giving me excellent advice on my own physical welfare, especially on the dangers of an occasional over-enthusiastic intake of alcohol.

For the next few years I began my further education in some of the special skills of the military profession. There was a course at the School of Military Intelligence in Sussex and the Russian language course at the School of Slavonic Studies at London University, part of which involved a period in Paris living with a White Russian family. Here I not only improved my Russian, but also developed a lasting taste for such delicacies as mushrooms in sour cream and for the custom of starting each evening with a plate of *zakooski* (Russian *hors d'oeuvre*) and a glass or two of vodka poured from a bottle encased in a block of ice.

The Army Staff College at Camberley, to which I was posted in 1950, was a much more sedate affair designed to prepare officers for the serious responsibilities of command and staff appointments. The teachers (or directing staff as they were properly called) were for the most part bright and highly professional lieutenant-colonels, and a year at Camberley under their expert guidance was an essential stage in the career of army officers hoping to reach high rank. We worked hard, but here, too, there was time for riding, drag-hunting, rugby and cricket. Here, my achievements were somewhat uneven. Although I was captain of the College rugby XV and won a County cap for Berkshire, my most memorable cricket game was one in which I dropped the easiest of catches off the bowling of an officer who was subsequently to become Chief of the Defence Staff – not exactly a career-enhancing occasion.

In 1951, having completed my Russian interpreter course and passed the Camberley Staff College course, I was posted to join my regiment for duty in Eritrea. I had been married for less than three years, and I hoped to take my wife, Mona, with me. No one seemed to know much about Eritrea, and we knew nothing. The atlas indicated a strip along the Red Sea far from anywhere. An army friend already in Asmara, the capital of Eritrea, wrote to say that it would be very difficult to get permission to take my wife unless I had a house to go to. However, he said that we could give his address and hope to find somewhere to live when we got there. We set off, full of hope, but without knowing that houses were not easy to find.

After over two weeks in a cramped troopship we arrived in Massawa – the hottest place in the world! We were directed to an armoured train to climb 8000 feet to Asmara. It was all appallingly uncomfortable, but at thirty-one years old it seemed rather exciting. When we arrived in Asmara I was summoned at once to meet my Commanding Officer, a tall, handsome bachelor who was said to dislike wives. He looked at me fiercely and said, 'You want to watch it young man – you lose your hair, your teeth and your wife in this part of the world if you are not careful.' In fact, he turned out to be a delightful friend and later married and had three children, without losing his hair or his teeth.

We spent a few days in a transit camp and quickly discovered that houses to rent really did not exist. Our plight was soon known among the army officers already serving there. A colonel in another regiment immediately offered us a room over his garage. I had a batman, a soldier servant, a car and a driver, and Mona had engaged a housekeeper. One room was going to be luxury indeed.

It was a big room with an alcove for a bed and a small bathroom, that was all. We created a kitchen outside. It consisted of three wooden boxes on which sat three primus stoves. My driver and soldier servant had, of course, accommodation in the barracks. What became of Zara, our beautiful statuesque black housekeeper each night I have no idea, but she was cooking breakfast by five o'clock every morning in her long silk dress. I left for my military duties at 5.30 every morning, leaving a somewhat bewildered wife to search for somewhere to live. She made remarkable progress and soon announced that the local airline had offered us an empty 'flat' above their office. I don't know how, but a small man with a wheelbarrow appeared and offered to bring us whatever furniture we required. It was an incredible performance. The wardrobe, in fact a wooden cupboard, was too big for the wheelbarrow. Soon the little man appeared bent double with the cupboard on his back!

Remarkably quickly a furnished flat was created. Chairs were covered, silk lampshades fitted and polished floors laid. Fortunately, my doctor wife has all the skills of a handyman and interior decorator. A friend balanced precariously on the balcony wall to fix an aerial and soon had the radio working. A minor drawback was that when the plug was removed in the bath, the water often came up in the kitchen. It really did not matter. It was a different world and an exciting challenge.

Eritrea having been an Italian colony was in some ways very sophisticated, but in other ways backward beyond belief. The Italians had built some remarkable roads and created some beautiful orange and lemon groves. Soon we also had tennis courts, polo fields and hard-mouthed horses that rarely went where we wanted to go, but it was a huge challenge and great fun. At 8000 feet, the climate was glorious with hot days and cool evenings. The sun shone for over forty weeks of the year, the sky was clear blue by day but night fell at 6.00 p.m. It was a strange life which only a few wives were willing to try. We had to make our own lives. Mona came out shooting with my soldiers and soon became a good shot.

I took my company on a training exercise down to the Mansura plain, 4000 feet below Asmara. Mona and one of the other wives came. We slept under the stars with our soldiers and their vehicles in a circle to prevent the camels from walking on our camp beds. We shot for our food and cooked it over charcoal. It was a hard life but a wonderful life, which very few will ever know.

We soon discovered that the forerunner of British Airways – BOAC – had its East African HQ in Asmara. They were a delightful collection of young pilots and their wives. Together we found a beautiful small theatre, obviously abandoned by the fleeing Italians after the Battle of Keren in 1941. It was a strange life for young soldiers and so we did our best to involve them in our lives. We soon found lance-corporals who were delighted to build scenery and become lighting experts or stage hands. A strange man in the Governor's office, the senior civil servant, became a great friend and supporter of our theatre efforts. At one stage, to my wife's horror, he offered to finance me to go on the stage. It would certainly have been a choice between the stage and my wife, and for some reason I chose my wife! We produced almost professional theatre – we found more than one former actress among the BOAC wives. As a very Welsh Welshman, I enjoyed nothing better than playing Danny in Emlyn Williams's *Night Must Fall*.

With a certain amount of time on my hands, I was able, as well, to insert myself into the Asmara Dramatic Society where I eventually played the leading part of Hugo Barine in the society's last production, Jean-Paul Sartre's *Crime Passionnel*. It was produced by Frank Stafford, the immensely civilised senior member of the Governor's staff, and he derived a certain mischievous enjoyment from directing an officer of Her Majesty's forces in the role of a disaffected communist intellectual who had never fired a gun in his life and who was hopelessly indecisive – *quando premere sul grilletto* – *ecco il suo dilemma*.

Asmara, the capital of Eritrea where we had our base, was an Italian colonial town of mainly white buildings and spacious boulevards lined with crimson bougainvillaea and scarlet hibiscus. The main street was surprisingly beautiful – a wide road with palm trees down the middle and with the glamorous name Viale Roma. There were one or two excellent Italian restaurants and there was, as usual, plenty of time for games and sports – in this case mainly riding and tennis. By the simple expedient of getting paired with the best tennis player in the regiment, I got my name on the national doubles trophy, to the somewhat demonstrative chagrin of an Italian pair who clearly felt that their national honour was at stake.

The relaxed and relatively peaceful atmosphere of Eritrea was conducive to some of the schoolboyish horseplay which is never far from the surface in army life. Our Commanding Officer, Charles Cox, was a man of impeccable appearance, not only in uniform, but in what we referred to in the army as 'plain clothes' also. Part of his accoutrement when out of uniform was a bowler hat purchased from a celebrated hatter in St James's. He was inordinately proud of this piece of headgear and was rash enough to wear it when visiting my house in Asmara for a drinks party on Guy Fawkes day. Our evening was made, and his ruined, when his hat was removed from the hall and placed on the lawn with a large firework, known in the army as a thunderflash, under it. When this exploded, the hat was blown about thirty feet into the air; the black outer part was blown into small fragments while the white silk lining slowly descended, parachute-like, and landed at the Colonel's feet. The atmosphere in the officers' mess was cool for several days.

At a more serious level, we fought a desultory and not especially demanding campaign against the *shifta*, the local terrorist group, until 1952 when, under the terms of a United Nations resolution, Eritrea was handed over to Ethiopia and its colourful emperor, Haile Selassie. In the meantime, King George VI had died and on 6th June 1952 we mounted a ceremonial parade, trooping the regimental colours to celebrate the Queen's Birthday. Finally, on 15th September, the battalion formed a guard of honour as the Union Flag was lowered. A few days later we embarked for home, the last British troops to leave Eritrea. It had been an interesting interlude, but not one of great professional significance.

When we returned to Wales we were given a civic welcome and, having been granted the freedom of the Borough of Brecon, we were able to march through the streets of the town with 'colours flying, bayonets fixed and drums beating'. We then moved into a camp nearby for a period of rest and retraining before the next move, which was to the British Army of the Rhine in Germany. However, I was not included in these plans. Instead, I was instructed to join the intelligence staff of BAOR, and on 5th December 1953, my thirty-fourth birthday, I arrived at Bad Oeynhausen to take up my new post.

There also occurred at about this time an event so terrible that, even now, I hesitate to record it. I do so purely because I am sure that it had an impact on our lives so profound that we ourselves cannot entirely measure it. Our daughter, whose arrival my wife and I had longed for with the excitement shared by all expectant parents, died in particularly traumatic circumstances shortly after her birth. It would be foolish to try to describe our feelings here, not least because even the passage of time has only distanced, never fully healed, the pain involved. Although we loved the company of children and my wife, as a paediatrician, was dedicated to the care of the young, we decided not to have more children ourselves.

This decision is worth recording here because it had significant implications for our lives thereafter. On the one hand we have no doubt suffered a deprivation in not having children of our own but, of course, we were freer to work in circumstances where having a family might have been difficult. Much more importantly, we seem to have acquired through friends a number of surrogate children over the years, in whose company and progress we take a very active interest and – almost always – a genuine delight.

4

Back to the Jungle

On arrival at Headquarters, British Army of the Rhine, I was promoted to the rank of major and took charge of the Soviet Army section of the General Staff intelligence section. Contrary to a widely held belief, this branch was not staffed entirely by officers who wore their hair terribly long and affected suede shoes with uniform; it was, in fact, a disadvantage to be of this persuasion since it made contact with the more virile branches of the General Staff a slightly delicate undertaking. On my staff at this particular time, I had two White Russians, one Czech, one Turk, a Canadian major who drank dry martinis for breakfast, the descendant of a grandee of Spain and an officer of the Household Cavalry whose sole function appeared to be to give the whole extraordinary assembly a veneer of social grace.

In the day-to-day business of collecting and processing intelligence, their brains, nurtured at Heidelberg, the Sorbonne, Cambridge and McGill, dealt effortlessly and incisively with the problems presented to them. Let a brief be required on the predilection of some Iron Curtain statesman for smoked salmon and malt whisky, and a paper of consummate skill, documented and authentic, would be produced at the drop of a hat. But let one of them be required to sharpen a pencil, and the office was at once full of blood, shavings and strange Slavonic oaths.

One of my favourite and least predictable officers was George, a White Russian of majestic mien who, when addressing everyone, including the Commander-in-Chief, used the royal plural. He was generous, autocratic, corpulent and, one can only say, entirely unco-ordinated. He possessed a small and almost completely hairless dog of quite squalid habits, and it was his custom to proceed pontifically from the mess to his office, preceded by his infinitesimal dog on a very large and heavy leather leash. The imperial progress was halted only once daily, and that was in the morning, when George would ceremonially halt at the main gate of the headquarters and allow his dog to perform an entirely natural function upon the small sign which read 'Chief of Staff', hereby availing himself by proxy of an opportunity for which many of the junior staff officers of the establishment would have given a great deal.

Now George had, in another member of my staff, a *bête noire* – the other White Russian. The antipathy between the two was a legacy of some obscure social distinction dating from pre-Revolutionary days and it was the habit for each to refer to the other as 'an ill-bred peasant' when talking to other people. When talking to each other, however, their manner of address was liberally seasoned with compliments and honorifics, and a good deal of bowing from the waist was used as punctuation. Alex, my other White Russian, was as volatile and puckish as George was phlegmatic and majestic, and it was, I suppose, inevitable that sooner or later there would be a monumental clash between them.

The occasion was reasonably solemn, or at any rate it was intended to be. Our headquarters was being visited by a delegation from the Soviet Army Mission to the Allied Forces, known officially by its acronym, SOXMIS. I had been asked to entertain some of the delegation at dinner on the night of their arrival and for various reasons, most of them devious, I had invited some members of my remarkable staff. George, it must be explained at this stage, was, amongst many other achievements, a superlative cook, and it had been agreed that in addition to being a member of the dinner party, he would arrange a memorable meal in honour of our guests and, with the palsied assistance of my locally enlisted cook, supervise its preparation before joining us at dinner. Amongst my other guests I had included, by what I now see was a grotesque miscalculation, the mercurial Alex.

The early part of the evening was comparatively free from

incident. It is true that Alex caused one of the guests to bite a piece out of his glass by proposing the health of Nicholas II, and George's dog had mistaken one of a pair of immaculate field boots for a lamp-post; but compared with what was to come, this was merely the small change of social currency. The inevitable champagne had been dispensed and conversation, in several languages, was flowing with satisfactory smoothness, when the door was suddenly flung open with great drama and considerable violence, to disclose framed in the entrance the majestic figure of George, bearing high in the air a tray of the most delicious food of which the central feature was an enormous confection of sugar, contrived most ingeniously in the shape of the Kremlin. With a sense of drama which never deserted him, George advanced slowly down the centre of the room, his intention being to place the food, with its sycophantic centrepiece, on a small table at the far end. Having, however, a large tray under the lowest of his three chins, he was unable to see the ground immediately in front of him, and consequently failed to observe that his dog had curled itself into a ball directly in his path, and was sleeping off the effects of a large glass of vodka administered to it by Alex. The scene which followed had a dream-like quality.

The only person near enough to halt George was Alex, who had no intention of doing anything of the sort. The rest of us, for the few seconds preceding the cataclysm, were too fascinated to move. Inevitably, one of George's enormous feet descended upon the unfortunate dog and in a moment there was a scene of wild disorder. The belated cries of warning from the petrified assembly coincided with the unbelievably loud noise emitted by George's dog; into George's episcopal features there entered a look of pure astonishment as he slid forward and, with the precision of a high-class scrum half, deposited the Kremlin into the arms of the head of the visiting mission. For a second, the General stood there, his arms full of cake, and a sad litter of sandwiches at his feet. After what seemed an appreciable pause, there followed the sound of George's arrival on the floor and peals of uncontrollable laughter from Alex.

The work of the Soviet Army section was, for the most part, a satisfying intellectual challenge. It involved collecting intelligence from various sources, secret and otherwise, on the organisation, movements and training of the Group of Soviet Forces in East Germany, processing and analysing this information and disseminating it to the operational staff with the principal aim of providing early warning of any Soviet move against West Germany. Apart from the daily routine, this involved frequent visits to Berlin to keep in touch with our small intelligence staff there and with the British Mission to the Soviet Forces (BRIXMIS). This meant somewhat spooky train journeys through East Germany in carriages with the windows totally obscured in case we might acquire any information about military installations or movements on the way.

Staff work at Bad Oeynhausen was, as might be expected, relieved by the usual army off-duty activities – sport, dinner parties and amateur theatricals. Once again, I played the part of Danny, the Welsh psychopath, in a production of Emlyn Williams's *Night Must Fall*, a role which in the opinion of my brother officers came perilously close to type-casting.

After two years of this congenial existence, I joined my regiment in Germany when it was preparing to go off to Malaya, once more on counter-terrorist duties. The Commanding Officer, Richard Miers, was planning the advance party. He invited me to join him. As he was taking his wife he said that Mona could accompany me and be useful with a group of raw recruits.

It was a terrible trip. We took four days to reach Singapore, stopping at Beirut, Karachi, and Calcutta en route. Our soldiers were young, pale and easily got sick and unhappy. However, we reached Singapore on a hot, humid evening and I took my apprehensive young soldiers to Kota Tinggi Camp in Malaya for training. I cannot remember what happened to Mona, but she usually managed to take care of herself.

We arrived in Malaya in the eighth year of a state of emergency which had begun in 1948 with the formation of a terrorist group calling itself the Malayan Races Liberation Army, dedicated to the removal of British rule from the Malayan peninsula and the establishment of a communist régime. By now, these communist terrorists (or CTs) had been reduced to between 2000 and 3000 men and women dispersed around the jungle in 'branches' of twenty to thirty. They operated from deep jungle camps, raiding rubber estates and murdering planters, ambushing convoys and terrorising Malayan villages into providing them with food and shelter.

Our task was to destroy them, using the special techniques of jungle warfare, long-range patrols, ambushes and surprise attacks on their camps. After a brief period of training at Kota Tinggi, we moved to the Kluang area of Johore and took over operational responsibility for an area of swamp and dense jungle, roughly twice the size of Glamorgan. Three months of reconnaissance and patrolling in Malaya did much to change my attitude to life in the jungle. Around the world there are various types of jungle, or rain forest, and the distinction between 'primary' and 'secondary' jungle is of special interest to anyone involved in military operations. Primary jungle consists of tall, straight trees, fairly widely spaced, with a clear, sometimes grassy, jungle 'floor' between them, and overhead a canopy of broad-leaved foliage. This creates a sombre, cathedral-like atmosphere, its silence broken only by the occasional cry of a bird or the rushing noise of monsoon rain on the canopy. If the trees are cut down or the primary jungle is cleared in any way, the tropical sun then stimulates a 'secondary' growth, a dense tangle of bush, creeper and grass which rapidly becomes infested with leeches, insects and snakes.

The misery of fighting against the Japanese in the jungles of northern Burma had arisen partly from the fact that much of it took place in this kind of secondary jungle, through which it was often necessary to hack a way with *machetes* or *parangs*. In Malaya we operated mainly in primary jungle, in day-time using compasses for direction-finding. At night movement was impossible and we formed temporary camps by clearing a circular patch of jungle floor, removing twigs, dead bark and earth so that we could move within the circle without noise. The men of the patrol would then sleep around the circumference of the circle, protected by a sentry and the tracker dog which accompanied most patrols. Even if there were terrorists in the same piece of jungle, they could not move without noise and there was something uniquely peaceful about night-time in a jungle camp, with its total silence and total darkness, broken only by the faint glow around the perimeter of the camp caused by the phosphorescence from the decaying vegetation cleared from the centre.

After six months in the jungle, I was so proud of my young soldiers that I asked if Mona could come and stay in my jungle camp for Christmas. My Commanding Officer agreed. Mona, having travelled from Europe with these pale and somewhat apathetic young men, was not too enthusiastic. Somewhat impatiently I suggested she should come and see what they were like now. She rather tiresomely said, 'Would you please tell those young men that your wife does not like soldiers' language and she will be living in the camp.' Of course, I said it was a ridiculous request to young soldiers in the jungle. However, I told them that she was coming and laughingly added her request. They were remarkable young men. My company had changed from pallid youths to tough weather-beaten soldiers and to my utter amazement during her three-week stay not an audible swear word was uttered!

When I returned for a brief period of 'rest and recreation' to Singapore, Mona had acquired a rather horrid modern flat while she looked for a better place. As usual, she meant to do some medical work but was told that as I was operating against terrorists it would be too dangerous. However, the faculty of medicine in the University of Malaya was in Singapore and she was invited to join the staff as a university lecturer. At first she refused on the grounds that she had never been a lecturer and secondly because she did not think that she deserved such a big salary. Needless to say, the Singaporeans found a dour Scot rather difficult to understand and asked what her terms were. She offered to work for six months on a low salary and would then review the situation. In fact, she loved the work and found that teaching a hundred of the most intelligent students of South East Asia was both a challenge and a great pleasure. In many ways it was a great addition to our lives. I spent most of my three years in the Malayan jungle searching for terrorists and, while many soldiers had bored and lonely wives in Singapore, mine was fully occupied and becoming very much part of the Singapore life.

There was, about this time, one particularly unpleasant operation which took place in a combination of swamp and secondary jungle. One of the leading terrorist commanders in the area had set up his headquarters in a swamp approachable only by a concealed causeway. After long planning sessions with our Special Branch adviser, who had provided the intelligence about the existence of the terrorist camp, it was decided that I would lead a large patrol into the area, confirm the exact location of the terrorist camp, and then, by radio and other means, guide a squadron of bomber aircraft to the spot. After a false start which caused us to spend a night lying in a foot of swamp water, the operation (code-named for some inscrutable reason 'Kingly Pile') began with the air strike. In his book on the Malaya campaign, *Shoot to Kill*, our Commanding Officer, Richard Miers, has described the scene: 'All at once a great rectangular rent opened in the backcloth of the jungle, the ground trembled under our feet and through my field-glasses I could see in the cloud of dust and rubble, broken lengths of tree being tossed in the air as though they were matchsticks.'

As I and my patrol were, at that moment, wading through chest-high swamp, I have never quite understood where the dust came from, but the air strike was certainly a complete success. When we eventually reached the terrorist camp we found the bodies of thirteen terrorists, including the commander, a much feared political commissar.

From Kluang, the small Malayan town which had been our base since our arrival, we moved sixty miles north to Segamat, where I mounted a few successful ambushes, including one which involved hiding for several hours curled up in an old coffee bin in a shed known to be used by the local terrorist commanders. We were hoping to entice Yap Kow, a well known local CT officer, out of his hiding place in the swamp, and Special Branch had identified a particular rattan hut, used for collecting coffee beans, where Yap Kow was regularly re-supplied.

Five of us mounted the ambush after a difficult journey through several miles of tracks criss-crossing the rubber estates and plantations. After a number of wrong turns we arrived at the hut shortly before dawn. I shared the coffee bin with another soldier while three others hid under piles of old sacking and broken boxes. Meanwhile two Malayan Special Branch officers, who were dressed as plantation inspectors, swept the hut and generally pretended to be going about their business. In so doing they discovered a package containing cigarettes, a pair of trousers, some rubber-soled shoes, and food – all left for Yap Kow to collect.

Three hours later, they were still sweeping the rubbish around the hut and the two of us crammed in a coffee bin were beginning to wonder whether we would still have the use of our legs when our visitor finally appeared. It was hard to know whether the lack of movement from beneath the old sacking was the sign of high-class jungle training or an indication that the others had finally expired from lack of oxygen and the copious clouds of dust generated by the Special Branch sweepers. We then heard, above the noises of the swamp, some distinct human cries.

It soon became clear that Yap Kow was circling the hut at a great distance, calling out in expectation of some sort of password. The policemen continued to sweep, pretending not to notice, knowing that they were in an extremely exposed position, easy targets for any suspicious CT. Yap Kow's circling drew nearer, but just as we were preparing to break out of hiding, he disappeared into the swamp. Half an hour later, as I was about to call the whole thing off, he reappeared and approached the hut, nervously holding his rifle. He seemed to be torn between the need for food and his sense that something was wrong; his suspicions proved too strong and he retreated once again.

This time we decided to move to a bamboo thicket some twenty-five yards away, since it was clear that Yap Kow had no intention of entering the hut while the police officers were working there. A full hour later one of the patrol signalled that there was someone in the hut, though we had not seen Yap Kow emerge from the swamp. We quickly surrounded our former hiding place in which, sure enough, someone was frantically looking for something. We were particularly anxious to capture Yap Kow because of the information he would have on CT supply lines, which were becoming an increasing problem for the organisation. When the patrol was in position, we called on whoever was inside to surrender, but Yap Kow ran for the swamp and, when he was brought down by a bullet, tried to get a grenade from his pack. He died shortly afterwards.

Many of these operations required meticulous planning, none more so than the operation to capture Ming Lee, the leader of a particularly effective CT unit. We had received intelligence of a rubber tappers' shed which Ming Lee was known to visit to collect supplies and harangue the unfortunate tappers with revolutionary wisdom. Although there was no clear indication of how long it would be before his return, such hard intelligence was comparatively rare and we decided to act on it. I decided to command the ambush party myself because I genuinely preferred this to directing operations from base, although it must be admitted that I was ambitious enough not to be unhappy if this came to the attention of my superior officers.

Having reconnoitred the area we discovered that the shed was surrounded by flat ground with no obvious place for an ambush party. The only possible site was a small clump of bushes, which had the disadvantage of being only a few yards from where the tappers would be working. It would be difficult to sustain an ambush party undetected in these circumstances for any length of time, but, since we had no date for Ming Lee's arrival, we had to be prepared to spend up to ten days there, falling back into the jungle only at night after the rubber tappers had finished their day's work.

Following our usual practice, we built a replica of the hut

and the bushes in a field near our camp. I selected five men whom I knew to be not only fine marksmen, but experienced enough to withstand the strain of this lengthy period of hiding. We then began a whole week of rehearsals, culminating with a full dress rehearsal in which some of the battalion dressed up as rubber tappers, clearly relishing the chance of a theatrical performance. The serious point behind the role-playing was to establish exactly how far forward in the bushes we could afford to be without being detected.

Our patrol moved out before dawn, with feet wrapped in sacking to limit any noise and to avoid leaving any footprints. We took up our positions in the bushes before the rubber tappers arrived for work. When they did they seemed even closer than we had expected and the risk of detection became acute. Whereas on other ambushes we had waited in silence for several days, on this occasion we were lucky. At about 11.30 a.m. on the first day I heard a slight commotion in the shed.

I had made a sufficiently large hole in the foliage to be able to keep an eye on the clearing, and I could now see tappers converging on the shed from all directions. On the track outside were two khaki-uniformed terrorists, complete with neatly rolled puttees, cap and red star badge. I was disappointed to see that neither of them was Ming Lee, and I signalled to the patrol that we would wait. After an hour of agonising tension, the CTs began to shoulder their weapons. It was clear that they were leaving.

I gave the signal and we sprang out and shot the leader; his colleague slipped out of his heavy pack and ran into the jungle. He was soon brought down and by the time I reached him he was obviously seriously injured. A quick look at his wounds showed me that he was dying, but with a massive concentration of effort he was trying to hide some documents which he had pulled from his jacket. His final exertion, almost with his last breath, was to spit in my face. It emerged from Special Branch that these two were well known senior members of Ming Lee's group. The one carrying the documents had been the CT leader's personal bodyguard and it was only the good luck of an injured foot that had kept Ming Lee himself away from the shed that morning.

It was for this and other activities in Malaya that I, along with many other colleagues in the regiment, was decorated – in my case with the Military Cross. I hesitate to mention this, not through any false modesty, but for two more substantial reasons. First, anyone who has been involved in active service will know that operations invariably depend on teamwork, and therefore to say that singling out individuals is unsatisfactory is more than a self-deprecating cliché. Second, any soldier faced with recounting his experiences is liable to fall into one of two traps: either he will be modest to the point of saying that he did nothing at all, or he will give the impression that he won the war single-handed. My niece, Ann, one of the most faithful members of my fan club, who was later to accompany my wife and me to Buckingham Palace when I received the decoration from Her Majesty the Queen, was convinced that the latter was somewhere near the truth.

All this sharp-end soldiering came to an end in the summer of 1957 when I was recalled to England to attend a course at the Joint Services Staff College, then at Latimer House near the Chalfont villages in Buckinghamshire. I did not see Malaya again for twenty-five years when, by way of a postscript to this episode in the jungle, Mona and I returned to southern Johore in 1980 to re-visit some of these sites. The clearing which had formed our base camp was now a four-star hotel, but further into the jungle the rubber tappers' hut which we had ambushed was still there. It was a little more decayed but otherwise unchanged; we sat and had some jungle rations, more nourishing than those which had been available the first time around. We then returned to Singapore to pay a call on the Prime Minister, Lee Kuan Yew, another actor from that period of history who had become a good friend over the years. We concluded an unashamedly nostalgic trip with a dinner to celebrate Mona's birthday, which was served with extravagant ritual at a lone table in the garden of the Raffles Hotel.

The Joint Services Staff College, which has since undergone

changes of name and location, was then an institution designed to train officers already qualified in the staff work of their own services for staff appointments on joint service staffs and for higher staff appointments in their own services and, to quote the directive from the Chiefs of Staff, 'in so doing to develop mutual understanding and a common doctrine between the services and to evolve a standardised system of staff work'. All this sounds formidably earnest but, as I wrote in a special edition of the College gazette in 1983, Latimer was not an institution of unrelieved solemnity. The pursuit of intellectual enlightenment was tempered with a realisation that much of the human condition is irretrievably ridiculous; and that there are few spectacles *more* irretrievably ridiculous than that of a body of middle-aged men in pursuit of intellectual enlightenment. Yet behind the self-deprecating refusal to take life too seriously lay a basic purpose which was very serious indeed. Latimer was, for many service officers, the first real experience of self-generated intellectual enquiry. The service academies, the single-service staff colleges and the specialist institutions, all tend to be pre-occupied with the acquisition of useful knowledge, the indispensable stock-in-trade of the professional officer.

This is not to suggest that useful knowledge was an entirely unknown commodity at Latimer. It is inconceivable that all those distinguished visiting lecturers were not transmitting *something*, although it was not always easy to identify precisely what it was. In parenthesis it is interesting to reflect upon the manner and style of some of those visiting lecturers. Every Latimer graduate will readily recall the politician of radical persuasion, overcompensating earnestly for a sense of unease at being exposed to the military establishment. 'Every man,' said Dr Johnson, 'thinks meanly of himself for not having been a soldier.' Then there were the newspaper editors and academic strategists, secure in their cocoons of intellectual certainty – 'My mind is made up: please do not confuse me with the facts'; and occasionally the urbane, worldly figure, often a diplomat or Oxford don, dispensing perceptive and subtle reflections, often without reference to a single note. It was one such visitor who demolished the author of a particularly asinine question with a single Delphic comment. 'Upon an assumption so precarious,' he declared, 'it would be difficult to erect a logical edifice of any substantial proportions.'

As interesting as these visitors were to the amateur social scientist, it was when the College closed its doors upon the world and turned inwards that it became most interesting. The examination of problems in syndicates often provided bizarre insights into the complexities of group and individual psychology. Leaders emerged, much to the dismay of those whose principal aim was a quiet life; thinkers displayed such prodigies of lateral thought that they never went anywhere but sideways; some of the contributions to logical enquiry were in direct line of descent from Humpty-Dumpty's Olympian assertion that 'Words mean what I want them to mean, neither more nor less.'

Over all these activities loomed, if that is not too sombre a word, the shadow of the directing staff. These somewhat equivocal figures – not quite instructors but much more than just observers and assessors – established the intellectual and academic climate of Latimer, often with remarkable impact. The course upon which I imposed my own disruptive influence was blessed with at least one DS of quite remarkable qualities. Although he was a Gunner, he was a man of civilised tastes, subtle wit and great compassion. It would be invidious and possibly embarrassing to identify him, but it would be wrong to allow his influence to go unrecorded. Although he had a relentless eye for the mediocre or the undistinguished, his strictures were never hurtful or dismissive; and he was able to find something funny even in such apparently unpromising concepts as 'the fleet in being' or the distant application of military power. It was this relaxed mixture of self-parody and the pursuit of excellence which, for at least one Latimer graduate, made the Joint Services Staff College such a rewarding and significant experience. It was not so much the acquisition of a new level of understanding about strategic doctrines, defence policy, or the highest direction of war; it was rather a confirmation that the profession of arms need not be enclosed or philistine; that 'intellectual' was not necessarily a term of abuse; and that the unlimited liability of the serviceman did not absolve him from the duties and concerns of the citizen.

The JSSC was, in a sense, a substitute for the university education which the war had denied me. For the first time I became interested in the idea of an academic life. Although I suspect that I would have been constitutionally unsuited to a career devoted entirely to book-work, I was able to develop interests in philosophy and military history which had previously been confined to a few leisure hours during active service.

It was at Latimer that I began, for the first time, seriously to shape and organise some of the analysis of the threat posed to the West by the USSR, which was to occupy my thoughts and preoccupations in the future. Indeed, in the course of the 'foreign studies' phase of the curriculum I wrote, ostensibly from the point of view of a Deputy Secretary of the Communist Party of the Soviet Union, a report on the long term policy of the Soviet Union addressed to the Central Committee. This analysis of Soviet foreign policy, which drew favourable comment from the directing staff, contained a section on disarmament which was to have a considerable resonance in my negotiations with the Soviet Union ten years later. My immediate responsibilities, however, were to be of a different kind. At the end of the Latimer course, I was posted to the 1st Battalion of the Royal Welch Fusiliers, which was about to leave for a tour of duty in Cyprus.

<h1 style="text-align:center">5</h1>

Notes from a Small Island

Cyprus, a Mediterranean island of great beauty, which has since become an international tourist resort, was at this time in the grip of a profound political and military crisis. The island had been under British administration since the end of the nineteenth century and had, indeed, been annexed to the British crown in 1914, when war broke out with Turkey. In 1931, a movement demanding *enosis*, or union with Greece, gathered momentum among the Greek Cypriot population and there were some civil disturbances. The movement became more serious and highly organised after the war, when Archbishop Makarios, the patriarch of the Orthodox Church in Cyprus, emerged as its leader. Civil unrest gave way to violence in the 1950s when the National Organisation of Cypriot Struggle (in Greek *Ethniki Organosis Kypriakou Agonos* or EOKA) led by a former Greek Army officer, Colonel Georgios Grivas, began a campaign of terrorist attacks on British military establishments, servicemen and their families.

Sir John Harding was appointed Governor in 1955, emergency regulations were introduced and in March 1956, Archbishop Makarios was arrested and deported to the Seychelles. When I arrived in Cyprus with the Royal Welch Fusiliers in the spring of 1958, the terrorist activities had taken on a new dimension with the intervention of the Turkish Cypriot community demanding partition of the island. I took my company straight to Kakopetria, a village 3000 feet up in the hills, known to be a centre of EOKA activity. I set up my headquarters and began a programme of internal security operations involving patrols, ambushes and 'cordon and search' of neighbouring villages.

61

The basic minor tactics were similar to those we had evolved in the jungle. The great difference was in what is known in military language as 'the terrain'. Cyprus is an island of clear skies, mild winters, hot summers and low, erratic rainfall. Operations in this environment were usually pleasant and, for disciplined and intelligent troops, reasonably undemanding, except for those moments of extreme danger and crisis inseparable from any confrontation with well-armed and determined guerrilla forces.

Our operations took us from the Troodos Mountains, rising to Mount Olympus at over 6000 feet, to Kyrenia Harbour on the north coast of the island with its twelfth-century castle, the beautiful abbey of Bellapais and a crusader castle overlooking the sea. The mountains were often snow-covered, and one of the great joys of our recreation times was to ski in deep powder at Troodos in the morning, travel down the mountain roads to the coastal plain, arriving at Kyrenia in time for some water-skiing in the afternoon and an excellent dinner at the Harbour Club in the evening.

Even the counter-terrorist operations, which could be as violent and unpleasant as any in Malaya, Northern Ireland or Kenya, were not without their lighter moments. The most spectacular and violent phase of the emergency in Cyprus came just before its end. At the time I was in command of a small mixed force of armoured cars, Royal Marines and infantry. We were carrying out anti-terrorist operations in and around a group of remote villages in the Troodos Mountains. In particular, one of these villages, small, squalid and sinister, was known to be a base and centre of communications for a mountain group of EOKA.

Apart from the mountain group itself, which took to its hiding places in the hills at night or at the approach of any of our patrols, there was, in this village, a strong support group which provided food, shelter, clothing and information for the terrorists. It was organised and dominated by two colourful characters whom we came to regard with a mixture of exasperation and affection. Between them, Sophie and Father

Andreas caused us more trouble than all the armed terrorists in the area.

Sophie, so called by the troops for her resemblance to a celebrated film actress, was the acknowledged leader of the village women. She was young and pretty and was employed, when she was not engaged in harassing the security forces, by a large industrial firm in Nicosia. Unlike the less sophisticated village women, she dressed like a fugitive from a coffee bar, in sweater and short, brightly coloured skirts. She was quickly on the spot if a military operation took place in the village, organising the women into some form of activity designed to make our task as difficult as possible. In addition to being an accomplished agitator, Sophie was a most eloquent spitter. Her favourite gesture of contempt for the security forces was to spit, with astonishing accuracy, just close enough to a soldier or vehicle to be intolerably insolent, but never so close that we could do anything about it.

Father Andreas was the village priest, a tall and elegant man, his blue-black beard and smooth brown face giving him an air of youthful distinction. He was known to hold an important post in the underground movement. His attitude, unlike Sophie's, was one of scrupulous politeness. In all his dealings with us he was invariably bland, non-committal and courteously obstructive. Up to this time it had suited the authorities to leave him at large – it was always a delicate matter to arrest a priest, even when he was suspected of being an EOKA supporter, and in any case Father Andreas had often, quite unknowingly, given us useful information by his movements and activities. However, an all-out assault on the local terrorist organisation was now being mounted as part of an island-wide operation, and one day we received instructions to pick up Andreas and his village group and to keep them out of circulation for a while.

So, one warm and moonless summer night, we left our silent mountain camp and moved quietly across the hills, through the pine trees and the vineyards, to the sleeping village. Quickly we surrounded it, and when the sky grew pale and the village below us began to stir, I took a small party in through the cordon. First, I toured the narrow village streets in my scout car, which had joined me at dawn. Ahmed, my interpreter, using an electric amplifier, made the formal announcement that the village was surrounded, a curfew was in force, and no one was to leave his house until ordered to do so. I then took a small detachment to the village school and prepared to set up the organisation for screening the entire male population of the village. Screening was the term used for the procedure of questioning the inhabitants of a village and examining their identity cards and passes. This would be done by a team of police and intelligence officers who would arrive later in the morning. It was designed in this case partly to ensure that no known EOKA men were living in the village, and partly to conceal until the last moment the main object of our visit.

As soon as this was underway, I again toured the village, which by now had a pair of beady and hostile eyes at every shuttered window. This time I ordered all men between the ages of sixteen and sixty to report to the village school, and soon a procession of sullen, unshaven Cypriots trailed through the dusty streets in the grey dawn. They passed into the wired enclosure set up for screening and resigned themselves to yet another of those familiar and dreary operations known as 'cordon and search'. I sat on the front of my scout car and watched them. Suddenly, my sergeant major touched my arm. 'Been hiding the detonators under the altar, I expect,' he said, as the bland and bearded priest submitted impassively to a search and went to sit amongst his flock.

Soon everything was ready and as the sun began to climb over the vineyards there was a familiar sound from the east and a helicopter sailed over the hills, circled the village and landed expertly on the football field, a half a mile away. My Land Rover had gone to meet it and soon it returned with the intelligence team from police headquarters all freshly scrubbed and starched.

'No policewoman?' I said, as they moved toward the screening enclosure.

'No, sorry,' said the senior police officer. 'They are all required at the Nicosia end – I tried to get one, but nothing doing.'

'A pity,' I said. 'We are about to have trouble from Sophie today – especially when we pick up the holy man.'

The screening now went on quickly and methodically, while I sent out patrols to enforce the village curfew. Soon the main screening enclosure was emptying rapidly. Most of the villagers were passing straight into a second enclosure to await the end of the operation before returning to their homes, but a handful of hard-faced young men were kept separately under guard. They were suspected EOKA contact men, to be taken away later for further interrogation.

Suddenly everywhere – amongst the soldiers, the policemen and the villagers – there was an almost imperceptible heightening of tension. Father Andreas, having been screened by the intelligence team, was being led over to join the guarded group of suspects. An excited, threatening murmur, like a crowd scene in a play, broke out amongst the men of the village. At the same moment there was a shout from my signaller; I went over to the scout car and picked up the radio headphones. It was the platoon commander from Sophie's sector of the village.

'Sophie's out,' he said. 'She's persuaded some of the women to break curfew. There's not much I can do.'

He was right. There *was* nothing to do except to get the operation finished and get Father Andreas out of the village before the entire female population descended on us and began their systematic attempts to turn a smooth and uneventful operation into a shambles of bad temper and frustration.

But we were too late. Over the brow of the hill behind the schoolhouse came the familiar rabble of women, making the peculiar nerve-racking noise which only a collection of Cypriot women know how to make – a dissonant confusion of screeches and hisses and wails. They were, of course, being led and encouraged by the shrieking, spitting figure of Sophie, swinging her bright yellow skirt and tossing her long black hair. When they saw Father Andreas in his little group kept apart from the rest of the men, they knew immediately what was happening. There was a moment of comparative silence as they absorbed the fact, then the deafening chorus started up again.

Quickly I called up a reserve platoon which I had kept waiting behind the church. They lined up, shoulder to shoulder, in a tight cordon around the village men. The women, by now a hundred or more of them, pressed forward to within about five yards of the cordon. There they stood, waving their arms and quacking insanely; Sophie, dancing up and down in a disjointed sort of way, hurled abuse at the unimpressed soldiers.

I told my interpreter to tell the women that if they kept quiet and went home, the operation would soon be over and their men would be released. If they did not, I said, I was prepared to stay there indefinitely and see who got tired first. When he had finished, the uproar diminished by a few decibels and Sophie came towards me. My batman, a tough and taciturn North Welshman, moved towards her with the purposeful air of a man about to put a badly behaved child in its place.

'It's all right,' I said. 'Let her come.'

Sophie walked up to me, spat automatically at a point about three feet from my left foot, and said, 'We shall not go home until you release our priest.'

I informed her, coldly, that I did not propose to bargain with her, and that if she did not go home at once and take her Amazons with her, I would be glad to set up camp in the village and wait until they came to their senses. Her reply, in Greek, was loud and penetrating. There was a stunned silence from Ahmed, the interpreter.

'Well,' I said, 'what did she say?'

Ahmed's face was deep red. 'It is very difficult to translate, sir,' he said. 'In any case, what she suggests you should do to yourself is physically impossible.'

I turned away and gave some instructions to the reserve platoon commander. A lorry was brought through the cordon and Father Andreas and his companions were put aboard it. At once Sophie reacted. She shouted at the women and quickly they crowded on to the narrow road, the only road leading from the village. There, some sitting, some standing with arms folded, they waited.

This, I thought, is very difficult. If I ordered the lorry to drive towards them they might break; but if they didn't, I would have to order it to stop and then we should all look very silly. I could use tear gas, but that would cause an uproar in the press and EOKA would make great propaganda out of it. I could, of course, put on a really big show and go through the solemn ritual known as 'dispersing a riotous assembly'; but the final sanction in this case is to open fire if all else fails, and the women knew as well as I did that I had no intention of doing that. However, every minute in which I did nothing would increase their confidence, and I might eventually be faced with the equally unpleasant alternative of using force against the women, or releasing the priest. Suddenly, as I looked at the defiant Sophie, I had an idea.

I seized the microphone of the wireless set and spoke for a few moments to the pilot of the helicopter on the football field. Almost at once his engine started and soon he soared into the air over the village, climbed to about two hundred feet and drifted gently over our heads. Then, gradually, he began to come down – very, very slowly, towards the crowd of women on the road. Under Sophie's militant glare they stayed firm as the noise of the whirling rotor blades grew deafeningly loud. Sophie now began to look worried. The helicopter was about fifty feet above her head, still sinking gently and she was not quite sure what we were up to. The troops, to whom a helicopter was as familiar as a three-ton truck, knew what to expect and were looking on with expressions of scarcely contained delight.

Suddenly, the helicopter reached the critical height for which we had all been waiting. The violent down-draught from the rotors hit the ground and at once pandemonium broke loose. The air was full of dust, small stones and loose bits of female attire. Sophie, directly under the helicopter, tried frantically but vainly for a while to prevent her short full skirt from flying over her head, but eventually she broke and ran. Shrieking wildly, in a cloud of dust and lacy underwear, she made for the shelter of the schoolhouse. At once the women, leaderless and defeated, fled from the whirlwind and, keening like frightened geese, ran for their homes. The helicopter climbed again and circled lazily over us while we quickly, but deliberately, drove away the priest and his companions, dismantled the screening enclosures and sent the men of the village back to their homes. We then withdrew, with dignity and unconcealed triumph, from the village.

I returned there a few days later with a routine patrol. As my scout car turned the first corner into the village, Sophie was walking along the street towards us. She saw us, stopped, hesitated and then turned and scuttled into a nearby house, followed by the unsympathetic laughter of the soldiers in the lorry behind me. She didn't even stop to spit.

During many operations of this kind we were fortunate to have as Governor of Cyprus, and our political master, Sir Hugh Foot, one of the sons of the radical liberal politician, Isaac Foot. Hugh had been a colonial administrator since 1929 and, to quote the *Dictionary of National Biography*: 'for over thirty years he had moved with authority in lands of daunting complexity and engineered their metamorphosis from colonies into free countries, working as a mediator rather than a ruler.' This is a more accurate and perceptive assessment of Hugh Foot's career and achievements than Harold Macmillan's later somewhat disobliging description of him as 'a colonial governor who ran out of colonies'.

In Cyprus he practised his long-held principle that the way to teach people responsibility was to give it to them. He respected the natural dignity of the Cypriots, both Greek and Turkish, and became a familiar, if slightly eccentric figure, as he appeared amongst the villagers, with a minimum of security and protocol, often on his horse, a massive grey almost as impressive as the Governor himself. He had a relaxed and understanding relationship with the military units on the island and was a welcome guest at many service functions.

Later, in 1964, when the Wilson government took office, he

was appointed a Minister of State, elevated to the House of Lords and sent as Permanent UK Representative at the United Nations. As I was appointed a Minister of State at the same time and had to attend the UN General Assembly, confusion inevitably arose. At one official dinner in New York at which I was the main speaker, I was introduced by the chairman of the event as Lord Caradon. He later apologised saying that the speaker was in fact Lord Chalfont, 'but, in any case, most of you will know him better as Sir Hugh Foot.'

During this period, Hugh and his wife also provided the stage for one of George Brown's memorable cameo performances. On a visit to the UN when he was Foreign Secretary, George, having been liberally refreshed at a dinner party given in his honour by the Permanent Representative, began to eat, absentmindedly but with apparent relish, the plastic imitation grapes which formed part of Sylvia Caradon's lovingly arranged table centrepiece. Having crunched his way happily through a number of these objects, George sat back looking rather pleased with himself. Lady Caradon's reaction was one of total bewilderment, but Hugh rose to the occasion with an appropriately delicate allusion to the grapes of wrath. Hugh Caradon's stern, even puritanical moral sense was not allowed to inhibit a sparkling and irreverent sense of humour or the smile which transformed his normally craggy and impassive face.

Caradon was one of the few really *good* men who cross one's path from time to time on the international scene and it was largely due to his efforts that, after years of violence, unrest and frustrating diplomacy, Cyprus eventually won independence in 1960, with Britain retaining two sovereign bases on the island. Meanwhile, the Royal Welch Fusiliers returned home and I had been posted to the War Office, with the rank of lieutenant-colonel, to take charge of the department which was planning the long-term manpower requirements of the army in the wake of the famous Duncan Sandys reorganisation set in train by his 1957 Defence White Paper.

The War Office was a formidably austere and anonymous building. There is a story, possibly but by no means certainly apocryphal, of a Foreign Office official walking along Whitehall during the war and being asked politely by a visitor which side the War Office was on and replying with equal courtesy, 'Ours, I hope.' Although this possibly went a little too far, there was always in those days something of a mystery about what went on in that massive complex of buildings. When I arrived there to assume my new appointment (officially described as General Staff Officer Grade 1, Staff Duties 4) the officer from whom I was taking over greeted me with the words, 'The most important thing to realise about this place is that it is a government department, not a military headquarters. Its entire dissimilarity to the latter will quickly become obvious to you.'

He was, of course, absolutely right. I spent the next two years more as a civil servant than a staff officer. Although the business of manpower planning involved a good deal of routine number crunching, it opened up for me the whole Whitehall world of Treasury arm-twisting, interdepartmental horse-trading and the stratospheric hypotheses of the Foreign Office planning department and the Joint Intelligence Committee.

It was fashionable for serving officers to regard their posting to Whitehall as a tedious necessity, something to be endured on the way up the military ladder. My own attitude was rather different. Although there was certainly a good deal of bureaucracy to contend with, my time in the War Office was invaluable in filling gaps in my experience, much as the JSSC had done in its own way.

For the first time I was faced with the detailed economic consequences of the military activities of a peacetime army. This forced me to add to my consideration of the strategic uses of military power the essential component of the public finances, a good preparation for political arguments in this area. At a more mundane level, I was forced – somewhat against my natural inclinations – to take notice of the details of balance sheets, a good preparation for business, even if I did not always apply this new-found skill as assiduously as I might have done.

My labours were enlivened by the collaboration of two remarkable Royal Artillery officers. Harry Tuzo went on to complete a distinguished military career as Chief of Staff Northern Army Group and General Officer Commander in Chief Northern Ireland. Harry became, and remained until his death in 1998, a firm friend. His successor, Paddy Victory, was less fortunate and less successful but, in his own way, just as supportive and entertaining. A nine to five job at a desk in Whitehall does, after all, call for occasional light relief. However, in the summer of 1961, my days at the War Office and at the same time my service career, came to an unexpected end.

6

Printing House Square

When I left the army in 1961 to become the defence correspondent of *The Times*, my interest in military strategy and my acceptance of the use of armed force as an instrument of foreign policy had not yet been clouded by any idealistic thoughts of general disarmament or even any sophisticated theories of arms control. Everything I wrote in my early days at Printing House Square was based on the simple premise that, as I wrote in a leading article in the summer of 1961, there was a need 'for strong conventional forces to complement Britain's contribution to the nuclear deterrent'.

My translation from the army to *The Times* was almost as unpremeditated as my subsequent conscription into politics. One morning, as I sat glumly in the War Office contemplating some arcane problem of war and peace establishments, my telephone rang and the caller identified herself as the secretary to the Editor of *The Times*. Would I, she would like to know, accept an invitation to luncheon with the Editor, who wished to discuss with me a matter of some importance.

In those days service officers did not consort much with journalists, who were regarded as a somewhat dubious lot, not on any account to be trusted with information more sensitive than the time of day or the state of the weather. However, I had met John Grant, the defence correspondent of *The Times*, on several occasions and had found him knowledgeable and sympathetic about the problems which faced the armed forces in the years following the abolition of national service. Assuming that his Editor wanted to pursue some matter of this kind, I accepted the invitation and was required to present myself at the Ritz Hotel at the appointed time and date. The choice of the Ritz was explained, somewhat apologetically, on the grounds that the Editor's club, the Athenaeum, was closed for the holiday. Knowing a little of the catering arrangements at the two establishments, it was a circumstance which I was prepared to accept with a degree of equanimity.

It was my first meeting with Sir William Haley, who had become Editor of *The Times* in 1952 after eight years as Director General of the BBC. He had been the last defender of the Reithian faith in an organisation which now tends to derive its values more from show business and tabloid journalism. Haley was a man of disarmingly modest appearance and manner. His voice was quiet, with a slight lisp, and I was reminded of an encounter at the other Ritz, in Paris, a half a century earlier, between Edmond Jaloux and Marcel Proust after which Jaloux remarked that 'one felt that one was in the presence of somebody who was both a child and a very old mandarin.'

When we were seated in the restaurant at a table looking out over Green Park, he asked me if I would like wine with my lunch. This seemed a reasonable enough suggestion, but when I said that I would, he informed me austerely that he did not take alcohol but that he would not mind if I did. His brief instructions to the *sommelier* resulted in the appearance of what must have been the smallest bottle of claret in the Ritz cellars, rather like those dispensed by the British Airways cabin crew on a flight to Brussels. Consuming even this modest beverage induced in me a sense of wild dissipation as Haley delicately dissected a small portion of sole and sipped his mineral water.

After a desultory conversation about the state of the universe in general and of the British army in particular, he told me that he was proposing to promote his defence correspondent to a higher editorial post and asked me if I would be interested in resigning my commission and taking his place on *The Times*. He said that he had read some articles which I had written in service journals and had decided that I was potential *Times* material. He reflected that the last military correspondent of the paper to have been an ex-officer was Basil Liddell Hart. He considered this to have been a successful appointment and added, with only the faintest hint of mockery, that *The Times* would regard it as a considerable triumph to have recruited a colonel instead of a mere captain.

After lunch I was driven back to the War Office in Haley's large and opulent editorial limousine. On the way he suggested that I take a few days to think about his proposal. If I wanted to discuss salary and other terms of employment, which he seemed to regard as relatively unimportant factors in arriving at a decision, I was to speak to the General Manager, who was responsible for such housekeeping matters. As I stepped out of the car at the Whitehall entrance of the War Office, a general of fearsome eminence emerged, accompanied by his aide-de-camp and another staff officer, clearly about to embark on some military errand of great national importance. He stopped, regarded me for a moment with the astonished air of someone confronted with an unnatural phenomenon, and then swept by, conferring with his ADC in a manner which hinted that explanations might be in order at some future date.

Haley's approach had, in fact, come at a critical juncture in my military career. I had just been gazetted as a brevet lieutenant-colonel, a modified form of accelerated promotion which was generally accepted to be reserved for officers destined eventually to reach high rank in the army. I had already passed through the Staff College and the Joint Services Staff College and confidently expected that when I came to the end of my tour of duty in the War Office, I would be given command of the regular battalion of my regiment, the South Wales Borderers, with whom I had served for over twenty years. It must be remembered that in those days, the principal ambition of every infantry officer was to command his regiment; any preferment after that was just icing on the cake.

At this moment, however, I was informed that a brother officer had been selected to command the regiment. Although his professional qualifications were comparatively modest, his place in the regimental family gave him the precedence of favourite son. I was offered command of a battalion of the

King's African Rifles. Incidentally, I was subsequently informed that the regimental sergeant major of this battalion was a warrant officer named Idi Amin; and although this would have meant nothing to me at the time, with hindsight it might have had some interesting implications. The Military Secretary's Department, which dealt with officers' postings, explained to me with all the unconvincing enthusiasm of a used-car salesman trying to get rid of an old banger, that this was a challenging appointment more likely to lead to rapid promotion than the routine business of commanding a British infantry regiment based in the United Kingdom. So, when Sir William Haley appeared in his black and yellow Rolls, his proposition had to be considered against the alternative of three years in East Africa, commanding African troops, with whom I had never served before, and the knowledge that I would never command my own regiment.

There followed a few days of heart-searching as I contemplated the potential hazards of life outside the structured, protective family life of the army. Eventually, I decided to pay a call on the General Manager of *The Times*, a jovial and friendly man who explained what my terms of service would be. The size of the salary which he mentioned brought back memories of the bottle of wine at the Ritz. Indeed, it reinforced Haley's unspoken but clear implication that writing for *The Times* was to be regarded largely as its own reward. I was to be paid £1750 a year, with an expense allowance of £250. I would be entitled to four weeks annual holiday.

Eventually, in spite of this modest remuneration, the opportunity to write on military matters for what was still, in those days, a great national newspaper, proved to be more attractive than the rival charms of East Africa, and I went back to the Editor to tell him that I would like to accept the appointment. I then went through the formalities of resigning my commission and on 1st June 1961 presented myself at Printing House Square. Opinion on my decision to leave the army was not universally approving: a former colonel of the regiment, generally known to his soldiers as 'Pop', declared that 'Jones obviously wants his arse kicked.'

On the following day there appeared the first article by the new defence correspondent, announcing a visit by the Minister of Defence, Mr Harold Watkinson, to the British Army of the Rhine, and commenting on the reasons for it. The only immediate reaction was a disagreeable comment from the Army Public Relations Department who in those days reacted tetchily to any newspaper report which they had not initiated themselves.

The old Printing House Square was a building of Dickensian aspect and, for a national newspaper, somewhat limited facilities. My first impression was one of quite remarkable confusion and disarray. The entire place was littered with copy paper, discarded cuttings, teacups and back numbers of *The Times*. To someone accustomed to the almost clinical tidiness of military establishments, my first day at *The Times* gave rise to distinct feelings of foreboding. They were, however, dispelled to some extent by the appearance of the court correspondent, Dermot Morrah, dressed in knee-breeches, silk stockings and all the trappings of ceremonial grandeur. He had, in fact, just returned from a great occasion at Buckingham Palace, but for some time I remained convinced that this was the normal working dress for the court correspondent of *The Times*.

My own appearance was a source of some interest and occasional amusement to my new colleagues. I had not yet abandoned the traditional London dress and accoutrements of an army officer – dark pin-striped suit, striped shirt with a stiff white collar, regimental tie, tightly rolled umbrella and a bowler hat, the last item essential for returning the salute of the sentry on duty at the Horse Guards. I only began to abandon this in favour of more relaxed apparel after a comment by Sir William Haley who had invited me to lunch with him to talk about my early contributions to the paper. When I appeared in his office for the occasion attired in my habitual version of what the army refers to as 'plain clothes', he glanced briefly at my umbrella and said very gently, 'You know, Mr Gwynne Jones, I scarcely think it will be raining in the Athenaeum.'

The office which I had been allotted in Printing House Square was a smallish room with an open fire place, four desks and piles of inevitable journalistic clutter. I shared it with three other 'specialist writers', one of them a sardonic Irishman who wrote most of the main political leading articles. Owen Hickey was a master of graceful and incisive prose and a stimulating conversationalist with a gently deflating sense of humour. It was by an assiduous study of his style that I soon began to acquire a certain facility in the tropes and cadences of the authorised *Times* syntax.

There were two other main influences on my developing journalistic style. One was the *Times Style Book*, a small pamphlet designed to inoculate the paper's writers against such diseases as split infinitives, unattached participles and double passives. The other was the Editor himself, who could detect a solecism in a piece of copy with no more than a cursory glance. He seemed to possess some kind of hidden syntactical geiger-counter which told him instantly that somewhere within the thousand words in front of him there lurked a hybrid derivative or an irrelevant allusion. My first encounter with his fastidious attention to glottologic detail came early in my apprenticeship. He was reading a draft of a leading article I had written and there was a moment when I detected a sharp intake of breath accompanied by an expression of acute pain. He pointed out that I had used the expression 'stemming from' when I really meant 'springing from' or 'arising from'. His brief dissertation on the etymology and correct use of the verb 'to stem' is still, more than thirty years later, vivid in my memory.

Even more impressive was his code of journalistic ethics, fiercely puritanical and uncompromising. At an editorial conference at the time of the Profumo affair, one of the leader-writers was adventurous enough to disagree with Haley on a matter of moral judgement, protesting confidently, 'But surely, Sir William, there are two sides to every question.' The Editor regarded him for a moment with a mixture of sadness and disbelief, and then said quietly 'No, Mr —, there are not two sides to *every* question. Some things are evil, and cruel, and ugly, and no amount of fine writing on your part will make them good, or kind or beautiful.' The first leading article in *The Times* the following morning was headed 'It *is* a moral issue.'

The Profumo story at this time was the subject of much debate in Printing House Square. In March 1963 I had been offered what could, I suppose, have been the 'scoop' of a lifetime. The source was Colonel George Wigg, a Labour Member of Parliament who had been a prolific provider of information for some time. He had a particular interest in the army and set himself up as a guardian of its interests. He would soon alert me if he or his colleagues felt that anything was awry in the War Office. He was also fascinated – almost to the point of obsession – with security and secret intelligence and felt an irresistible temptation to interfere with its workings.

The flow of information was not one-way. George frequently asked for guidance on broader issues of defence and nuclear strategy, which he passed on to Harold Wilson and Labour Party policy-makers. I was more than happy to supply this advice, and did the same for the other political parties. I believe it was through this connection, and through George in particular, that my name was suggested to Harold as a suitable Minister to handle disarmament negotiations when he came to form a government. Indeed, as I have recorded elsewhere, Harold's opening words to me were, 'Well, you've been writing about this stuff for long enough, so it's about time you *did* something about it...'

George was an extraordinary character: rough in almost every aspect. He later became the Labour government's security guru and had a reputation as an unscrupulous political fixer. In his favour it must be said that, despite his fascination with the world of espionage, there was nothing shady about his political manoeuvring. He was an up-front rogue and did his spin-doctoring with a sledgehammer.

It was therefore no surprise to get a call from George one day in March 1963, asking me to meet him at a seedy pub in

Leicester Square. In these grimy but, for his purposes, suitably murky surroundings, he told me that Jack Profumo, Secretary of State for War, was involved in a sexual relationship with a Miss Christine Keeler, who was simultaneously involved with a Russian diplomat. Both these affairs were being conducted in a flat belonging to a Dr Stephen Ward, who also had a villa on Viscount Astor's estate at Cliveden. MI5 believed that Profumo would be forced to resign because of the security implications, but that he would be allowed to do so discreetly and to retire gracefully into a new life in the City. However, after a bizarre incident in which shots were fired at Christine Keeler's flat, letters were found there, written to her by Profumo on War Office notepaper. These were now in the hands of the newspaper then known as the *Sunday Pictorial*, now the *Sunday People*.

I relayed this moderately sensational piece of information to the Editor, and it is an interesting reflection on the changing standards of journalistic ethics that, in spite of the total reliability of my sources of information, we decided not to publish anything without first contacting Profumo. Pursuing an excessively formal approach, Oliver Woods, an assistant editor, wrote to the Secretary of State seeking a meeting and received a reply dated 14th March, a week after my meeting with Wigg, saying that he, Profumo, would contact *The Times* when he 'had got the Army Estimates out of the way'. However, the following day his resignation was reported in the *Daily Express*, whose procedures were less stately than those of Printing House Square. Haley was totally unconcerned that *The Times* had stepped back from a remarkable scoop. There were, he insisted, more important considerations for the Editor of a serious newspaper.

This moral dogmatism was, however, the full extent of Haley's editorial hegemony. For the next three years I had the freedom to write on any military or strategic matter which attracted my attention. I was writing two or three major articles a month, dealing with nuclear strategy, the control of nuclear weapons, the importance of strong conventional forces to raise the 'nuclear threshold', the strength and composition of Soviet armed forces and a number of issues directly involved with the strength and effectiveness of Britain's armed forces. Articles in this last category often aroused predictably strong feelings in the military establishment, with senior officers conveying to my Editor their feelings of distress, usually 'more in sorrow than in anger', at some of my critical comments.

In the summer of 1963 I wrote a five-part series of articles on 'The American Strategic Revolution', which *The Times* subsequently published as a monograph entitled *The Sword and the Spirit*. This arose from a two-month tour of the United States, arranged by the State Department as part of what they rather flatteringly called the Foreign Leader Program. My visit had been set up by Henry Kissinger, whom I had met in London the year before. Henry was then at the Center for International Affairs at Harvard, but obviously already had his hands on some of the levers of power and influence at the State Department.

Kissinger was to become a regular contact over the years and without question one of the most dynamic intellects active in public life. He was not widely known for his sense of humour, but I found that he could be extremely funny, albeit in a rather heavy way. Most impressively, he matched the quickness of many politicians with a corresponding depth of reflection. He had taken the time to consider – and therefore understood better than most – the uses of military power as an instrument of foreign policy.

Henry remained an academic, even at the heart of the political establishment. I remember an occasion, some years later, when we were at a meeting in Paris to discuss the war in Vietnam. In a typically elegant and slightly irrelevant interlude, our host asked the assembled guests to speculate on the impact of the French Revolution on the development of their respective countries. Henry produced a dazzling and beautifully rounded little lecturette, with erudite quotations from de Tocqueville. Our host then turned to the Chinese representative whose eminence and political seniority were, in line with Chinese custom, marked by his extreme age. When faced with the same question he simply remarked, 'It is too early to say.'

My trip began in the first-class cabin of PanAm Flight 107 to Philadelphia, in an ambience of *luxe, calme et volupté* which I have never since been able to enjoy on any airline. There were only three passengers to occupy the sixteen seats with the result that we each had our own personal cabin attendant. The dry martinis were real American martinis, the claret with lunch was excellent, and for the rest of the journey a bed was made up on the three empty adjoining seats. My diary for the day consists of a single appreciative comment – *This is positively the life!*

The rest of the trip, although perhaps not so unremittingly sybaritic, was beautifully organised into a series of meetings and visits which did much to influence my perception of American military and political thinking. After a meeting in Washington with Paul Nitze, the Assistant Secretary of Defense, I went on to see the British Ambassador, Sir David Ormsby-Gore, later Lord Harlech. It is perhaps a little ironic to recall that even in those days the 'European idea' was already alive and well, and living in Massachusetts Avenue. In the course of a brief conversation on the subject of the Multilateral Force, Ormsby-Grove suggested that some of the problems of nuclear control might be simplified when Britain became a member of a European community committed to 'some form of political integration'.

I also had a fascinating meeting with President Kennedy in the Oval Office. The exact details of military strategy which we discussed escape me, but the occasion remains in my memory for another reason. At the time I had a fondness for Havana cigars, a weakness long since purged by my chief medical adviser, who is also my wife and who understandably disapproved of such an unhealthy activity being pursued beneath her own roof.

Someone had obviously told Kennedy about this because he made some allusion to my being a cigar-smoker and offered me a fine-looking Dutch specimen. Noticing my surprise he said, 'I suppose you were expecting it to be a Havana?' and then proceeded to explain with some solemnity how he could not possibly contemplate the promotion of Cuban tobacco. A cordial meeting followed in which I was impressed – as most visitors were – by Kennedy's quick mind and thorough grasp of strategic ideas.

About a week later, when I was back in London, a magnificent box of Havana cigars was delivered to my home in Chelsea, with the compliments of the President of the United States.

It was during this American tour that I came upon some alarming repercussions from the Profumo affair. Before his unfortunate and sensational departure from the political scene, the Secretary of State for War had visited several military installations in the United States, and the circumstances surrounding his resignation provoked a great witch-hunt in American intelligence and security circles. American doubts about the effectiveness of British security, never far from the surface, were now widely canvassed, and in several of my conversations with politicians and officials in the United States, our security arrangements in the United Kingdom were described as being 'as full of holes as a sieve'.

It is unlikely that Profumo's relationship with Christine Keeler ever carried any real security risk in terms of the leakage of secret information. There was always something faintly comic about the scenario in which Profumo was supposed to have discussed details of nuclear strategy with Miss Keeler, who then solemnly passed them on to her Soviet client. If there was any danger to security it lay in the possibility that the Secretary of State had made himself vulnerable to blackmail. This always seemed to me to be most unlikely.

I knew Jack Profumo quite well from my position at *The Times* and, previously, in the War Office. He was a first-class Secretary of State and an impressive man. To my mind, the whole affair was, quite simply, a sex scandal and I wrote to Profumo to express my own regret at the situation in which he found himself. It was the assiduous George Wigg who almost single-handedly turned the affair into a security issue, making much political capital for the Labour Party. His campaign was so successful that in June the government set up, under Lord Denning, a judicial inquiry 'into the events leading to Mr Profumo's resignation'.

While the issue played well for Harold Wilson, it was at the expense of more important relationships. So far as the Americans were concerned, I came to a conclusion which was to have a substantial influence on my thinking when I came later to consider, as a Minister of State at the Foreign Office, matters of Anglo-American strategic relations. My conversations in Washington convinced me, for example, that in the aftermath of the Profumo affair, the US administration would have been reluctant to agree to the transfer of sensitive information on nuclear systems to European countries, including the United Kingdom, while security was seen to be so ineffective.

I had some sympathy with the general unease expressed by the Americans during those years. At the time of the Vassall case I received briefings from contacts in MI5 and MI6 (in fact, I was given remarkably thorough access to the intelligence services throughout my career at *The Times*); these led me to the conclusion that the security services were in some disarray and, in particular, were hampered by a deteriorating relationship between MI5 and MI6.

The conduct of the intelligence services was only part of my brief. One of the more satisfying perks of the job was the chance to indulge in further study of military history and grand strategy. In this I was particularly inspired by the example of my illustrious predecessor in the job, Captain Basil Liddell Hart. He became a good friend and a generous source of advice, and my frequent visits to his home were among the highpoints of my years at *The Times*.

Basil was a fascinating character, quite regardless of his brilliance as a military writer. He was immensely vain and his appearance was extraordinary: he dressed with extreme formality and great attention to detail. During our conversations he would frequently go through the ritual of lighting his pipe, with the absence of only one of the normal requirements for such a process: tobacco. He must have been the only pipe-smoker in existence who smoked matches exclusively. For this and other reasons his delightful wife Kathleen treated Basil as something of a child, which never seemed inappropriate.

But in the area of military doctrine, Basil was exceptional. He was certainly loquacious and at times his brain moved faster than his tongue; he allowed little time for interruption. But 'the captain who taught generals' had an unrivalled grasp of strategy and became a great influence on me as a correspondent, not least because I admired his determination to combine real substance with an attention to elegance and style in his writing. Basil had acquired an almost legendary status, even amongst those who disagreed with him, and he would often feed back to me the verdicts passed on my articles by his many eminent contacts in the military. It always amused him when yet another Whitehall figure would 'blow up' over my comments.

I was given a vivid illustration of Basil's eminence during one of my visits, when he informed me that Enoch Powell would be arriving to join us later in the day, as he wished to discuss a subject similar to the one with which I was concerned. When the door bell rang, Kathleen opened it to discover a rather dusty and bedraggled Enoch, and asked him where he had left his car.

'I have no car,' declared Enoch with his inimitably lugubrious solemnity. 'I have come on foot, as befits a disciple visiting the master.'

It was always hard to tell with Enoch, but I suspect that he was only half joking.

7

From *The Times* to the Foreign Office

It would be difficult to imagine a more stimulating experience than my three years with *The Times* in the early 1960s. The paper was still, in those days, the sort of institution which Trollope had in mind when he wrote in his political novels of the power and influence of *Jupiter*, the Thunderer. Under William Haley's stern moral and political guidance, *The Times* was not only an indispensable newspaper of record; the views expressed in its leading articles were taken seriously by the policy-makers of Whitehall and Westminster, both in government and in opposition. Its news values were strict and uncorrupted; its ethical approach to such matters as the right of people to have their private lives respected was governed by the highest principles. It had not allowed circulation wars to debase its standards of accuracy, reliability or presentation.

In the course of my relatively brief time at Printing House Square, my output seems to have been alarmingly prolific. Between the summer of 1961 and my departure in 1964 I wrote, apart from frequent news reports on defence matters, over fifty major articles on such issues as nuclear strategy, the defence of Western Europe, United States defence policy and co-operation in the Western Alliance. There were also a number of series including a three-part analysis of the British Army of the Rhine, five articles on the American Strategic Revolution and a two-part critique of the Multilateral Force.

Many of these articles provoked strong reactions among military and political circles. Senior officers in the armed forces occasionally became seriously agitated and General Sir John Hackett, a thoughtful and perceptive soldier, told Oliver Woods, one of the assistant editors, that one of my articles had 'cut him to the quick'. In June 1964 I wrote a leading article in which I commented on the phenomenon of 'overstretch' – a problem which has not been solved to this day – and which I concluded with the words: 'The choice that faces the Government hardly needs spelling out. If the number of tasks entrusted to the armed forces cannot be reduced, the number of men to fulfil them must be increased.'

This reasonably unexceptionable proposition, which I have continued to this day to advance in one form or another, drew a severe reprimand from Major-General Monckton (now Viscount Monckton) then Director of Army Public Relations. I wrote a fairly pompous reply, of which Trollope's Quintus Slide would have been proud, and which Gilbert Monckton took in good part. Thirty-five years later we sat together on the crossbenches in the House of Lords, directing co-ordinated fire against governments of all complexions.

Writing on defence and strategic matters involved a fair amount of travel, often under the auspices of the service ministries and their public relations departments. On one of my first visits as defence correspondent to an army training exercise, a delicate situation arose when I discovered that, on arrival at the training area, suitable buses, barges and other forms of mechanical transport had been arranged for the correspondents of other newspapers, while a separate car and boat had been provided for the gentleman from *The Times*. I was fortunately quick enough on my feet to decline this special treatment, which would have been distinctly unpopular with my colleagues, perhaps especially with Chapman Pincher of the *Daily Express* who regarded himself as the doyen and guru of this particular branch of newspaper work.

My contract with *The Times* did not debar me from writing for other publications, with, of course, the consent of the Editor, which was never once withheld. In August 1963 I interviewed the Foreign Secretary, R. A. Butler, for BBC2 on his return from a visit to Moscow, and an edited version appeared in *The Listener*. My fellow interviewer was James Mossman, and in retrospect it seems to me that the interview was characterised more by an almost obsessive urbanity than by any disclosure of significant views or information. Butler was a supreme master of the art of the parliamentary reply. That is one giving no information which was not already available. In response to one of my questions about the Soviet threat, he said, 'Mr Khrushchev said to me that he didn't want ideology to separate us, and I think that is a very sensible statement.' It was also, of course, a statement which meant absolutely nothing.

Perhaps the most significant change in the policy of *The Times*, so far as I was concerned, was the gradual erosion of the practice of anonymity. Indeed, I was to some extent responsible for this, as the Editor had agreed that I should appear on current affairs television programmes identified as '*The Times* Defence Correspondent'. I took part in a *Panorama* report on the Cuba missile crisis in 1962 in which Richard Dimbleby asked me unexpectedly at the end of the programme whether we were about to become involved in a nuclear war. I prophesied incautiously, but, as it turned out correctly, that the Soviet Union would not risk provoking the United States that far. I took the somewhat cynical view that if I was right, I would be credited with admirable foresight; whereas if I was wrong there would not be many people left to point out my mistake. From that moment there was not much point in trying to conceal the identity of the man from *The Times*.

It was the beginning of a close association with the BBC. I was engaged as defence and foreign affairs consultant for BBC Television Public Affairs, the head of which was Paul Fox, a consummate television professional who was to play an important part in my life ten years later. I also became, in 1963, the anchorman of the BBC's weekly political programme *Gallery* and worked on a two-part film called *Overkill* on nuclear arms control and disarmament. This provoked strong reactions from the emerging 'peace' movement, and an appreciative letter from a former colonel of my regiment who congratulated me on a performance 'well up to regimental pantomime standards'.

For BBC Radio, I broadcast a series of interviews called *Man at the Centre*, mainly with senior military officers, including Field Marshal Montgomery, whose biography I was later to write; and in 1964 there was a somewhat strange correspondence with Stanley Kubrick, whose remarkable film about nuclear war, *Dr Strangelove*, had also, for rather different reasons, raised the blood pressure of the Campaign for Nuclear Disarmament.

By the autumn of 1964 I had achieved a certain success in the world of newspapers, radio and television and was looking forward to the challenge of reporting on and analysing the defence policies of Harold Wilson's new Labour government. It was at this moment that the call to Downing Street interrupted my glass of champagne at the United Hunts Club and I accepted the Prime Minister's invitation to join his administration as 'Minister of Disarmament'. This involved a reduction in income almost as drastic as that which I had had to accept on leaving the army, but, as the Editor of *The Times* commented at the time, it was too interesting a challenge to turn down.

The press coverage in the following days was on balance positive and sympathetic. One enterprising photographer succeeded in getting a shot of me with some barbed wire in the foreground, making for some colourfully obscure symbolism. The *Evening Standard*, in a diary piece on political outsiders which linked my appointment with those of Sir Hugh Foot and Sir Charles Snow (the writer C. P. Snow), referred to a 'disclosure' by Woodrow Wyatt that I had advised the Liberal Party on defence policy, thus planting the seed of a story of political opportunism which even today still comes to the surface from time to time. My own newspaper reported these world-shaking events with commendable and characteristic absence of drama and, like a few of the other serious newspapers, reminded its readers that, in spite of the newly-minted title of my appointment, my terms of reference were, in fact, to continue to do what a succession of Ministers of State at the Foreign Office had been doing for years, namely to represent Britain at international disarmament negotiations not, as some of the dottier elements in the peace movement seemed to assume, to disband this country's armed forces.

There then followed a process which has also given rise to a number of interesting rumours, most of them without foundation – the business of choosing a title for my introduction into the House of Lords. This involved a series of visits to the College of Arms, an elegant and unpretentious building behind ornamental iron gates in Queen Victoria Street. Here I was courteously received by the Garter Principal King of Arms, and we entered into an esoteric discussion about titles. Before I could be introduced into the House of Lords, it seemed, it was necessary to decide upon the style by which I was in future to be addressed.

'Garter', as he is known to his colleagues, was politely dismissive of the idea of simply using or adapting my name and prefixing it with a title. It was, he murmured gently, a mistakenly egalitarian notion which was unhappily gaining currency, especially among life peers. He implied, without ever actually saying it, that if there *had* to be life peers, they might at least try to behave like the real thing. We therefore considered a number of interesting possibilities. Some were rejected on arcane grounds of precedence, and one – the name of a perfectly respectable Welsh village – on the grounds that much of my government work was likely to be done abroad. 'Just imagine,' said Garter sorrowfully, 'a Belgian civil servant trying to get his tongue around *that*.' His own politely formulated preference was for a title with English territorial or geographical associations, possibly with a reference to my Welsh background which would not be too exotic to be understood. Eventually, after a few cups of Earl Grey (a beverage named after a nobleman who seems to have ignored the preferences of an earlier Garter), it was decided that Lieutenant-Colonel Alun Arthur Gwynne Jones would henceforth be known by the style and title of 'Baron Chalfont of Llantarnam, in the County of Monmouth.'

It was by this grandiloquent style that I was introduced into the House of Lords in the traditional ceremony; and on 17th

December I made my maiden speech from the Despatch Box. In it I announced that the government's major preoccupation was prevention of the spread of nuclear weapons and extension of the partial test ban to include underground testing. I also announced that I intended to establish an Arms Control and Disarmament Research Unit (ACDRU) in the Foreign Office; this group of officials provided research, briefings and position papers throughout my six years as a Minister.

I also said that I wanted to assemble an advisory panel of outside experts from the academic and business world, announced predictably in the press under the headline 'Lord Chalfont's Brains Trust on Disarmament'. Among those I approached was Michael Howard, subsequently Regius Professor of History at Oxford. Although he declined to take part on the entirely reasonable and understandable grounds that he would not be able to give it the necessary time, I have had the good fortune to enjoy his friendship over many years and have the greatest admiration for his work. He has surely been one of the most influential commentators on military matters of the past thirty years, not least because he has such a fine grasp of the uses of military power as an integral part of a country's foreign policy. A greater understanding of the subtleties involved in this approach to power would, I think, have saved many governments from unnecessary crises over the past two decades.

In my maiden speech I went on to say something which, in the light of later experience, had a faintly surrealist air. Speaking of proposals for a freeze on levels of nuclear weapons, I delivered the following summary of the Government's policy. 'This would be a first step in general and complete disarmament and part of the first step in the complete elimination of all missiles, all bombers and all armed forces. Our final objective, of course, is world government with an international peace-keeping force firmly in its hands.'

This uncharacteristically utopian declaration was made after a series of briefings and meetings in the Foreign Office where I had made my first appearance on the Monday after my appointment. It was my first encounter with that silky, steely and beautifully articulated machine, the diplomatic service.

It was said of the Marquis de Norpois, one of Proust's most engagingly ridiculous characters, that in the course of a long career in diplomacy he had become imbued 'with the negative, methodical, conservative spirit called "governmental", which is common to all governments and, under every government, particularly inspires its Foreign Office'. It is difficult, as with so many of Proust's mordant ironies, to suppress a smile of delighted recognition. Yet, whatever might be said of the mandarins of the Quai d'Orsay, it would be unwise to deliver such a dismissive judgement upon our own diplomatic service, which has recently celebrated the two hundredth anniversary of the Foreign Office.

There have been many attempts to capture the flavour of diplomacy in some lapidary phrase, from Sir Henry Wotton's definition of an ambassador as 'an honest man sent to lie abroad for the good of his country' to John Kennedy's devastating description of the American State Department as 'a bowl of jelly'. One of the aphorisms which has come closest to the heart of the matter is that which referred to the art of diplomacy as 'letting the other side have it all your own way'. The favourite dictum of the Foreign Office itself originated with Talleyrand, but is more suited to the temperament of the English diplomat than the French – '*surtout pas trop de zèle*'. Yet there is much more behind the elegant façade at the eastern end of St James's Park than any of these somewhat facetious observations might suggest.

From the outside, the Foreign Office is an elegant and pleasing construction. Seen from the Foot Guards War Memorial on the open side of the Horse Guards' Parade, it has something of the serenity and charm of a Venetian palace, complete with *campanile*. At one corner is a gracefully curved and pillared balcony, behind which lies the office once occupied by the Secretary of State for India and which was to become my own office for the next six years. It is an oval, panelled room of exquisite proportions, with Mogul prints on the walls and a cunning system of entrances and exits originally designed to prevent embarrassing encounters between arriving and departing envoys. When I first occupied it, it had in cold weather two coal fires, one at each end of the oval, replenished at intervals by a messenger bearing a brass coal-scuttle. These were probably essential for the comfort of Indian potentates visiting London in mid-winter, but seemed archaic in the Foreign Office of the 1960s.

To get into the Foreign Office it is necessary for the visitor to cross the quadrangle from a gate in King Charles Street, at the end of which a monument to Clive of India looks inscrutably out over St James's Park. It was once possible to enter direct from Downing Street, but the great iron gates are now locked. Unkind rumour has it that the orders for this were given by George Brown in a despairing attempt to keep Harold Wilson's spies out of his manor. At the main entrance, under a forbidding portrait of the third Lord Salisbury, an equally awe-inspiring lady fills in a temporary pass, and the visitor is conducted to his appointment through the echoing corridors. There are, of course, other entrances to the Foreign Office – some reserved for officials, others for visitors to less publicly-accessible departments. There is, too, the Park Entrance at the corner of the Horse Guards' Parade, through which I entered on my first day as a Foreign Office Minister. Its most memorable feature was a lift, evidently designed in the early days of mechanical engineering, which rose and descended with great deliberation and alarming crepitation, much as though it were manually operated. It took Ministers to their offices and distinguished visitors to the Ambassadors' Waiting Room, an impressive if somewhat gloomy apartment, furnished with leather chairs, a great mahogany table and one copy of each of the quality newspapers. Mr John Kenneth Galbraith, an American diplomatist of great height and laconic manner, was once heard to comment, as he waited at the top of the lift shaft for the ancient conveyance to appear, 'Say, we have trees in the States that come up quicker than this thing.'

The interior of the Foreign Office was, in those days, a bizarre mixture of opulence and squalor. At the top of the main staircase were five great wall-paintings (often inaccurately described as frescoes) by Sigmund Goetze, depicting Britannia discharging a number of her symbolic duties. Of these racy portrayals, *Britannia Nutrix* remains most vividly in my mind. It is intended to depict Britannia the bride becoming a mother and rearing a sturdy race of children. If symbolically it seemed a trifle obscure, anatomically it left little room for speculation. The corridors of the main floor of the building were either paved with mosaics or silenced with burgundy carpets. Some of the offices were, quite simply, magnificent. Apart from the old India Office, there is the splendid room of the Secretary of State, gilded and spacious, with magnificent views over the Horse Guards' Parade and the Park.

Outside the glowing, hushed domains of the Ministers and Under-Secretaries, the rest of the Foreign Office of the 1960s suggested that to achieve its unique brand of brutal neo-realism Franz Kafka must have been turned loose in the drawing office of the Ministry of Works. Lining the corridors were a succession of identical doors, each giving the strong impression that it could not be shut without a clanging noise. Behind the doors were small overpopulated rooms, often uncarpeted, full of safes and filing cabinets, stark tables with tea-cup rings and languid young men in shirt sleeves wearing red felt braces. George Brown, whose impact on the Foreign Office when he was appointed Foreign Secretary was something like that of a killer-whale introduced into an embassy swimming pool, was notably unimpressed with the working conditions. 'People,' he wrote in his memoirs, 'still work in what must have been once upon a time intended to be cupboards.'

There is, among the connoisseurs of these matters, much profound argument about where the real power in the Foreign Office lies. The received wisdom is that it is certainly *not* with the Foreign Secretary or his junior ministers, those transient political vagrants who have the same effect on the diplomatic service as passengers have on airlines, or war has on the armed forces – they prevent the professionals from getting on with their legitimate business. It was put to me that officials regarded new Ministers as an oyster regards a piece of sand: an irritant accidentally acquired and with only the remotest possibility of producing anything of value.

Sir Alexander Cadogan, once Permanent Under-Secretary at the Foreign Office, described politicians in words which would find an echo at many a luncheon at the Travellers Club: 'They embody everything that my training has taught me to eschew – ambition, prejudice, dishonesty, self-seeking light-hearted irresponsibility, black-hearted mendacity.' This jaundiced view of politicians has been current since it was expressed with such timeless precision in Plato's *Republic*. 'When they go to the administration of public affairs, poor and hungering after their own private advantage, thinking that hence they are to snatch the chief good, order there can never be; for they will be fighting about office, and the civil and domestic broils which thus arise will be the ruin of the rules themselves and of the whole state.'

Some think that the real power in the Foreign Office is wielded by the Under-Secretaries, a closely knit and exclusive body, most of whom have recently been, or are about to be, ambassadors abroad. One of these *eminences grises* was once overheard giving instruction to a junior colleague on the basic techniques of drafting an answer to a Parliamentary question addressed to the Foreign Secretary: 'It should be brief; it should be accurate; and it should give no information that was not previously available.' Others attribute almost sacerdotal influence to the Private Secretaries, those high-flying younger diplomats, generally of silken tongue and elegant aspect, who control the private offices of the Ministers. These clairvoyant and omniscient acolytes, often marked for the highest ranks of the service, act as advisers, companions, confessors, wine-waiters and travel agents to their political masters, steering them clear of the denser thickets of Whitehall intrigue and inoculating them against the dangerous belief that international problems might actually have solutions.

It is arguable, however, that if it were possible to isolate one vital nerve centre in the complex organism of the Foreign Office, it is the Third Room, in more leisurely days the scene of elegant tea parties, complete with Dundee cake and Lapsang Souchong, but now more austerely refreshed. The Third Room is the location, in every department, of the most junior officials of the service. It is here, as Lord Gladwyn has described in his engaging *Memoirs*, that bright young men commit to paper the fledgling thoughts which, after passing through the hierarchical filters of Head of Department, Assistant Under-Secretary, Deputy Under-Secretary and Permanent Under-Secretary, might emerge as a ministerial speech, or a telegram to an overseas post. (Incidentally, *every* telegram to embassies abroad, of whatever degree of importance, bears the signature of the Secretary of State; so that even a message concerning the grade of lavatory paper in a minor consulate bears the intimidating subscription 'Curzon', 'Callaghan' or, most imperious of all, 'Carrington'.)

The process of upward submission is at the heart of the system designed by the Foreign Office for educating its political masters. When a Minister is about to make a speech, negotiate with a foreign government, or argue a case in Cabinet, he is presented, whether he likes it or not, with a 'submission', distilled from the combined brainpower of the Foreign Office staff. It is almost always lucidly presented and persuasively argued; it is also, with only an occasional exception, unadulterated by reservation or dissent. These are carefully ironed out at the official level, and what is presented to the Minister is the considered, agreed Foreign Office view. Almost invariably, too, it has been the subject of consultation at the official level with other appropriate government departments. This is especially true of briefings for Cabinet meetings; if a Minister is ever surprised by the views of one of his colleagues in Cabinet, his officials are considered to have been deficient in their briefing.

This system has obvious advantages. It means that Foreign Officer ministers are almost always formidably well-prepared for conferences, meetings and debates. If they are not, it is usually their own fault. The main *disadvantage* is that Ministers sometimes complain that they are not presented with a range of options from which they are able to select a policy consistent with their political judgement. They are usually confronted with a single recommended course of action; and if they reject it the whole submission process has to be gone through again; and, in the rare case of a Minister so self-opinionated as to wish to initiate policies of his own, the Foreign Office machine is capable of being shifted into a very special low gear, kept in reserve for distasteful contingencies of this kind. It must be said that this view of ministerial impotence is held mainly by politicians; the officials modestly disclaim any policy-making hegemony.

It is by no means certain that the Foreign Office and diplomatic service will, or should, continue to survive indefinitely in its present form. There are powerful arguments, in an age of instant communications, supersonic travel and electronic handling of information, for a system of overseas representation of a radically different kind. Mr Pierre Trudeau, when Prime Minister of Canada, said that the whole concept of diplomacy today was outmoded. 'I believe,' he declared '[that] much of it goes back to the early days of the telegraph, when you needed a despatch to know what was happening in country A, whereas now you can read it in a good newspaper.'

This is, of course, a vast over-simplification. Even with the benefits of modern technology and the assistance of omniscient journalists, a diplomatic service is an indispensable system for conducting foreign policy. The special function of the diplomat is to interpret the policies and interests of his own country to the government of that to which he is accredited; and to interpret the policies and interests of the foreign country to his own government at home. The Foreign Office, although still too infuriatingly 'conservative' for some tastes, has, in fact, moved further than many people might think into the post-imperial world. Its officials have a clearer view of Britain's diminished status than most politicians or journalists.

This may have something to do with the willingness of diplomats to engage in reflection and study on a theoretical level, seldom allowed in other Whitehall departments. Needless to say, this is likely to be carried out in suitably civilised settings: Wilton Park in the case of official Foreign Office policy discussions, or Ditchley Park, for more independent and free-ranging exchanges. I have visited Ditchley more times than I can remember, and it still continues to make an important contribution to national policy-making, under the wise guidance of such directors as Sir Michael Quinlan. There is some merit in the criticism that, in its early days, Ditchley was almost too genteel; pampered by the atmosphere of a country house weekend, participants were so keen to avoid confrontation and polemics that they tended to side-step awkward issues.

The impeccable academic and intellectual ancestry of the Foreign Office and the diplomatic service may be judged from the fact that the first Foreign Secretary, two hundred years ago, was Charles James Fox (an Eton classicist) and the first Under-Secretary was Richard Brinsley Sheridan (an Harrovian dramatist). Sheridan, as the first official head of the department, set, during his brief tenure, formidable standards of literacy and wit; while Fox began to lay the foundations of modern foreign policy, discarding the Machiavellian conceptions of the earlier eighteenth century for a more civilised diplomacy. 'War,' he said, 'should never be undertaken when peace can be maintained without breach of public faith, injury to national honour or hazard of future security.' It is a precept which still echoes in the corridors of the Foreign Office, although it is perhaps more audible nowadays to diplomats than to their political masters.

Not everyone has been as ready as I was to inhale the unique incense of official wisdom in the Foreign Office. One of the favourite stories circulating in the building is that of Ernest Bevin who had been Foreign Secretary in Clement Attlee's 1945 administration. At the end of his first week in the Office, Bevin found on his desk a large pile of papers, with a note from his Private Secretary saying, 'The Secretary of State may care to peruse these documents over the weekend.' When the Private Secretary came in on Monday morning he found the pile untouched, and his own neat message annotated in Bevin's untidy scrawl – 'A kindly thought, but erroneous!'

8

Arms Control and Disarmament

I was met at the Park Entrance on my first day at the Foreign Office by the official who was to be my Private Secretary. Paul Buxton was a man of dauntingly academic aspect and background. Before joining the diplomatic service he had been at Rugby and Balliol, and three years in the Coldstream Guards had done nothing to blunt the edges of a formidable intellect. He was, indeed, the personification of that special Balliol presence once described as 'the tranquil consciousness of effortless superiority'. Much later, after a somewhat acerbic difference of opinion about the meaning of a word in a draft telegram, he presented me with a copy of William Empson's *Seven Types of Ambiguity*, inscribed on the fly-leaf with the words 'in case of any lingering belief that words mean what they say'. For the next three years this sardonic and disenchanted figure was to be my indispensable link with the official establishment of Whitehall, as well as my guide and companion on all my visits overseas.

This brings to mind memories of another Private Secretary, later in my time at the Foreign Office, who provided me with some hair-raising and hilarious moments. In those days the Minister was expected to remain at his desk until summoned for an overseas visit: the Private Secretary arranged everything from cars and flights to despatch boxes and appropriate briefings. The Minister was not expected to think of such minor details. The Foreign Office maintained the self-deprecating and elegant fiction that this was to allow Ministers to dwell on the great matters of state, without being troubled by trivial or mundane thoughts. Cynics observed that the practice also coincided with the general Foreign Office line that the fewer thoughts allowed to make the brief journey across a Minister's brain, the better for the national interest (the latter being indistinguishable, of course, from the Foreign Office's interests).

On this particular occasion I was due to address a conference overseas. I was ushered down to a waiting car by the Private Secretary, driven to London Airport, and escorted on to the plane. After an agreeable flight, during which I had assiduously studied my papers for the conference and prepared my speech, I heard the captain's voice over the intercom system asking us to fasten seatbelts as we were about to make our descent to Fiumicino Airport, Rome. Unfortunately, the conference which I was due to attend was in Brussels. The embarrassment caused was mildly reassuring for a Minister – at least, I thought, Foreign Office officials are human. Needless to say, the Private Secretary involved was, in fact, a fine diplomat and rose to an important position in the service.

As I later wrote in a foreword to Geoffrey McDermott's book *The New Diplomacy*, the first trial of strength between a political minister and the Foreign Office *curia* is often no more dramatic than the perfunctory handshake of two boxers; but it often decides whether the politician is eventually able to exercise some control over the machine and use it effectively, or whether he falls into the works under the benign gaze of his officials and comes out at the other end bearing a remarkable resemblance to a rubber stamp. In my own case, any potential conflict was quickly defused when, barely a month after arriving at the Foreign Office, I went to Washington for talks with the Head of the United States Arms Control and Disarmament Agency, William C. Foster, and for a meeting of the four Western powers represented on the Geneva Disarmament Committee – the United States, Canada, the United Kingdom and Italy.

My diplomatic support was formidably impressive. In addition to the cautious murmurings of my Private Secretary and the Head of the Foreign Office Atomic Energy Department, I had at my disposal the advice of Sir Harold Beeley, the immensely able and experienced Head of the British Delegation at Geneva and, of course, of Lord Harlech, the British ambassador to the United States and his staff. David Harlech, formerly David Ormsby-Gore, was a career diplomat of great distinction and an inspired choice as ambassador to the United States of John Kennedy and subsequently Lyndon Johnson.

The principal issue of the day, as far as the talks with the Americans were concerned, was a bizarre concept known as the MLF, or Multilateral Force. This was a well-meaning attempt by the United States to share the control of nuclear weapons with other members of the Western Alliance. It had passed through several phases of modification since its emergence at Nassau in 1962, and at the NATO meeting in Ottawa in the spring of 1963 it had taken the form of a fleet of surface vessels armed with Polaris intercontinental ballistic missiles, jointly owned by those nations of the Alliance willing to subscribe to it, collectively managed by an international staff, manned by mixed crews, the crew of each ship to be drawn from the nationals of at least three NATO countries.

Political control was to be by a small international consortium within the Alliance, each member having a veto over the use of the force. It had been originally suggested that the MLF should consist of merchant ships, but this idea was soon abandoned in favour of a fleet of warships, possibly of the frigate type. The American theory was that this mixed-manned force was to be an alternative to proliferation – the spread of national nuclear deterrents, especially to Germany, a possibility which was regarded as especially dangerous and destabilising. There were substantial reservations to the concept among the European members of the Alliance, who were not slow to point out that the Americans, while having the right of veto over the use of the MLF, would still retain a massive nuclear striking force of their own over which NATO would have no control.

However, the political arguments were, with some reservations, accepted by the British government. On the one hand, the Ministry of Defence and the Chiefs of Staff argued that the Multilateral Force would add nothing to the military capabilities of the West, and that it would be expensive and unacceptably vulnerable to Soviet countermeasures. There was less rigid opposition in the Foreign Office, where there was some sympathy with the American belief that, so long as Britain and France continued to pursue declared policies of total nuclear independence, there was a growing possibility that extreme political elements might be able to manipulate feelings of national inferiority in Germany and to arouse enthusiasm for similar policies there.

The Americans, furthermore, were brutally direct in dismissing any illusions that Britain could prevent the MLF from coming into being by refusing to co-operate, and by the autumn of 1965 the British government had agreed to take part in discussions aimed at the establishment of the force; and the Foreign Office view was that it would be pointless to enter the talks without a constructive purpose. At this stage, it seemed likely that a treaty embodying agreement on the force would be drafted by the spring of 1964 and that the fleet might be substantially operational by 1967.

This timetable, however, proved to be optimistic, and the project, already regarded with something approaching derision by some strategic analysts, was further complicated in the summer of 1964 when the British government put forward a plan under which the multilateral concept was to be extended to cover *all* medium- and long-range nuclear weapons, including the British V-bomber force which would be manned by mixed NATO national aircrew in units and squadrons. It did not go as far as to propose the mixed-manning of individual aircraft. This initiative was, predictably, regarded by the Americans as a sort of 'wrecking amendment', and Britain came under heavy pressure from the US who wanted a MLF treaty ready for signature in time for the presidential election in November 1964.

It was against this strategic and diplomatic background that, in July 1964, I had written two long articles in *The Times* analysing the political and strategic rationale of the Multilateral Force idea. My conclusion was that, although there were powerful military arguments against the concept, the political case for it was persuasive. I pointed out that, with a general election due in the autumn, the attitude of Harold Wilson's Labour Party was of some importance; and I advanced a proposition, the significance of which, from a personal point of view, I was then in no position fully to appreciate.

'Unless,' I wrote, 'there is some unexpected change or delay [in the MLF programme] the British Government which takes office in October or November will therefore be faced almost at once with the need to take a decision that will affect the whole structure of international power relationships – the future of the Atlantic Alliance, Britain's place in Europe, the developing *détente* between Russia and the West, and, not least, relations between Britain and the United States throughout the whole spectrum of international politics.'

Not content with this oracular pronouncement, I had then offered some unsolicited advice to the Labour government when it duly came into power after the autumn general election. In an article on British nuclear policy, and the MLF in particular, I pointed out, perhaps unnecessarily, that the new government would have to choose between the conflicting views of the Ministry of Defence and the Foreign Office. 'The Chiefs of Staff,' I wrote, 'continue to damn the whole project of the surface fleet as expensive military nonsense which would use vital specialist manpower and seriously distort the structure of the Navy. The Foreign Office point to the political dangers of affronting Britain's most powerful ally and of being left in isolation if the force should come into being in spite of British opposition.'

My conclusion was that, given the context of imminent elections in the United States and Germany, a government decision on the MLF by the spring of 1965 was virtually essential. This was my last article as Defence Correspondent of *The Times*. It appeared on the morning of 23rd October – the day on which the new Prime Minister invited me to Downing Street. Four weeks later I was in Washington, acutely aware that pontificating about these issues from the cloisters of Printing House Square was relatively simple; doing something to resolve them on the diplomatic battleground was altogether a different matter.

Most of the Washington visit was devoted to a review of progress at the Eighteen Nation Disarmament Conference (ENDC) in Geneva, and to the essential business of co-ordinating American and British policies on arms control and disarmament in the light of Russian threats that, if the MLF came into existence, there would be no hope of any further progress in this field. At this stage, Western priorities were directed to agreements on the proliferation of nuclear weapons and the extension of the partial nuclear test ban treaty which was then in force.

There was the usual quota of 'glittering occasions' inseparable from official visits of this kind, including a very elegant dinner party at the British Embassy, a Washington film première in aid of the English Speaking Union's Churchill Statue fund, and an enormous reception at the Blair House attended by Dean Rusk, the American Secretary of State, Robert McNamara, the Defense Secretary and the Head of the CIA, the French and Italian Ambassadors, and a fair sprinkling of figures who were to play leading roles on the international stage in the coming years, among them, Cyrus Vance, Walt Rostow and George Ball. There was also the unforgettable Angier Biddle Duke, the American chief of protocol, a man whose aristocratic demeanour and studied elegance left no doubt in our minds that he regarded his function as that of lending tone and gravitas to what might otherwise have been a routine diplomatic clambake.

A few days after my visit, Harold Wilson arrived in Washington, accompanied by the Defence Secretary, Denis Healey, and the Foreign Secretary, Patrick Gordon Walker, whose tenure of this great office of state was sadly cut short by his regrettable inability to win a seat in Parliament. At the meetings with President Johnson and Dean Rusk, the Prime Minister rehearsed British objections to the MLF and tried out on the Americans the concept which became known as the Atlantic Nuclear Force (ANF) which would have four components: the British V-bomber force; all the British Polaris submarines; at least an equal number of American Polaris submarines; and some kind of mixed-manned contingent in which the non-nuclear powers could take part.

Most American strategists, with some justification, regarded the ANF as no more than a typically crafty British device designed to sink the MLF. The Conservative Party, however, saw it as a threat to the 'independent nuclear deterrent', and when the Prime Minister returned from America there were, predictably, indignant debates in both Houses of Parliament, in the course of which the Prime Minister said that in fact Britain had no independent deterrent 'because we are dependent on the Americans for the fissile materials for the British warheads'.

Whether the notorious ANF *was*, as the Americans firmly believed, a smart torpedo conceived and eventually fired by the Foreign Office must remain a matter for speculation, both informed and otherwise. It is more likely that the idea of mixed-manned and collectively controlled nuclear forces eventually sank under the sheer weight of its own fatuity. As I had written in *The Times* in the summer of 1964, for a time it had seemed unlikely that the idea would survive the ridicule that greeted its formal appearance in 1961. 'Fred Karno's Navy' and 'The Conning Towers of Babel' were only two of the more decorous tributes to its eccentricity. Yet there was, in fact, never any insuperable difficulty in the international manning of ships, whatever may have been said in the Ministry of Defence by otherwise responsible admirals about the grave culinary difficulties of preparing meals at sea for crews of mixed nationalities.

Technically, the multilateral force and the ingenious variations to which it gave rise were not entirely impractical. The real objection was political, and it sprang from the very genesis of the idea – the desire to give non-nuclear powers (specifically West Germany) a share in strategic nuclear decision-making. In fact, of course, no European member of NATO would have been able to do more than apply a safety catch to a small element of the Western nuclear striking force, while the United States, France and Britain would still have been able to use their own national nuclear weapons if they perceived it to be in their national interest to do so. It was, to say the least, unlikely that this state of affairs would satisfy any West German really interested in achieving influence over the control of nuclear weapons. On the other hand, any arrangement which promised a *real* share in nuclear decision-making to the Germans would have aroused in the Soviet Union even more violent opposition than that with which they had reacted to the initial MLF proposal.

The issue was therefore clear from the beginning. Either the Multilateral Force was to be operated permanently on a basis of unanimity, in which case it would satisfy no one and might, on the other hand, arouse a dangerous sense of resentment as the West Germans realised that they had been the victims of a confidence trick; or the principle of unanimity was to be abandoned, thus providing the possibility of a real voice for Bonn in nuclear decision-making, in which case the survival of *détente* between Russia and the West would have been put at risk and the pursuit of serious nuclear arms control agreements with the Soviet Union indefinitely delayed.

It was against this strategic background that I began to get to grips with the intellectually stimulating but politically frustrating problems of arms control and disarmament. On my return to London from the United States I had my first meeting with Soldatov, the Soviet ambassador. The supply of vodka at the Soviet embassy was lavish and Soldatov deployed the familiar Russian mixture of bonhomie and bullying. He rehearsed the predictable arguments against the Multilateral Force, and left me in no doubt that in the two areas of arms control then under serious discussion – a non-proliferation agreement and a comprehensive nuclear test ban – negotiations would be conducted by the Soviet Union strictly according to calculations of national interest.

In March I was back in the United States for more talks with the State Department. On my way to Washington, I spent a few days at the United Nations in New York where Lord Caradon was now the United Kingdom representative. As Hugh Foot, he had been a most effective Governor of Cyprus during the years of EOKA terrorism, and he and I had been elevated to the House of Lords at the same time by Harold Wilson. This man of high principle, imposing presence and resonant voice was already well known in UN circles as principal adviser to the United Kingdom delegation, a post he had held between 1961 and 1962, and which he had resigned as a result of a disagreement over British policy in Central Africa.

He conducted me briskly around the United Nations building on the East River, arranged a series of meetings on arms control matters with other delegates and accompanied me on a courtesy visit to U Thant, the UN Secretary General. He also put me on the endless merry-go-round of the United Nations social circuit, where organisers of dinner parties vied to attract the latest visitor to the UN. These were invariably packed with American celebrities, from the insufferably arrogant Leonard Bernstein to the charming Jacqueline Onassis, a genuinely fascinating and engaging hostess. To be fair, a good deal of networking and some serious business was conducted through these dinners, which were often attended by more senior State Department figures and Russian delegation officials than could readily be found at the United Nations.

Caradon was a great believer in the United Nations as a force for good, and a steadfast admirer of U Thant. These were sentiments which I did not wholly share. The whole place struck me then as being a fairly harmless but impotent talking-shop, presided over by an amiable but ineffective international civil servant. It is an impression which has remained with me ever since, modified only by a feeling that it has become less harmless than it used to be.

It seemed to me then, as it does now, that the reality of the global distribution of power is such that the United States will remain the basis of our security and defence. However reluctantly, that superpower will have to accept the role of international policeman – in so far as such a thing is needed – and we will have to support and influence her policy. I have discussed elsewhere the shortcomings of a common European defence and foreign policy (a notion that is only marginally more credible now than it was then). Of course there have always been suggestions that a military force could be assembled under the direct control of the burgeoning, corrupt and hopelessly inefficient United Nations bureaucracy. Anyone who has sat through the tortured wranglings and posturing of a General Assembly session will see that as a nightmarish vision.

If the United Nations itself was something of a disappointment, some of its expensive subsidiary bodies veered between the ludicrous and the alarming. In the 1980s I became involved in a campaign to persuade the British government to withdraw from UNESCO, which its critics described as a veritable shambles of bureaucracy, incompetence, and gross maladministration, rounded off with ideological prejudice. As it happened, the government did not need much persuading to pull out of UNESCO, once the Foreign Office had despaired of getting any real reform.

At the time of my first visit to the United Nations, with the General Assembly in customary disarray over the costs of peacekeeping, the reconvening of the General Conference, the Eighteen Nation Disarmament Conference (ENDC), had become a matter of some urgency. I went on from New York for talks with the State Department in Washington. We were in agreement with the Americans that the ENDC, adjourned in September, would at least provide a forum for contacts which would maintain the current atmosphere of *détente*. The Russians, on the other hand, took the pragmatic view that there was no point in meeting in Geneva unless there was something substantial to talk about. As British governments have been known to take a similar view when it suits them, it was difficult to deploy any convincing arguments against it. The Americans and ourselves therefore set about drafting a constructive agenda, including not only non-proliferation of nuclear weapons and a comprehensive test ban, but also a start on talks about chemical and biological weapons, as well as some more esoteric matters such as nuclear weapons on the seabed and in outer space. Some of these initiatives were described by an incurably cynical Foreign Office official as 'measures to prevent people doing things they either cannot do or have no intention of doing'. It seemed clear, however, that these small steps – then described in the jargon as 'partial measures' – were essential if any serious momentum was to be created and maintained.

While I was in Washington I had the quite remarkable and memorable experience of being formally introduced on the floor of the Senate. After listening to some notably sceptical debate on disarmament matters, I was duly presented to the assembled senators by Senator Clark who delivered a speech which sounded at times rather like an obituary. However, he ended on a note which seemed to me to reflect my own aims and aspirations, which were somewhat different from those attributed to me by certain sections of the British press. After referring to my earlier military career, the Senator said, 'I should think this would give him an intimate and personal idea of the desirability of disarmament, or at least drastic arms control.' It was with these words, if not exactly ringing in my ears, at least indelibly fixed in my mind, that I returned to London to prepare for what was to be a long and often dispiriting battle.

9

Dealing with the Nuclear Deterrent

In December 1964, as I have already recorded, I had been entertained to lunch at the Soviet embassy, a heavily guarded establishment in Kensington Palace Gardens. Soldatov, the ambassador, was a typical Soviet *apparatchik* of those days, outwardly gregarious and convivial, but coldly calculating and professional when serious matters needed to be addressed. My first meeting had left me in no doubt that the USSR regarded arms control negotiations as very much a matter of give and take – the West giving and the Soviet Union taking.

The main centre of arms control negotiations at this time was Geneva, where the Eighteen Nation Disarmament Conference carried on its business. The ENDC consisted of the delegations of five countries of the Warsaw Pact, five of NATO and eight non-aligned or neutral countries whose main function, according to some observers, was to find ways of bridging the gap between East and West. The reality was that they formed a club of nuclear have-nots who often seemed to regard the possibility of any agreement on arms control or disarmament between East and West as little better than a plan devised by two groups of alcoholics to impose total abstinence on everyone else.

The Eighteen Nation Disarmament Conference was in many ways a microcosm of the global power structure of the day. China and France, two of the nuclear weapons powers and also permanent members of the United Nations Security Council, chose not to be represented at Geneva, although France was technically a member of the ENDC. The two superpowers therefore faced each other across the table, the United States supported by her NATO allies, the United Kingdom, Canada and Italy, and the Soviet Union by her Warsaw Pact partners, Poland, Czechoslovakia, Bulgaria and Romania. These Cold War adversaries had to argue their case not only to each other but to the eight neutral or non-aligned countries, of which two (India and Sweden) were especially active and influential.

I began my preparations for entry into this disputatious assembly by attending a discussion on British defence policy at Chequers, under the chairmanship of the Prime Minister, in preparation for his forthcoming visit to the United States. Here the problem of the spread of nuclear weapons and other arms control issues were briefly discussed, although the collectively pugnacious presence of Denis Healey, the Defence Secretary, Lord Mountbatten, the Chief of the Defence Staff, and the three service Chiefs of Staff, ensured that disarmament was not exactly the flavour of the day.

As Defence Secretary, Denis Healey was quite understandably suspicious of disarmament proposals, suspecting that the Foreign Office secretly wanted to disarm the United Kingdom. He almost automatically disputed any proposals for our nego-tiating position at Geneva and seemed nervous that we might make too much progress. But our personal relationship was good and Denis's style was refreshingly forthright. I gained a good insight into this after a particular meeting at which Denis had floored a colleague with characteristic directness. In fact he had reduced her to tears. When I raised an eyebrow at this in the direction of Harold Wilson as we broke up from the meeting, Harold took my arm: 'My dear boy, you have to understand that every Prime Minister needs a thug. Denis is my thug.' As the years have gone by, Denis and I seem to have moved in opposite directions. I became gradually more pessimistic about the prospects for disarmament and more cynical about Soviet intentions; Denis found himself in a party which favoured a degree of unilateral nuclear disarmament.

Immediately after this meeting, I went to Washington, partly to prepare the ground for the Prime Minister's forthcoming visit, but principally to discuss policy and tactics with W. C. Foster, the Head of the United States Arms Control and Disarmament Agency. Bill Foster was a big, amiable Southerner whose patrician demeanour and casual style concealed an acute political brain and an encyclopaedic knowledge of the arcane minutiae of disarmament negotiations. He later became a close friend and collaborator, but this was our first meeting and we shared two main concerns – how to deal with the new Soviet leadership over such matters as a nuclear test ban treaty and how to resolve Anglo-American differences over the concept of a NATO nuclear surface fleet, the now notorious MLF or Multilateral Force.

I had to tell Foster that the British government was opposed to the whole idea, mainly on the military grounds which I had outlined in my last article in *The Times*. Indeed, Harold Wilson had made this clear in a House of Commons speech on the day of my arrival in Washington, and on the eve of the Prime Minister's own arrival, President Johnson, in a speech at Georgetown University, recognised 'the reasonable interests and concerns of other allies – those who have nuclear weapons of their own and those who do not'.

All this was closely linked to the question of the Soviet approach to arms control, especially as the Russians had let it be known that if the MLF came into existence it would mean an end to all hope of disarmament agreements. There were further discussions on Western policy and tactics at a meeting in Washington of the NATO members of the Eighteen Nation Disarmament Conference. Although the French maintained their empty chair policy at the formal meetings, Hervé Alphand, the French ambassador in Washington, came to a reception given by Bill Foster for the occasion. Here I had my first meeting with the formidable McGeorge Bundy, Special Assistant to the President, Dean Rusk, the US Secretary of State and Robert McNamara the Defense Secretary, as well as the heads of the Canadian and Italian disarmament delegations who were to be my colleagues and friends in the disarmament negotiations which lay ahead.

In the summer of 1965, I had, as I have already recorded, set out in a maiden speech in the House of Lords some of the possible approaches to international arms control. I had also set up a panel of eminent people outside the government machine to whom I could turn for scientific and other advice, and a research unit inside the Foreign Office charged specifically with examining new approaches to disarmament and arms control.

At this stage, no meetings of the Eighteen Nation Conference were being held, the Soviet Union, which shared the chairmanship of the Geneva talks with the United States, refusing to agree to reconvene the conference. In March 1965 at a meeting in London between the Foreign Secretary, Michael Stewart, and Andrei Gromyko, the Soviet Foreign Minister, I put forward a strong case for the resumption of the talks. The conference had been in abeyance for some time and my first priority was to get it reconvened. When Mr Gromyko came to London in March 1965, Michael Stewart and I pressed him hard to agree to a resumption of the negotiations. He agreed that this was desirable in principle, and gave us a list of arms control measures (then called 'partial measures of disarmament') which he would want the conference to discuss, a non-proliferation agreement (to prevent the spread of nuclear weapons) and a comprehensive nuclear test ban, as well as some measures of conventional or non-nuclear disarmament. Mr Gromyko, making an effective debating point, suggested that there was some inconsistency in a British position which advocated disarmament and measures to prevent the further spread of nuclear weapons and at the same time proposed the establishment of an Atlantic Nuclear Force which would, in Soviet eyes, put nuclear weapons into the hands of the West Germans.

The position of the Soviet Union at this stage still seemed depressingly negative, but there was an unexpected development soon after Gromyko's return to Moscow. The government of the USSR proposed an early return to the Geneva talks, which were duly resumed on 27th July. In my introductory speech on 29th July, I emphasised the importance of concluding a treaty to prevent the further spread of nuclear weapons and this was to be a recurring theme in the twenty or so major speeches I was to make at the ENDC over the next two years.

My contact with the Soviet delegations at Geneva was one of the more heartening aspects of an otherwise slightly sterile experience. Semyon Tsarapkin, the first leader of the Soviet team, was a delightful character. An obscure disease had given him an extraordinarily enlarged face and hands to the point that people found it quite hard to look at him. But he was a man of great warmth, with a fine sense of humour, who could invariably find something to laugh at, even in Soviet foreign policy. His successor, Roshchin, was a very different character, a smooth, polished diplomat with a dazzlingly sharp intellect, but an equally congenial companion.

I had for some time regarded the spread of nuclear weapons outside the existing nuclear powers (the United States, the Soviet Union, China, Britain and France) as one of the principal threats to international stability. In the course of my first reconnaissance patrol through the minefield of real politics, I delivered a speech at Salisbury in February 1965 on the occasion of the first by-election of the new parliament. In it I suggested to the electors of this archetypal garrison town that we were spending a great deal of money on defence but that as long as armed force remained an instrument of international politics, we should be looking for ways of making the world a safer place to live in. I went on to argue that the most urgent task in this context was the need to stop the spread of nuclear weapons, an urgency underlined by the recent Chinese nuclear test.

In April 1965, in a speech made to the United Nations disarmament commission in New York, I had outlined the risks implicit in the further spread of nuclear weapons, including the danger that 'in the event of a nuclear free-for-all ... weapons might get into the hands of people wanting to upset the established government of their own country. The idea of nuclear revolution may be too horrible for some men to contemplate, but we should not deceive ourselves. It is one of the logical ends of the unrestrained spread of nuclear weapons.' Even then my mind was much occupied with the appalling possibility of nuclear terrorism.

In an article written in June for the Welsh national daily the *Western Mail*, I said that I intended to give priority to arms control measures which were urgent and which at the same time offered the best chance of agreement, a fairly uncontroversial approach. I went on to write: 'The first of these is a pact to prevent the further spread of nuclear weapons. The Chinese nuclear explosions are bound to create pressure on other governments to embark on nuclear weapons programmes of their own.'

In October, I outlined the government's policy at the General Assembly of the United Nations, saying that Britain would not embark on any action which was not compatible with non-proliferation, but making it clear that: 'we are equally determined to safeguard the cohesion and strength of the Western Alliance until we have begun the process of general disarmament under international supervision and control.'

Given this preoccupation with the spread of nuclear weapons, it is not surprising that one of my first policy moves when I went to the Foreign Office after the 1964 election had been to begin serious work on a draft treaty to prevent what was then called 'dissemination' and later 'proliferation' of nuclear weapons. Previous governments had done some valuable work on the problem, and we had inherited a wealth of analysis and research. By the beginning of June 1965, we had agreed internally on a legally drawn draft treaty which we then showed to the Americans, Canadians and Italians as well as to the Germans who, although not members of the ENDC, were especially concerned with the problem and its implications for European security. At the end of July I went to Paris to present the draft to the Atlantic Council and then on to Geneva for the opening meeting of the ENDC, where a long and often frustrating series of discussions on non-proliferation was about to begin.

Although, as the leader of a delegation from the NATO bloc, I was naturally regarded as a member of the Western, pro-

American camp, I saw my role also as that of a broker between the United States and the Soviet Union. I had a good relationship both with William Foster, the leader of the American delegation, and with Semyon Tsarapkin of the USSR and, as the representative of the only other nuclear weapons power at the Geneva negotiations, I had a special position, especially in discussions about the spread of nuclear weapons. I used this to urge both the Americans and the Russians towards a non-proliferation treaty. Much of the opposition to this came from the non-aligned, non-nuclear powers who regarded the concept as a discriminatory device to perpetuate what they regarded as 'the existing nuclear hegemony'. At the same time, the Soviet Union and its allies insisted that such a treaty was not possible so long as the concept of nuclear sharing, as reflected in the MLF and ANF proposals, continued to be discussed in NATO.

Throughout the next two years attitudes of this kind persisted, preventing any progress on the non-proliferation issue. Between my first appearance at the ENDC in July 1965 and my last in May 1967, I record with some dismay that I delivered twenty-two major speeches, every one of them including a reference to the need for a non-proliferation treaty. At a meeting of the Western members of the ENDC in Paris in January 1966, I warned our allies that until we had resolved the nuclear sharing issue in NATO, the Soviet Union would not be prepared to enter into serious negotiations on such a treaty; and at the opening of the 1967 ENDC session I read a statement from the Prime Minister declaring that a treaty to prevent the spread of nuclear weapons was 'the most urgent of the Committee's tasks'.

At this stage, we were awaiting the tabling of a joint US/USSR draft treaty. At a meeting of the United Nations Disarmament Commission in New York in the spring of 1965, Adlai Stevenson, the United States permanent representative at the UN, had proposed that the drafting of a nuclear non-proliferation agreement should be given the highest priority by the ENDC and that its main provisions should be that nuclear powers pledge themselves not to relinquish control over nuclear weapons or provide non-nuclear states with assistance necessary to their manufacture; and that non-nuclear countries should agree not to manufacture or otherwise acquire control of such weapons. On behalf of the United Kingdom, I strongly endorsed Mr Stevenson's initiative, supported by, among others, Italy, the Netherlands and Denmark, and the Commission adopted by eighty-five votes to one (Albania) a resolution based on the American proposals. It was not, however, until now, the summer of 1967, that the United States and the Soviet Union submitted a draft treaty to the ENDC and, despite persistent objections to certain features of the draft by India and other Asian countries, the treaty was eventually successfully negotiated and came into force on 6th March 1970. It was described by the United States President as the first big step from confrontation to negotiation and a lasting peace, and Mr Kosygin, the Soviet Prime Minister, said that it was a substantial step towards the prevention of nuclear war.

Although I had been closely engaged in the negotiations leading up to the agreement and had, indeed, contributed substantially to the final draft, I was not to be involved in the last stages. In May 1967 it was announced from Downing Street that I was to take charge of negotiations for British entry into the European Community. The press reaction to my new appointment contained a number of familiar examples of newsspeak such as 'bombshell' and 'U-turn' and one tabloid columnist mysteriously attributed my selection for this task to the fact that I had 'a wistful expression and a good tailor' neither of which would, I thought at the time, be altogether powerful weapons to deploy against General de Gaulle.

Although the EEC portfolio was clearly a prospect too challenging to resist, it was with some regret that I moved out of the world of defence and disarmament. After more than twenty years in the army, including courses at two staff colleges and three active service campaigns, followed by three years as defence correspondent of *The Times* and two years of arms control negotiations, I had formulated some reasonably coherent ideas about the use of armed force in international relations. They were, as I explained to a moderately sceptical audience in

Top: Llantarnam Church. 'I had stood in the church-yard of Llantarnam as a very small child and watched the soldiers of the regiment salute the grave of Private John Williams' – the last VC from Rorke's Drift.
Above: West Monmouth School, Pontypool. 'A new world for a small boy from a small village'.

Right: 'Lamb white days'. In the garden aged 3½.

Left: My sister and three brothers in the 1940s.

Below: After the battle for the Mayu Tunnels, Burma 1944. 'From the ugliness and bloodiness of war came my conviction that it is a grotesque and indefensible way of conducting relations between states. … I came to feel that a nuclear capability could actually prevent others from going through the same experience'.

With Mona and our niece Ann after my investiture of the Military Cross by the Queen.

Mona as an officer in the Royal Army Medical Corps.

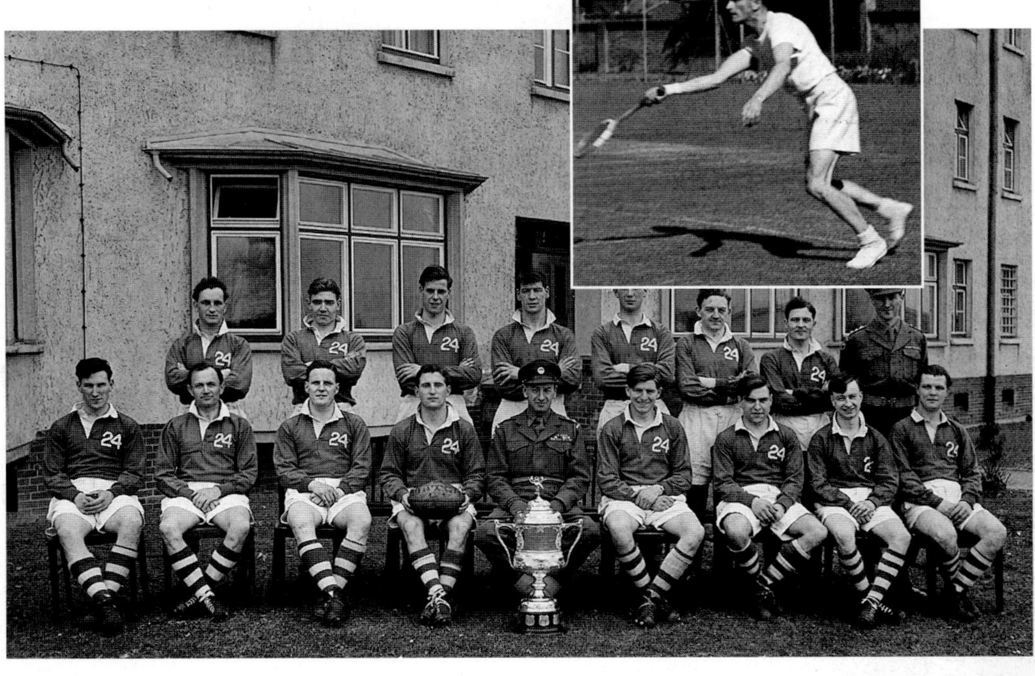

Right: Staff college 1950.
below: Regimental Rugby XV.

B Company Asmara.

Eritrea 1951– kicking for touch on a makeshift pitch.

Playing Hugo Barine for the Asmara Dramatic Society, in Sartre's *Crime Passionnel*. 'A disaffected communist intellectual who had never fired a gun in his life and who was hopelessly indecisive'.

With Mona at home on the announcement of my ministerial appointment and barony, 23rd October 1964. 'When we arrived back home in Chelsea late at night, it was to find our house under siege by a bombilating swarm of reporters and photographers.'

William Haley, the editor of *The Times*. As I resigned from *The Times* he said, 'You will miss two things. One will be your freedom of action; the other will be your influence on government policy'.

My introduction into the House of Lords with Garter, King of Arms and two supporters, Lord Kennet and Lord Shackleton. Harold Wilson had said 'Well you've been writing about this stuff for long enough, so it's about time you *did* something about it'.

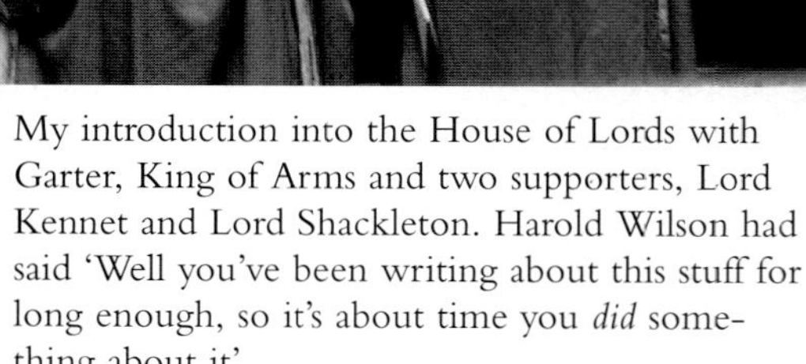

The invasion of Czechoslovakia crisis, 21st August 1968. Arriving at Downing Street for the emergency meeting called by Harold Wilson who had broken off his holiday in the Scilly Isles.

Top left: With Michael Stewart, Foreign Secretary (left) and Andrei Gromyko, the Soviet Foreign Minister.
Top right: George Brown and his wife, December 1966.
Middle left: Interviewing Willy Brandt in Bonn in 1970 for the BBC. 'Perhaps the most impressive politician and statesman I had the pleasure to deal with. He was a delightful companion and conversationalist … immensely civilised'.
Middle right: With Mona and Henry Kissinger. 'A regular contact over the years … he could be extremely funny, albeit in a rather heavy way'.
Bottom: The Royal Family of Iran.

Robert Thomas with his sculpture of me, designed for the Llangollen Eisteddfod.

With the Prince and Princess of Wales at the International Eisteddfod 1985.

On *Britannia* with the Queen and the
Duke of Edinburgh as minister-in-
attendance, 1968. 'The atmosphere
on board was relaxed and convivial'.

The Chadlington children; our
extended family.

Mona and I on our way to a
Royal garden party, *c* 1985.

'One of the concerns which has been at the heart of most of what I have said and done and written in my adult life is that of the liberty of the individual human being. I have opposed, as far as I was able, any political system or philosophy which attacks or erodes the right of an individual to act freely according to his own conscience, provided always that in doing so he does not inhibit the freedom of others to do likewise'.

the Royal Marines Church at Eastney Barracks in March 1965, based principally upon the Christian concept of 'the just war'. More than thirty years later this concept remains at the heart of my thinking about war and peace.

Then, however, I had to turn aside to less philosophical concerns. Having been thoroughly briefed by the Foreign Office Common Market team – most memorably by the acerbic and Euro-omniscient Con O'Neill – I went to Brussels in July on what was described by my advisers as a 'familiarisation visit'. Con O'Neill was a remarkable influence within the Foreign Office. He had the most acute mind of any official I ever worked with and his enthusiasm for Europe was impressive. I suspect that even in those early days he privately entertained a vision of an integrated or even federal Europe. Just as I saw Michael Quinlan as the intellectual father of the British nuclear strategy, so Con was undoubtedly the driving force of British policy on Europe. They were impressive twin pillars of policy-making in Whitehall in the 1960s, whose influence went far beyond that of many of their less able political colleagues.

My visit to Brussels was a fairly concentrated affair during which I met Jean Rey, the President of the Commission, and several of his Commissioners, as well as the Belgian Foreign Minister. My wife and I also visited the flat which was to be our official residence in Brussels and I was able to inspect the building which was to house my negotiating team. The British Ambassador at the time was Sir Roderick Barclay, who was later to experience the full Force Nine impact of a George Brown visit. He orchestrated my own low-key and incident-free programme with his customary urbane skill.

George Brown, the Secretary of State for Foreign Affairs at the time, already had a considerable reputation for eccentric behaviour. At his desk in the Foreign Office he used one of those chairs which spins on a central pedestal, and George was accustomed to begin spinning disconcertingly, often in the middle of a sentence which was not, even without this gyratory diversion, entirely comprehensible. On one occasion, a meeting of Ministers and senior officials had been summoned to be addressed by the Foreign Secretary on some issue of national importance. Unfortunately, it took place immediately after an official lunch at which the government hospitality people had dispensed imprudent quantities of champagne.

The Secretary of State entered the room, which was already full of his expectant minions, sat at his desk and immediately embarked on a more than usually vigorous spin, with the result that he revolved rapidly for what seemed like several minutes while we all waited with decreasing optimism, for some pronouncement on the direction of British foreign policy. Eventually the Foreign Secretary came to rest, facing away from his audience, gazing expectantly across the Horse Guards' Parade, as though seeking inspiration from Admiralty House. At last he turned towards the group and dismissed it on the grounds that we had all had too much to drink at lunch.

There were, and have been since, various explanations advanced for George Brown's disconcerting behaviour, many of them to do with drink. The effect of alcohol on individual behaviour is, of course, a complicated medical problem and in George Brown's case it was suggested that there might have been some deficiency in his body's enzyme system for metabolising alcohol. Whatever the reason, his behaviour certainly became erratic even after one or two drinks and this frequently made diplomatic intercourse and even serious negotiations difficult to sustain in his presence. This was especially regrettable as, when completely sober, he was quick to master a brief and was formidably articulate and persuasive in expounding it. This sometimes tended to be a wasted asset as when, for example, he once summoned me to his side as he was apparently engaged in conversation with a distinguished French statesman and said loudly, 'Here, Chalfont, you speak this man's silly language. What's he on about?' The fact that 'this man' also spoke almost perfect English had evidently escaped his notice.

It was under the direction of this somewhat Rabelaisian character that I began my attempt to negotiate Britain's entry into the Common Market.

10

A Brief Interlude in Europe

The greater part of the month following my appointment as 'Mr Europe', as several tabloids confusingly described me, was spent reassuring delegations from anxious Commonwealth countries. New Zealand was particularly keen to secure its agricultural export markets in the event of British entry into the EEC, and Australia, India, and Pakistan voiced similar concerns. I then returned to Europe, where my first official visit to Brussels was followed by a tour of the capitals of EEC member states, the 'Six', in early September 1967. While we awaited the official report from the Commission on the British application, we hoped to discuss with political leaders any potential fears or objections in advance of the next meeting of the Council of Ministers in October. Our position was straight-forward: we could see no reason why the Council should not decide to open negotiations immediately. While Britain was not prepared to settle for anything less than full membership of the Common Market, the government was ready to negotiate on specific areas of concern, notably the role of sterling as a reserve currency.

The first and most important courtesy call was to Paris, still the focus of opposition to British membership. I was received in the splendour of the Quai d'Orsay by the Foreign Minister, Couve de Murville. Diplomatic relations need not mirror personal feelings, but it is certainly true that M. Couve's character did not make for a genial relationship. He was dry to the point of desiccation.

He repeated old fears that the admission of Britain and others would 'dilute' the EEC and that an enlarged union might be incorporated into a larger Atlantic community aligned more closely with the United States; this, he argued, would have the effect of prolonging the division of Europe. I gave the obvious assurances that Britain and the other applicants (Denmark, Ireland, and Norway), were intending to join the EEC as it then stood, leading to a bigger but no more 'diluted' community. Further, we hoped that a larger community would play a greater role in an Atlantic partnership, but as a government at the forefront of attempts to achieve a thaw in East–West relations we were hardly going to work against that goal once inside the community. M. Couve de Murville gave little indication of what the French position would be at the Council but we proceeded on the assumption that British membership was ultimately inevitable, even if French objections could cause a considerable delay. In fact this delay was not to be broken until after the resignation of the ageing General de Gaulle some two years later.

In an effort to build some momentum in the run up to the Council of Ministers' meeting, I addressed the Consultative Assembly in Strasbourg a few days before the Commission's report on our application was due to be published. It was a deliberately tub-thumping speech in which I promised that 'we shall go on sounding the British trumpet while there are still people who believe that Europe can be made without us.' We certainly hoped that by making it clear that we would not take 'no' for an answer the other five member states would, at the very least, put pressure on the French not to veto the application. As if to underline the point that we would not go away, whatever the Six decided at their next meeting, the Foreign Office leased an apartment in the Ixells quarter of Brussels for the princely sum of £25 per week. Our official residence, the property of a widowed Belgian aristocrat, offered fine views over the Bois de la Cambre on one side and a monastery garden on the other. I hoped that our tenancy would be as short as the projected negotiations, and Mona wisely decided not to give up her job in a London teaching hospital until the Six had finally agreed to talk.

Our arrival in the Avenue Jean Duray coincided with the publication of the report into the application by Britain and other nations to join the EEC. It was a classic example of the Commission's work, listing a clear balance of advantages in favour of Britain and other applicants joining the EEC and yet unable to give a firm opinion on the merits of British entry. The report stated that it would be appropriate to open negotiations to explore the problems raised, but in a passage on financial and monetary difficulties the tone switched from confidence and optimism to severe criticism. It was generally agreed that the influence of the French Commissioner, M. Raymond Barre, was discernible in the harsh critique of structural weaknesses in the British economy.

The unwillingness of the French government to move towards negotiations was further reinforced when de Gaulle summoned the British ambassador in Paris, Sir Patrick Reilly, to the Elysée Palace. Sir Patrick's pessimistic assessment was then passed to George Brown in Scarborough, where he was preparing to do battle on Europe at the Labour Party conference. The conference backed the application to join the EEC solidly but by no means unanimously: Manny Shinwell's contribution to the debate, 'damn the Common Market', was representative of a significant group within the party. More importantly for those of us preparing to negotiate, George succeeded in getting support for the government's approach to Europe without hampering our negotiating position with pre-conditions or restrictions; Labour had effectively abandoned the 'Gaitskell conditions' agreed by the party in 1962.

The preliminary rebuff to our application delivered by M. Couve de Murville at the Council of Ministers' meeting in Luxembourg heightened the tension at home and delighted the anti-Marketeers, nowhere more so than in Fleet Street. It was against this background that I found myself briefing a group of journalists in a hotel room in Lausanne during an EFTA meeting in late October. Such was the impact of this fairly innocent discussion amongst the media and, to a lesser extent, the diplomatic community, that it became elevated to the status of the 'Lausanne Incident' or the 'Chalfont Affair'. The facts, as always, are a little less sensational.

I held two meetings with journalists on the evening of 27th October in my room at the Hotel Beau Rivage. The correspondents were keen to know what the British response would be in the event of a rejection of our application, although we did not regard Couve de Murville's speech in Luxembourg as a veto. Having laid down the ground rules for the discussion – that it was off-the-record and was not to be written up as a story, and certainly not to be attributed to any individual – I agreed to enter into a broad-ranging exchange of views with the journalists present. The tone of the conversation was philosophical and speculative and my opinions, as I repeatedly pointed out, were clearly my own and had not been discussed with other members of the government.

We teased out the political implications of a rejection of the British application, and several journalists pointed to a change in the public mood at home if Britain were 'snubbed'. Within this hypothetical situation we discussed the role of NATO and the possible development of Anglo-French and Anglo-German relations. It was, as the BBC correspondent later suggested, a throwback to the time when Ministers were able to have completely friendly and open discussions with experienced journalists in which the Minister listened to the ideas of the press as much as putting forward his own. It is a measure of how far the relationship of trust between the press and the government has declined that my confidence in the journalists with whom I was talking now seems somewhat naïve.

My first inkling that some of the group intended to ignore or break the ground rules came during dinner. As a result, I invited them back for a second meeting, again attended by my officials, at which I re-emphasised the basis on which the discussion had taken place. Several journalists who had not attended the first meeting were present at the second and it is an interesting reflection on their approach to the truth that they were subsequently among the most enthusiastic at reporting the first discussion, at which they had not even been present. Nothing appeared in the following day's papers but by Friday evening the first hint of trouble had reached the Foreign Office news desk and it became clear that, with one or two honourable exceptions, the journalists had apparently come to some sort of collective decision to ignore the conditions laid down for the conversation. In the process they had decided that the opinions I expressed were more than my own and that I must in some way have been meaning to 'fly a kite' for a major change of policy in the event of a definitive rejection by the EEC member states. This was simply untrue, but their remarkable capacity for self-delusion allowed the journalists to justify a breach of trust that was, in those days, comparatively rare.

The result was a series of front page stories on the Saturday morning grotesquely distorting what had gone on in Lausanne. It was suggested that the government was somehow contemplating a complete revision of her attitude towards Germany; we might withdraw troops from the Rhine Army and recognise East Germany and the Oder-Neisse Line. In short, I was supposed to have suggested a complete realignment of our strategic commitments and historical alliances. This was interpreted as a direct challenge, if not a threat, to de Gaulle, a position as unwelcome to our diplomatic efforts as it was encouraging to the anti-European press. Equally damaging was the inference in some reports that I had discussed divisions within the Cabinet over European policy, suggesting differences between the Prime Minister and the Foreign Secretary. These were not distortions or exaggerations: they were, quite simply, inventions.

I returned to London early on the Saturday morning and went to Downing Street to see the Prime Minister. He was seated, as usual on such occasions, at the Cabinet table and I sat down next to him and gave him a full description of the events of the Thursday evening. I felt that the situation might be so embarrassing to the government that I should resign and I told Harold that he should consider my position to be at his disposal. Harold would have none of it: we all have trouble with the press, he said, and having already heard from my officials, he felt that I had been badly let down by one journalist in particular and that the 'pack' had followed.

There was absolutely no question of my being allowed to resign and Harold added that, to demonstrate this fact, he would personally see me out of the front door and shake my hand in public, before I went back across to the Foreign Office. I was impressed not only by Harold's support but by his willingness – not always to be taken for granted among politicians – to show his loyalty in public.

The Prime Minister went on to mount a strong defence of me in the House of Commons when confronted by the Opposition, some of whom actually welcomed what they saw as my threat to 'turn nasty' on the Six. In the following days I drew on personal relationships built up with the 'Five' to reassure all of them, and particularly the Germans, that the stories said more about the British press than about the British government.

The Lausanne Incident also brought to a head a simmering tension between the government and the press over a wide range of issues from journalistic ethics to the coverage of Kim Philby, a ruthless traitor whom *The Sunday Times* was busily re-inventing as some sort of folk hero. The Prime Minister launched a number of attacks on the press, pointing to their shameless behaviour in Lausanne, where they had abandoned any semblance of trust in the interests of furthering their anti-European agenda. George Brown's response was, characteristically, more spectacular. He warmed up by roundly criticising the press at a farewell reception for one of his officials, attended by diplomatic correspondents. The party ended in some acrimony after George's choice remarks on the chairman of the Mirror Group, Cecil King, caused his son Michael to walk out. The following evening, at a Savoy dinner hosted by Lord Thomson, owner of *The Times*, George prefaced his prepared speech with a scathing personal attack on his host in which he questioned the press baron's honesty and integrity, as well as *The Sunday Times'* enthusiasm for furthering Soviet interests. As an excitable group of journalists swarmed around him after the speech George harangued them on their behaviour in Lausanne, describing the

British press, in Aneurin Bevan's words, as 'the most prostituted in the world'. He concluded by shouting, 'You can't do a Chalfont on me – full stop.'

The details of what was actually discussed at Lausanne tended to be overtaken by the wider argument about the rights and responsibilities of the press. In any case, events in Europe were moving on and demanding new policy initiatives ahead of the next Council of Ministers' meeting in December. In late November President de Gaulle held a press conference at which he was a good deal tougher than expected in his opposition to the British application. As the first reports came through the Secretary of State called a meeting at which the policy he intended to present to Cabinet was agreed: we decided to provoke the other five members of the Common Market to precipitate a crisis with the French at the December meeting, as a result of which they would force the French either to negotiate or to produce a veto. This strategy would be pursued through a series of bilateral meetings over the following fortnight.

After the meeting I remained behind to discuss some of the political implications with George Brown. It seemed to me essential to prepare the way for a veto and to look at policy beyond it, given that the General had, to all intents and purposes, already imposed that veto. George resolutely refused even to contemplate this, taking the stance of a trade union negotiator who gives nothing away until the last moment and does not even admit to any doubts in his own mind. I agreed, of course, to follow this policy but I told him that I regarded it as misguided. By the end of the evening a French spokesman had made it clear beyond any doubt that de Gaulle had meant that negotiations with Britain were out of the question. The formal veto followed at the Council of Ministers' meeting in December, despite the views and votes of the other five members.

The veto created an entirely new political situation and we immediately set about deciding what our next move should be. With the agreement of the Cabinet, we determined that we should leave our application 'on the table' while developing some form of communication between 'the Friendly Five' and ourselves. While privately accepting that our application was likely to remain blocked as long as de Gaulle was in power, we intended to by-pass the French and strengthen other European structures in readiness for our ultimate entry. The Five were open to this but had different ideas about the next step. Willy Brandt, the West German Foreign Minister, was keen to pursue some form of membership by stages and seemed particularly put out that the Italians had taken the initiative in promoting the '5+1' strategy.

These policy developments took place in an increasingly unsettled and demoralised atmosphere at the Foreign Office. The degree of distasteful political infighting also increased with every complication in Europe and, in December, my own rather equivocal personal relationship with George Brown was in danger of becoming unworkable. Ronald Brown, the Foreign Secretary's brother, had reported to me some political gossip to the effect that I was conspiring with the Prime Minister to undermine the Secretary of State's policy on the Common Market, a rumour hardly calculated to improve our relationship.

In fact I had given George considerable support in his enthusiasm for Europe, when Harold Wilson tended to take a more sceptical attitude. Our relationship was a little strained, not because of Europe or other aspects of foreign policy, but because the task of being George's unofficial minder, which Harold had quite clearly delegated to me soon after my appointment, was becoming a considerable challenge. Although many Foreign Office officials had genuine admiration – as I did – for George's intellect and political skills, and for his warmth and relaxed dealings with civil servants, a few senior officials and more than a few of his Cabinet colleagues were unhappy with his behaviour.

This was frequently embarrassing, and I was quite used to being taken aside by officials of other European countries, who would ask with some incredulity, 'Is this what the Foreign Secretary really wants us to hear?' I do not myself think that his erratic style did any serious diplomatic damage; people made allowances and the Foreign Office ensured that the wheels of serious diplomatic relations kept turning.

There were, of course, occasions of catastrophic embarrassment. One such took place during an official visit to Brussels. After a day of talks with the Belgian government, the Foreign Minister held a banquet in George's honour at his official residence. The Belgian Prime Minister, the Defence Minister, the Belgian Chiefs of Staff, and many other dignitaries were there and the meal, as one might expect in such a setting, was sumptuous. As usual I was keeping an eye on George from across the table and, after an uneventful meal, I realised that he was becoming a little 'tired and emotional' after partaking of the excellent wines with his customary enthusiasm.

I signalled to a Belgian official that it might be time to bring the proceedings to a fairly swift conclusion, and the party broke up. It was not in any case their custom to extend the evening with discussion over brandy or coffee. I then looked round to discover, to my horror, that George had disappeared from his place. He then made a dramatic appearance at the main door of the dining room, waving his arms in the air and shouting, 'Wait! I have something to say!'

We were as frozen with the premonition of embarrassment as were our hosts, and so George was able to continue before we could get to him. 'While we've all been wining and dining here tonight,' he said, 'who's been defending Europe?' This was clearly not going to be a rhetorical question. It scarcely had time to hang in the air before George answered it. 'I'll tell you who's been defending Europe – the British army, that's who!' Unfortunately, this was not the only question on his mind: 'And where, you may ask, are the soldiers of the Belgian army tonight? I'll tell you where the Belgian soldiers are. They're in the brothels of Brussels.'

The flourish with which George delivered this last piece of rather slurred alliteration gave us the chance to bundle him out of the room, leaving our dazed hosts behind. It had, of course, been a private joke amongst British and American officials that the soldiers of our NATO allies tended to go home for the weekend, presumably on the assumption that the Soviet armed forces kept office hours. But no one had quite foreseen such a public airing of the issue.

The evening did not end there. On our return to the British embassy George, having metamorphosed into his petulant child persona, sat down in Sir Roderick Barclay's sitting room and demanded a whisky. He then observed, 'There's no fire in this room. I'm cold. I want a fire.' Roddy, notwithstanding the trying evening he had suffered, observed that all the servants had gone to bed.

'Where's your wife?' asked George.

'Well, she's in bed as she normally is at this time.'

'Get her up,' commanded George.

In similar circumstances I might have suggested exactly where George could light his fire, but Roddy, one of nature's consummate gentlemen and a born diplomat, woke Lady Barclay, who dutifully laid a fire. It was at the end of days like this – particularly during foreign visits – that the undeniable compensation that 'life with George is never dull' began to pall a little.

But there certainly were lighter moments, even to overseas visits. I am sometimes quoted as the source for the Foreign Office's favourite George Brown story. I retell it here for completeness' sake, but in the knowledge that the passage of time and the inevitable developments of the 'oral tradition' have made me a little hazy as to the exact details. Suffice to say that George was attending a glittering diplomatic ball of the sort which, by the 1960s, were held only in Latin American countries or in those European states which still saw themselves as the descendants of the Austro-Hungarian empire.

As the evening wore on and George became a little worn himself, he spotted amongst the gold braid of dress uniforms and sumptuous evening dresses, a figure clad in scarlet watered-silk who caught his particular attention. Having lurched dangerously across the room, George asked with suitable courtesy, if he might be granted the pleasure of a dance. After a long and somewhat frosty silence, the guest replied: 'There are three reasons, Mr Brown, why I will not dance with you. The first is that I fear you have had a little too much to drink. The second is that this is not a waltz. The orchestra is playing the national anthem which is, perhaps, why the other guests are standing to attention. And the third reason why I will not dance with you, Foreign Secretary, is that I am the Cardinal Archbishop of Lima.'

To return to the more mundane reality of life in the Foreign Office, I discussed the general situation there with Michael Palliser, the Prime Minister's Private Secretary. We talked about the possibility of my moving to another post, even perhaps to a diplomatic appointment if that was the only means of escape from the political rat race. A similar conversation followed with George Wigg, the ubiquitous political fixer, and a number of government appointments were considered, with no particular conclusion. In the event, George Brown's extraordinary reign at the Foreign Office came to an end three months later. Having threatened to resign on countless occasions, most recently in my hearing at a pre-Christmas dinner hosted by the Argentine ambassador, his resignation during the international gold crisis in March 1968 was accepted and he departed for the back benches.

As it happened, the Argentine ambassador was well used to George's antics. I can vividly recall a dinner at his embassy attended by the Foreign Secretary, at which a fine steak was served as the main course. Staring at this magnificent cut of meat, George prodded it accusingly and then shouted at the ambassador, 'Where's this from, then?' His host, with some pride, replied, 'Argentina, Foreign Secretary.' 'I'm not eating this muck,' was George's diplomatic rejoinder and, as usual in these circumstances, he was not joking.

Whatever else might be said about George Brown, there has never been anyone quite like him in British politics. Whether this is a matter for regret or satisfaction depends on which facet of this remarkable character is turned towards the light of history – the bullying extrovert, compensating for basic insecurity with outbursts of childish petulance, and hair-raising social indiscretions, or the thoughtful politician quick to reach the heart of the most complex problem, generous, loyal to his friends and concerned for those to whom he might have caused distress.

I remember one particularly tiresome day at the Foreign Office walking out of the room in the middle of one of George's meetings, rigid with anger at an attack he had made on me in the presence of officials, some quite junior. After a period of quiet reflection in my own room – an essential part of any day at the Foreign Office in those turbulent years – I sent him a short note saying that I would like to see him privately. I was summoned at once and went back to the Foreign Secretary's room, ready for a fight.

George was alone and, looking up from his desk, he smiled ruefully and said, 'I suppose you've come to give me hell?' There followed a handsome apology and a glass of the darkish sherry which was used as balm on these occasions. At such moments, most people would have forgiven George anything – except, perhaps, that sherry.

His departure did allow some time for a review of the government's foreign policy. I put together a paper calling for a more imaginative and flexible approach beyond what appeared to me the tired certainties of the Cold War stand-off. I genuinely believed that the only way to break the deadlock in the arms negotiations was to take some risks in foreign policy initiatives. I sent my suggestions to Michael Palliser at No. 10, but they soon disappeared without trace in the depths of the Whitehall machine.

George's commitment to Europe had been unwavering and his insistence on maintaining the British application after the veto laid the foundations for further attempts and for final entry. In the two years after his departure we continued to develop structures for closer integration with European allies, notably through the Western European Union. The harmonisation of foreign policy and the strength this could bring were all the more desirable in the light of the Soviet invasion of Czechoslovakia. In a fit of pique the French began a boycott of the WEU in February

1969, but my appointment as permanent delegate a month later reinforced both our commitment to Europe and our refusal to bow to French notions of their hegemony.

With the resignation of President de Gaulle came the first real prospect of opening constructive negotiations. The Prime Minister decided that the Common Market negotiator should be in the Cabinet and appointed George Thomson to the post, allowing me to resume, with some misgivings and a growing weariness for politics, full responsibility for disarmament negotiations.

As I look back on the tortured process by which we eventually entered the Common Market, parallels with our current dilemma are all too clear. From the very first consideration of membership the principal attraction for me was the prospect of an economic union, a block which could become a major trading power and a significant rival to the United States economy. However, I was then – and I remain – opposed to political integration, primarily because I do not wish to see our political links with the United States weakened.

For reasons which may have become clear, I have always been an Atlanticist in foreign and defence matters: the simple reality is that our best interests in security will continue to lie with the United States for the foreseeable future. The notion of common European foreign or defence policies – ideas which have been talked or dreamed about since long before I was involved in European negotiations – seem to me to be fanciful, even now.

I am suspicious of a single currency, not because I doubt the efficacy of the currency itself, but because I cannot envisage a single currency without an effective central bank with control of fiscal policy across the whole union. I cannot easily see how national governments can maintain sufficient autonomy while handing over fiscal policy to a collective European body.

Having said this, I am sufficiently pragmatic to agree that entry into the single currency may become inevitable, once all the other member states are participating. Clearly, we must do everything necessary to prepare ourselves for this possibility –

should the country vote for it – and to this extent I am in agreement with government policy, so far as it can be clearly identified at the time of writing. The Conservative Party's present policy leaves me as bemused as the Labour Party's did, for different reasons, in the 1970s: the idea of closing down options for a period of two parliaments (longer presumably, if no preparations are to be made during that time) strikes me as politically disastrous and totally unnecessary.

I I

From Moscow to the Falkland Islands

One could be forgiven for thinking that six years at the Foreign Office were dominated in equal measure by the vicissitudes of European negotiations and the colourful presence of the Secretary of State. In reality, the landscape of international relations was overshadowed by the looming threat of the USSR and the Eastern bloc countries, the global stand-off between East and West which was finding its latest expression in Vietnam. It was against this background that the daily routines of a Foreign Office Minister, the parliamentary appearances and overseas visits, were undertaken.

My experiences in military intelligence for the BAOR had left me with few illusions about Soviet strategy or intentions. Negotiating face to face with Soviet leaders was, however, a different matter. My first encounter with Andrei Gromyko, the man who dictated Soviet foreign policy throughout most of the Cold War period, came during a visit to Moscow in November 1965. Seated at a large oval conference table on the seventh floor of the Foreign Ministry building, the Foreign Secretary, Michael Stewart, and I were confronted with the self-righteous inflexibility which I came to associate with the Soviet position throughout the following years of disarmament negotiations.

Gromyko was depressingly like his image in the Western media: tough, dour, and without much discernible warmth. It was often joked that '*nyet*' was his favourite word, and it is certainly true that his use of it was liberal, even if his political instincts were not. But he was an effective negotiator and an adversary to be respected.

At this stage the Russian view was that plans for a multilateral

133

NATO nuclear defence force would have to be abandoned before there could be any East-West agreement on a pact to prevent the further spread of nuclear weapons. Our reply was that, even if NATO decided to set up such a multi-national defence force – by no means a certainty – this would not amount to dissemination because actual control of nuclear weapons would remain firmly in the hands of the existing nuclear powers. It did not seem unreasonable that the NATO nuclear powers should discuss with their allies the possible uses of these weapons and, in any case, proliferation was far more than a European problem, as the Cuban missile crisis had demonstrated.

As so often, the three-hour meeting became a simple statement of positions, supplemented by a barrage of criticism over British support for American policy in Vietnam. Gromyko demanded a cessation of US bombing in North Vietnam but refused Michael Stewart's suggestion that Russia might use her influence with the North Vietnamese government to bring them to an international conference at which a sustainable peace settlement could be constructed. We left Moscow after the usual round of official lunches, protocol visits, and entertainments – on this occasion a performance of *Don Quixote* at the Bolshoi Theatre.

Vietnam remained the focus of discussions, for me at least, when I returned to Moscow some weeks later, in February 1966, accompanying the Prime Minister and a large delegation on a four-day visit. Our arrival was less than totally dignified after heavy fog forced our Trident aircraft to abort its landing at the last minute, pull back from the runway and fly on a further thirty miles to the airport at Sherematievo. For our hosts the arrival was even less dignified as they sped across country to meet us at the new airport, losing at least one official car on the icy roads en route. But it was clear from the scale of the guard of honour and the welcome by Prime Minister Kosygin that the Russians intended this to be a successful visit.

Despite progress in bilateral talks on technology and trade, Vietnam remained an immovable obstacle. Kosygin and his delegation were not prepared to move towards any kind of negotiated solution and Leonid Brezhnev, then Party Secretary, took an even harder and gloomier line. However, during the intervals of a performance of *The Fountain of Bakchisarai* at the Bolshoi Theatre, it became possible to get beyond official posturing; without his officials, except one interpreter, Kosygin discussed the situation freely with the Prime Minister and with me (I was also acting as Harold Wilson's interpreter).

We impressed on him our disappointment that the bombing-pause initiated by the Americans had not produced any positive reaction from the North Vietnamese. We were keen too that he should accept the sincerity of the US administration's desire for talks leading to a genuine and total withdrawal of American forces. Whether or not Kosygin accepted this, it became clear that Soviet influence over Hanoi was severely limited, particularly in the context of aggressive Chinese pressure. He did, however, surprise us by suggesting that he might be able to arrange a meeting for me at the North Vietnamese Embassy.

The circumstances of this meeting were quite bizarre. Halfway through a function at the Kremlin, I was informed that a visit to the North Vietnamese Embassy had been arranged. The conditions were quite strict: I was to go alone and the Russians insisted on driving me in an ageing black limousine, complete with KGB minder, through the darkened streets of Moscow to the embassy. It was an unsettling and somewhat sinister experience. I arrived to find what seemed to be a lively party in progress. Although I was expected, the North Vietnamese Chargé d'Affaires, Lee Chang, seemed slightly surprised that the meeting had been arranged – clearly the North Vietnamese had not requested it. The atmosphere at the meeting was surprisingly convivial, providing the occasion for a fairly informal exchange of views about the situation.

This was the first contact between a British Minister and a representative of North Vietnam, and I began by pointing out that the Prime Minister's interest in these discussions was evidence of our good faith and of the UK's willingness to help in the process of reaching a settlement. Above all, we wanted –

and we were convinced that the US government also wanted – a negotiated end to the conflict in Vietnam. We hoped that the irreconcilable public positions of the two sides could, by means of confidential discussions, be brought to a point where negotiations could begin.

There were, however, a number of clarifications needed. First, it was clear that the US government would be unlikely to respond to a proposal that involved either the exclusion of the South Vietnamese government or a privileged place for the National Liberation Front (NLF). Second, if the total withdrawal of US forces was envisaged before an agreement had been reached, this would be equally unacceptable. Third, if the North Vietnamese message meant that the US must agree, in advance of negotiations and irrespective of their result, that the NLF exercise supreme power in South Vietnam, then this was clearly unrealistic, destroying the whole point of negotiations. Finally, the North Vietnamese demand that US bombing should cease was only likely to be acceptable if reciprocated by similar concessions on the North Vietnamese side.

Throughout the long, five-hour session I stressed that I was not speaking on behalf of the US government but that my Prime Minister was prepared to act as an intermediary and recommend to President Johnson any process of negotiations that could realistically proceed on reasonable and honourable terms. The reply from Lee Chang did not inspire great hope that this would be possible. The North Vietnamese refused to believe that the US wanted to negotiate a peace settlement at all and argued that the recent American 'Peace Offensive' was merely a cover for further aggression. As for the role of the NLF, it was, they said, the sole genuine representative of the Vietnamese people and must have the decisive voice in negotiations. Having refused to settle for anything less than a unilateral cessation of military activity on the part of the Americans, the Chargé rounded off his reply with a general attack on the British position, accusing us of disregarding our obligations as co-chairman of the 1954 Geneva Conference on Indo-China.

This response was both disappointing and depressing and it

was difficult to see why the Russians had gone to such lengths to set up a meeting with so little prospect of success. We concluded with a slightly pointless exchange over the confidentiality of our talks; I told Lee Chang that it was unrealistic to suppose that their existence could be kept a secret, as the North Vietnamese wished, but I assured them that the contents would not be published. In contrast to this impasse, talks with Russian officials on disarmament issues, especially on non-proliferation, were warmer and more productive. By the end of the Prime Ministerial visit I had been invited to return to Moscow in March, my third visit in less than six months.

The warmth extended during the previous visit, when factory workers 'spontaneously' cheered our drive to the airport, was still felt in March. Indeed, the fact that a British visitor was received in the days immediately before the 23rd Congress of the Soviet Communist Party – the apparatchik's busiest time – was seen as significant. The two days of talks with Gromyko on non-proliferation reinforced this friendly atmosphere and moved us nearer to breaking the log-jam and clearing the way to a treaty. Observers were divided as to whether the Soviet leadership genuinely saw the UK as a useful channel to Washington or whether they hoped to reassure their own 'doves' before indulging in ritual imperialist-bashing at the Congress, where they expected to encounter further charges of revisionism and weakness from the Chinese.

Both Gromyko and I had come to an unspoken recognition of a state of affairs which I had confronted in Geneva: that General and Complete Disarmament (GCD) was going nowhere. It was therefore sensible to concentrate on the area of non-proliferation (preventing the spread of nuclear weapons) where there was a real prospect of concluding a treaty. For a change, the nuclear powers – excluding China, which took no part in the discussions – were in broad agreement. It was the 'near-nuclear' states or the non-aligned who were much against the idea. In the Moscow discussions we intended to address some of the concerns of these states and to agree ways of ensuring that co-operation between nuclear allies would still be possible under the treaty.

It was not, however, these meetings, or the endless round of disarmament negotiations in Geneva that were to be the defining moment of the Cold War for me. That watershed came in London late at night on Tuesday, 20th August 1968, when I received a call from the Foreign Office asking if, in the Prime Minister's absence, I would receive the Soviet ambassador at my home in Chelsea.

I knew Ambassador Smirnovsky well. He was a civilised and effective diplomat who had done more than most to improve relations between our respective governments. When he arrived at the door he was clearly embarrassed, ill at ease, and visibly upset. I offered him a drink, to which he replied, 'Perhaps you should hear what I have to say before you decide to be hospitable.' He then told me that he had been instructed by his government to inform us that Warsaw Pact forces were about to move into Czechoslovakia.

We had, of course, discussed this possibility at the Foreign Office and I spelt out to him our dismay. I hardly needed to tell him that this would seriously damage relations between our countries and escalate the crisis between East and West – he knew better than anyone the effect the invasion would have. Even as the ambassador spoke to me, Soviet paratroops were taking control of Prague Airport and some half a million Warsaw Pact soldiers were preparing to invade at first light.

The Prime Minister was on holiday in the Scilly Isles and the communication was such that it could not be passed to him even over the scrambler phone in his cottage. Instead he went to an office at the Customs & Excise building, which had a secure communications link. Having received the news he travelled back to London and arrived at Downing Street soon after 9.00 a.m., along with Foreign Secretary, Michael Stewart, who had also rushed back from a holiday in the West Country. Our statement of condemnation was sent to Lord Caradon at the United Nations and was probably the first issued by any country.

Parliament was recalled within a week and joined the international chorus of condemnation. But the feeling of Western impotence, combined with betrayal of the much-vaunted *détente*, was powerful. As news and intelligence reports revealed the ruthlessness with which Soviet forces put down dissent, the political implications became unavoidable. The Soviet Union felt entitled to intervene anywhere within what amounted to its 'empire' – the first example of a policy which became known as the Brezhnev Doctrine, which was to reach its brutal consummation in Afghanistan more than a decade later.

There had always been a serious debate in the country and in the Labour Party about the foreign policy objectives of the communist states. Whereas it was generally agreed that China was not expansionist, opinion was genuinely divided on the ambitions of Soviet communism. There were good arguments – only gradually eroded over the years – to support the thesis that the Warsaw Pact was as defensive and pacific as NATO.

Experience of Soviet negotiators like Tsarapkin and Roshchin in Geneva, and of diplomats like Smirnovsky, had encouraged me to sustain the hope that this might be true. But the invasion of Czechoslovakia changed that definitively. Just as I was beginning to lose faith in Soviet intentions at the arms talk, so the invasion and the intelligence material generated in those weeks, convinced me that I could no longer be confident that the Soviet Union had really satisfied her territorial ambitions. If there was a moment when I became a committed Cold War warrior, this was it.

There is an interesting postscript to these events which confirmed my opinions about the extent of Soviet ambitions. In 1975 I had a series of conversations, on which I based a string of articles for *The Times*, with Major-General Jan Sejna. He had defected from Czechoslovakia shortly before the Prague Spring and had been described at the time as the highest-ranking defector ever. But his significance was greater than even his rank suggested. For Sejna was the First Secretary of the Communist Party in the Czechoslovak Ministry of Defence, the senior party official in the armed forces. He was also a member of the

Praesidium, the ruling élite of the Czechoslovak parliament.

Sejna's position was such that he regularly attended the Warsaw Pact planning meetings and for ten years no significant military or political decision was taken in the country without his knowledge. Most importantly, he was involved in the formulation of the Warsaw Pact's strategic plan, designed to implement the foreign policy objectives of the Soviet Union from 1968 into the 1980s. Like all dissidents, Sejna had his shortcomings and there were those who doubted his veracity. But I found that little in his account conflicted with other sources of information on the intentions of the Soviet leadership.

The strategic plan was a massive undertaking: it ran to ten volumes, with individual studies devoted to each country of principal concern to the Warsaw Pact, including, of course, the United Kingdom. Even to someone who had regularly experienced the strategy of the Soviet Union at first hand, this was a breathtakingly cynical document. The first section was historical: Soviet planners explained how the Khrushchev policies of de-Stalinisation had created an opening to the West, and persuaded capitalist countries that the communists were now prepared to abandon military confrontation for economic competition.

The second phase of the plan, from 1960 to 1972, set as its key objective the promotion of disunity in the West and the acceleration of social dislocation in the capitalist world. In Western Europe the planners hoped to exploit fears of German nationalism and to exploit French nationalism so as to detach France further from NATO. In line with these aims, the communist parties of Western Europe were given appropriate guidelines. Trade union and student movements were to be used to exploit existing causes of social and industrial unrest and to stimulate new sources of internal conflict. In the United States the aim was to encourage the growth of isolationism, while, on the purely military side, the Warsaw Pact was to be strengthened as a hedge against the possibility of future arms control agreements.

Given that my interviews took place in 1975, perhaps the

most interesting section of the plan recounted to me by Sejna was the third phase, covering the period up to the mid-1980s. The main strategic concept of this part of the plan was to 'smash the concept of false democracy', and achieve the total demoralisation of the West. Co-operation with the United States would ensure maximum economic and technological advantage for the Soviet Union while undermining the belief of the West in the need for effective military defences. Withdrawal of the United States' presence from Europe would be the ultimate goal, against the background of a debilitated NATO.

The final phase of the plan, according to Sejna, was to be the creation of a period of 'global democratic peace' in the late 1980s, with the arrival in power of a 'progressive peace-loving administration' in the United States. With America isolated from Europe, the Warsaw Pact planners envisaged an intensification of the arms race, leading to a situation of overwhelming superiority for the communist forces and an ability to exert effective political control at will. During the two decades which followed the Prague Spring, there seemed to me to be little indication from Soviet sources to suggest that this plan had been altered, or its objectives abandoned. The depressing effect of the events in Czechoslovakia lingered as the reality of Soviet intentions began to sink in.

For me the gloom was lifted in November by my attendance on a State Visit to Brazil and Chile which was both successful and highly enjoyable. Although no announcement had been made in advance, I was also to visit the Falkland Islands on the way home, the first visit by a British Minister.

Appointment as Minister-in-Attendance on the State Visit gave me a fine opportunity to see two equally smooth machines, the Foreign Office and Buckingham Palace, working in flawless harmony. Schedules with precise timings and copious printed notes of advice were circulated in advance, including cautionary observations that 'the climate in Chile is said to be like Scotland in June', and that 'it is not customary to wear white dinner jackets in either country'. (This meant Brazil and Chile, not Scotland.)

After a pleasant but rather functional journey aboard an RAF VC10, including a stop at Dakar, the royal party arrived at Recife to join HMY *Britannia*. The reception in Recife was spectacular. Thousands of Brazilians lined the streets to the Governor's Palace and the music, dancing and shouting made our own street parties look decidedly staid. A power cut inside the palace added a dimension of mediaeval splendour as the Queen was preceded in her progress from room to room by attendants carrying silver candelabra.

The royal yacht itself was an oasis of calm; spotless decks and silent, air-conditioned cabins with stewards who would appear noiselessly and produce perfectly pressed laundry in record time. The atmosphere on board was relaxed and convivial, the ideal setting in which to prepare for the first stage of the visit. As a young (or youngish) Minister I became a good friend and reasonable deck tennis partner for a young naval officer called Jock Slater, who was subsequently to become First Sea Lord.

After a day's sailing south of Recife, flanked by the frigates *Danae* and *Naiad*, we entered the Bay of All the Saints; it was twenty-six years almost to the day since my last visit, on board a very different ship and in very different company.

The reception in the picturesque city of Salvador was equally ecstatic, as the whole town appeared to be in the streets throwing flowers. Matins in a tiny Anglican church on top of the hill was followed by a tour of the spectacular baroque Cathedral of San Francisco. By lunchtime we had left Salvador behind and began to prepare for the serious work of the visit in Brasilia; I discussed with the Duke of Edinburgh the drafts of speeches supplied by the Foreign Office for Her Majesty and our conversations turned to more philosophical matters concerning the use of armed force in international relations, in which the Duke was particularly interested and clearly very knowledgeable.

Once we had reached the Bay of Guanabara, with our escort now augmented by two Brazilian frigates, we went ashore and flew to Brasilia, where the visit became an exhausting round of official receptions, banquets and ministerial meetings. The popular affection for the Queen was apparent everywhere and quite moving to all of us in the royal party, particularly in Rio where she visited the slums of that sprawling city. I was deeply affected by the opportunity to see the monarchy functioning at close hand. It is difficult not to be depressed by the damage that has been done to that institution – though not to its present holder – in the intervening years.

After ten hectic days in Brazil we moved on to Chile, where the popular reception was equally warm but the political situation a good deal less stable. My job as Minister-in-Attendance was to divert any political missiles and to give any advice necessary on government policy. The Duke of Edinburgh and I discussed the speech drafts and decided to dispense with the somewhat bland offering from the Foreign Office intended for the Queen's address to the joint session of Congress. We replaced it with a speech on the theme of the dangers of apathy in a democracy and the forces capable of undermining the democratic system; this subject met with Her Majesty's approval and seemed to go down very well with the Chilean press and public. With hindsight, the message could hardly have been more apposite: within a decade, Chile had lurched through Marxist revolutionary government to military dictatorship.

The State Visit had been a remarkable personal success for the Queen but it also helped to revive interest in South America at home and brought several more tangible benefits. Chief among these was a major contract for nuclear reactors which the Chilean government agreed to purchase following the nuclear co-operation treaty which I had signed in Santiago.

As the royal party began the return journey, the Foreign Office announced my visit – the first by a British Minister – to the Falkland Islands. I left for Montevideo, where the icebreaker HMS *Endurance*, the Royal Navy's only ship stationed in the South Atlantic, was waiting to take me to the islands.

To describe the Falklands – in the words of the official guide to its wildlife – as 'not always easy to get to', was something of an understatement. It was indicative of the anomalous political situation that we could not travel the 300-mile journey from

Argentina, with whom there were no transport links of any kind. Instead we, in common with all visitors, communications and supplies, had to make the five-day journey from Montevideo, across a thousand miles of the world's roughest seas.

The journey did, however, allow me plenty of time to discuss our policy with Sir Arthur Galsworthy, the deputy Under-Secretary with responsibility for dependent territories, and Christopher Diggines, the head of the Latin American department. It was clear to all of us that Britain's changing position in the world, together with growing pressure from Argentina and, more recently, interest from the UN, called for a new initiative; the strategy of masterly inactivity which had served the Foreign Office so well for so long was not sustainable.

Our visit finally got underway in West Falkland, an area devoted exclusively to farming and remote even by the standards of the islands. As we approached from the sea, I was touched to see the quay lined with islanders holding placards – a charming traditional welcome, I assumed. As we got nearer, the words 'Chalfont Go Home' punctured any sense of hubris I might have had and I realised that this was going to be a difficult visit.

The biggest meeting of the day comprised sixty people in the village hall at Port Howard, where ladies served beer, sherry and cake. One local custom which I found less than agreeable was the 'smoko', a kind of barbecue where anyone who could not eat at least ten pounds of mutton at one sitting was considered something of a wimp. But the islanders themselves were unfailingly courteous and, despite the welcoming placards, the profusion of Union Jacks and 'Keep the Falklands British' banners was more than an expression of imperial nostalgia: the islanders clearly felt a deep insecurity about the future.

My purpose was not merely to reassure them, as I did, that there could be no change in sovereignty against their wishes. We genuinely hoped to persuade them that trying to maintain the status quo was not in their real interests; permanent isolation from Argentina and a refusal even to negotiate was damaging to their own economic interests and could, in the longer term, actually be dangerous. The islanders had to recognise the importance of the Falklands issue in Argentinian political life and to appreciate that 'keeping the Falklands British' in 1968 meant something very different from what it might have meant in 1900; Britain was no longer the great nineteenth-century imperial power. If the islanders could bring themselves to face the future realistically, they could rely on the British government to defend their rights and allay understandable fears about closer ties with a politically volatile Argentina.

The very isolation of the islands inevitably made such a perspective difficult for its inhabitants. As we reached Port Stanley on the following day a crowd of some 250 – about a quarter of the population of the capital, which itself was home to half the population of the islands – lined the harbour in icy winds holding 'We want to stay British' signs.

A series of meetings with various bodies, from the Sheep Owners' Association to the Executive Council, allowed us to set out the 'agreed position' which was within sight after eighteen months of negotiation with the Argentine government. This would allow practical steps to improve communications which both sides hoped would lead to a wider rapprochement; meanwhile the two governments would agree to disagree on the issue of sovereignty. This seemed the best chance of developing a future relationship between the islands and Argentina, and avoiding ultimate conflict; it was clear that many members of the Executive Council were opposed to any change whatsoever, but after a further day of talks a majority accepted our position with varying degrees of enthusiasm. In a radio broadcast to the islanders I repeated our assurance that no change in sovereignty could take place without their agreement, ultimately safeguarded by Parliament.

Despite the great kindness and warm hospitality of the islanders, our party left on board HMS *Endurance* with no optimism for their future and with a strong sense of the bizarre anachronism of their situation. By 1st December we had reached Buenos Aires, where an evening of talks over dinner with the Argentine Foreign Minister, Dr Nicanor Costa Méndez, did little to brighten the mood. The Argentine government continued to take a very hard line on sovereignty, refusing to accept the primacy of the wishes of the islanders and the principle of self-determination, particularly since many of the inhabitants had not been born on the Falklands. Talks continued, however, and in July 1971 the Conservative government was to sign an Anglo-Argentine Agreement along the lines of the 'agreed position'.

After this lengthy spell in the southern hemisphere I flew back to London to face ritual accusations of 'betrayal' from certain sections of the press and the opposition. Ironically – in the light of subsequent events – attacks on our policy of negotiating with the Argentinians were led by an indignant Lord Carrington, who accused me of saying that Britain could no longer defend the islands. I had, in fact, said no such thing, but over a decade later, when the invasion finally took place, our inability to defend the islands was inescapable. That is not to say that the crisis in 1982 could not have been averted. The British government could have been more flexible with Argentina and should perhaps have been prepared to take a stronger political position on the future of the islands, rather than simply handing control of policy to the islanders. While acknowledging the ultimate right of islanders to decide, successive governments need not have abdicated all responsibility: they could, for example, have advocated publicly the merits of some sort of lease-back agreement.

This position of persuasion could have been complemented by the judicious use of military force as an implement of foreign policy. Certainly, the warning signs should have been read and a firm military response initiated to demonstrate the government's commitment to the islands. Instead, Argentina – like many others – was left thinking that the United Kingdom cared very little for the Falklands, despite its rhetoric about sovereignty.

The moral and legal imperative to re-take the Falklands in 1982 did not alter the basic fact that the position of the islanders is politically and economically untenable in the long term. It is as clear as I write today as it was when I left the Foreign Office in 1970, that some accommodation with Argentina will one day be necessary.

My next visit to that continent was, as it turned out, my swansong at the Foreign Office. In May 1970 I was asked to undertake a lengthy tour of Central and North America, primarily to represent the government at yet another transfer of power in one of the Central American states. The compensation for a whirlwind, two-week tour of eight nations was that I would be accompanied by my wife.

Looking back, the Nicaraguan leg of the tour remains the most vivid memory, if only because of our encounter with its dictator, Somoza. After the exuberant friendliness of Costa Rica, Managua seemed subdued: even the Latin American spirit had apparently succumbed to the dreary nervousness of a military dictatorship. Although it may have been little consolation to his frightened population, Somoza was himself fearful to the point of paranoia.

When we visited him we were driven to his official residence in an armour-plated car so heavy that its axles groaned under the strain. The palace, which was closer to a fortified bunker than a house, was worthy of a James Bond film. Fabulous paintings vied for wall space with a huge array of humourless bodyguards. No doubt in a vain attempt to calm the nerves of those visitors who had begun mentally to assess their life insurance policies, Somoza had arranged for music to be piped through speakers in the ceiling of each room. The resulting mixture of sensations was quite disorientating: it was hard to know whether one was about to be assassinated in a supermarket or an undiscovered wing of the National Gallery.

Notwithstanding some ghastly despots in a continent which specialised in dictators, these visits to South America cemented my lasting interest in the region. A few years later I was asked to become president of the Hispano and Luso-Brazilian Councils, Canning House. This proved to be an extremely valuable forum for the exchange of ideas between interested business people, academics, civil servants, diplomats and politicians, at a time when Latin America tended to be regarded as something of a backwater by many of those groups.

Shortly before the general election of 1970, there was an

event which left an especially vivid mark on my memory. The three astronauts who had been to the moon on *Apollo 11* visited England and I was asked by the Prime Minister to entertain them. My wife and I took all three out to dinner and were given a memorable personal briefing on their remarkable achievement. Afterwards we were presented with a colour photograph, signed by the three men, of the landing module approaching the moon's surface, with the Earth, itself like a small moon, in the background. It was clear from our meeting that these men had been through an experience so profound in its impact that it was not possible to communicate it fully to anyone who had not shared it. Quite simply, they were like beings from another planet.

Much later I was to meet Neil Armstrong, the commander of the *Apollo* mission, as a fellow member of the Academy of the Kingdom of Morocco. He became a good friend, and although he has not lost his other-worldliness it has been overlaid by the pleasant, unassuming self-confidence appropriate to the persona of the first man on the moon.

12

Television Journalism

Labour's unexpected defeat in the General Election of 1970 introduced me to a new and not altogether comfortable experience of political life, as part of Her Majesty's Loyal Opposition. It also meant losing my ministerial salary, but this was not a matter of grave importance, since I could rely upon the support of a wife with a flourishing medical practice, and could also return to the world of newspapers, radio and television. The transformation, however, had other less welcome consequences.

For someone who had become a politician solely with the purpose of joining the executive and exercising real responsibility, opposition was at times a tiresome exercise. The ritual of constantly and automatically objecting was irksome, and I was expected to pronounce on subjects well outside my field of interest or expertise. The growing conflict in Northern Ireland was a subject on which I could make a useful contribution; street cleansing in central London, however important that might be, was not. I was even, at one point, a member of the opposition health team, perhaps on the basis that my wife was a doctor.

I had already been involved in a minor way in the events in Northern Ireland while at the Foreign Office, and had frequently been called upon to comment on the situation both in government and later in opposition. In 1969 the first bombings of the current period of 'the Troubles' had taken place – the destruction of electricity and water supplies in Belfast by Loyalist paramilitaries. By August the situation had deteriorated further and there were fierce riots in Londonderry; British troops were deployed on the streets.

The Irish government had reacted by setting up army field hospitals across the border in Co. Donegal, and announced the mobilisation of Irish army reservists 'to ensure they will be in readiness for participation in peace-keeping operations'. At the same time they launched a diplomatic initiative at the United Nations, asking the Security Council to send a UN peace-keeping force to Northern Ireland. This was never likely to succeed because, even if UN member states had been prepared to see their own troops assaulted or gunned down on the streets of the province – which they were not – our representative, Lord Caradon, pointed out that this amounted to interference in the internal affairs of a sovereign state. But the initiative satisfied the Irish government's need for action and highlighted the situation in an international forum.

The Republic's Minister for External Affairs, Dr Patrick Hillery, came to see me shortly afterwards. Lord Stonham, the Home Office Minister, and I held two hours of talks at which little real progress was made. We re-stated the position of successive governments that the unrest in Northern Ireland was an internal problem for the United Kingdom. We rejected the idea of a UN force as neither necessary nor appropriate, but we had no objection to the call-up of Irish reservists.

From a Foreign Office standpoint all this made perfect sense. But Hillery's argument that the increasingly unstable situation did have an impact outside the UK was difficult to gainsay. Moreover, the grim and increasingly bloody reality was that, even if the government of Northern Ireland was a purely internal affair, we – or rather those to whom Westminster had devolved power – were not making a good job of it. A week later, Dr Conor Cruise O'Brien brought an Irish parliamentary group to see me. They also proposed a UN force, though with more detail, since Dr O'Brien had himself led a UN peace-keeping force in Africa. Our discussion was livelier and friendlier, but the basic conclusion was the same.

These meetings took place while British troops were still welcomed by both communities. By the time I visited Ulster in January 1971, as an opposition spokesman and a journalist, this was beginning to change and changed decisively in that year, with the bungled introduction of internment and the events of Bloody Sunday in January 1972.

I wrote soon after that whatever the exact cause of the killings in Londonderry on that day, the disaster was almost inevitable, given the way in which the army was required to operate in the towns of Northern Ireland. The fundamental principles of employing armed forces in support of civilian power were being consistently violated. The classic and effective method – which I had experienced myself in counter-insurgency operations – was to keep them in reserve as an instrument to be used only when the resources of the police had proved inadequate, then to deploy them swiftly and decisively, using the minimum (but sufficient) force to restore the situation before handing control back to the civil power.

What I saw happening on the streets of Northern Ireland was a situation in which the army was, for all practical purposes, the civil power. Young soldiers were required to stand on street corners with high-velocity rifles and sub-machine guns, while mobs of children showered them with bottles, bricks and obscenities.

I concluded – and in this I was in full agreement with Harold Wilson – that in the long term, transition to a united Ireland would eventually have to be accepted as a practical policy. This was, however, distinct from the war against terrorism, which could be, and was, fought successfully. The fact that there could not be a *purely* military solution to 'the Troubles' did not mean that there could be no military solution at all. The tragedy was that for too long the efforts and sacrifices of the security forces were not matched by political movement. For that, terrorists on all sides bear most of the blame because, as always, terrorism hardened political positions and made conciliation all the more difficult.

Back in Westminster, the growing weariness with party politics which I had felt while in government was exacerbated by the inevitable party bloodletting after the election defeat. The focus for this was the debate over Europe, a fact which placed

me in a uniquely different position as the party's main spokesman on foreign affairs in the Lords.

It was clear that the Labour Party was drifting to the left on
Europe, as on so many other issues, and the anti-Europeans
were beginning to reverse the very policy under which I had
been pursuing British entry into the Common Market during
my time at the Foreign Office. It was absolutely clear to me that
the terms negotiated for British entry into the EEC by the Heath
government would have been broadly acceptable to our own
government in 1968. However, Harold Wilson faced a formidable task in trying to hold the party together and the price
was the eventual rejection of the European ideal at the party
executive in July 1971.

This left the party in general, and the opposition team in
the Lords in particular, in a mildly ridiculous situation as we
approached the 'Great Debate' of December 1971 – the longest
parliamentary debate since the war and one of the most momentous in history. While Conservative MPs were given a free vote,
Labour imposed a three-line whip which was defied by no less
than sixty-nine of the party's MPs. The situation in the Lords
was even more extreme: more Labour peers voted for entry
into the EEC than voted against. Several of us were former
Ministers, including George Brown and Eddie Shackleton, the
Leader of the Opposition in the Lords.

Matters came to a head in April of the following year, when
the party reversed the policy – only recently agreed at a Shadow
Cabinet meeting – of opposing a referendum on British entry,
and decided to support a Conservative backbencher's amendment calling for such a poll. It was now clear that what had
previously been an opposition to the terms of entry was becoming an opposition to the EEC on principle.

To many of us the idea of a referendum on Europe was a
constitutional absurdity and an abdication of responsibility.
More importantly, at least for the future of the Labour Party, it
was scarcely credible that those who precipitated the crisis
over the referendum did so to change the government's policy
towards Europe; in fact they ensured almost beyond doubt the

success of the legislation. The real objective was Labour Party unity, but a unity built around and dictated by the unions, and a unity which excluded pro-Europeans.

In early April Roy Jenkins and others resigned from the Shadow Cabinet and I wrote to Eddie Shackleton to ask him to release me from my appointment as a front bench spokesman. A situation in which the chief spokesman on foreign affairs could not speak on one of the most important foreign policy issues of the day had always been unsatisfactory, but an unwilling silence had been a reasonable price to pay for agreement on entry into Europe and party unity. The party's decision to support a referendum made the price too high and my position untenable.

One of the first letters I received after my resignation was – somewhat to my surprise – from the Prime Minister of Singapore. Lee Kuan Yew wrote to express his regret, noting that 'time will prove that it was not only principled, but was also right for Britain and for the Labour Party. It can also help the Labour Party win back the respect of fellow European socialist parties.' The last point was characteristically perceptive: it was clear that the debate over Europe was marking a sea-change in British politics and a fundamental re-alignment of left and right. The fact that the British socialist party was out of step with its European socialist and social democrat counterparts, and even with European communist parties, showed how far to the left it was moving. Later splits became inevitable.

My contact with Lee Kuan Yew had come through a television interview I had conducted with him the previous year, although he had not yet seen the finished product himself. It was the second in a series of programmes which began in 1970, when Paul Fox, then the Director of BBC Television, and one of his producers, Malcolm Brown, had been looking for someone to interview Willy Brandt. I dutifully obliged and our relaxed discussion at the Palais Schaumberg ranged across German economic policy, the idea of 'collective guilt' over the war, the dominant preoccupation with German unity, and the European ideal (Brandt was strongly against any notion of a European nuclear force, at least until Europe had a common foreign policy).

I knew Willy Brandt well from our meetings over Europe and he lives in my memory as perhaps the most impressive politician and statesman I had the pleasure to deal with. He was a delightful companion and conversationalist, and his stocky frame embodied an equally resolute and firm moral centre, which informed all his activities. Indeed there was a clear moral criterion to all his policy-making, yet this was accompanied by a gentle and kind personality rather than fanaticism or self-righteousness. He was immensely civilised, in the greatest tradition of German politicians, and he told me that, when bedevilled by an intractable problem, he would sit and listen to Mozart's Piano Concerto No. 21 (for purists this is the C Major K467); failing that he would play it in his head. The warmth of my relationship with Brandt and with Helmut Schmidt made governmental relations with West Germany easy and pleasurable.

The BBC seemed to like the programme on Willy Brandt and, more importantly, the ratings suggested that the viewers also enjoyed it. I was therefore asked to begin a whole series of interviews with world leaders, to be known as *The Chalfont Profiles*, which ran from 1970 until 1975. The intention was never to engage in the ill-mannered verbal punch-ups that constitute modern political interviews, much to the chagrin of some critics who wanted blood on the carpets of their favourite international hate figures. Instead, the programmes were intended to give some flavour of the leader's character and an introductory profile both of the personality and his or her country. As well as being popular with audiences, this approach frequently allowed subjects to reveal more about themselves than an aggressive grilling might have produced.

It was a matter of surprise and gratification to me that one should actually be paid for engaging in such a congenial occupation which, apart from the serious business of the interviews, included such fringe benefits as vodka and Imperial caviar in St Moritz with the Shah of Iran or a quiet drink with his placidly beautiful Empress at the seaside palace on the Persian Gulf; a walk around the streets of Singapore with the immensely energetic and impressive Lee Kuan Yew; a conducted car-ride around Jerusalem with its unforgettable mayor, Teddy Kollek; and tea with President Sadat and his family on a Nile houseboat which once belonged to King Farouk.

Along the way one picked up a mass of mildly diverting trivia: the Shah was allergic to caviar; Indira Gandhi did her own home decorating; Lee Kuan Yew drank twenty-five cups of Chinese tea every day and passionately hated cigarette smoke; and the extraordinary Imelda Marcos sang a very good version of 'Smoke gets in your eyes', with which she entertained us after a day's filming with the President.

I was left with two lasting memories of my visit to the Philippines. The first was of Imelda Marcos. It was not so much the shoe collection which she proudly showed me, or her missed vocation as a salon entertainer; what struck me most was the ease with which she dominated not only the centre of power at Malacanang Palace, but much of the country, too. It was abundantly clear that the diminutive figure of Ferdinand Marcos deferred to his wife at almost every level of decision-making. Moreover, as we travelled round the country it seemed that ordinary Filipinos had also absorbed the Imelda cult to the point where they regarded her as at least equal to the President.

The second memory is personal, although it was brought on by Imelda's penchant for wandering along the beach in the evening dressed in flowing gowns. When filming was complete she returned to the Palace, while the film crew and I stayed sitting in the beach house. In the following hours of convivial conversation so many insects took the opportunity to feast on me that I became unconscious and had to be rushed to hospital.

After the Marcoses came Indira Gandhi, and our conversation focused on her early life and on the refugee problems created by Pakistan's annexation of East Bengal or Bangladesh. She was the only world leader I have encountered who, to put it delicately, used her femininity quite so openly and effectively when confronted by an interviewer.

Lee Kuan Yew, who was initially so apprehensive that he

telephoned Willy Brandt to ask what the experience had been like, proved a natural interlocutor. His exceptional mind readily turned from economics to personal and political philosophy, and the discussion could have filled a whole series. I had lived in Singapore for over three years before its economic and political transformation and I was immensely impressed – as anyone would be – by Lee Kuan Yew's extraordinary achievement. He remained a good friend and retains even in advancing years an incredible intellectual energy.

The same could not be said of President Kenyatta, the subject of a profile in 1974. Having invited me and my film crew to Kenya to record an interview, Kenyatta proved elusive and only allowed us to film him from a considerable distance, usually while he was engaged in his favourite activity of building up his bizarre personality cult. He was, perhaps, understandably anxious not to discuss his 'Africanisation' policy and its implications for the large Asian population in Kenya.

We went ahead and produced a profile of Kenyatta, albeit at a distance, and provoked an angry protest from the Kenyan government as a result. I was declared a 'prohibited immigrant' and barred from re-entering Kenya – not, it must be said, a great deprivation at the time. With a feeling for melodrama that characterised the régime, the foreign minister called on all forty-two members of the Organisation of African Unity to ban me, while the Vice-President, Daniel Moi, proclaimed that I had abused the entire Kenyan nation by, allegedly, calling President Kenyatta a 'small dictator'. He *was* manifestly a small dictator, although I cannot recall ever saying so, and how this observation constituted an abuse of the entire Kenyan nation was difficult to see. For once, however, the critics were happy, even though, in their scheme of things, upsetting an African dictator seemed to earn fewer bonus points than upsetting a Middle Eastern potentate.

Further interviews followed with Gough Whitlam and Pierre Trudeau, the Prime Ministers respectively of Australia and Canada. Trudeau in particular took some three years to agree to take part, but turned out to be well worth the wait. He was an intriguing character, who had entered politics comparatively late, after a remarkable career as athlete, traveller, lawyer and philosopher. An admirer of Karl Popper's political thought, Trudeau was passionately concerned with the freedom of the individual. This made for a particularly interesting discussion because I arrived at a time when he was facing the greatest crisis of his seven-year premiership in the shape of a terrorist campaign mounted by Quebec separatists. His response had been a formidable quasi-military clampdown and our discussion centred on his ability to reconcile this with his own philosophy; his answers revealed an impressive moral toughness beneath the playboy image cultivated for him by the international media.

Perhaps my strongest memories of the interviews are of those conducted with leaders in the Middle East. It was a rare privilege, if, at times, a depressing one, to hold long and relaxed discussions with the protagonists of that turbulent region, some of whom were later to become its victims. President Sadat, King Hussein, Prime Minister Rabin and the Shah of Iran spoke at length, on and off camera, about the future of their region and about their own troubled countries. For many the starting point was their relationship with Britain, in King Hussein's case his British military education. But all of them – accustomed to the hysteria which surrounded the Middle Eastern debate in the West – seemed to welcome the opportunity to speak and to answer sometimes awkward questions in a relaxed and civilised setting.

Yitzhak Rabin and his wife Lea wrote to me independently to say how much they appreciated a profile of their country which was not melodramatic or sensational; they were pleased that Rabin was able to put his side of the story, for good or ill, leaving the viewers to reach their own conclusions. I became a good friend of Rabin's and his background as a soldier meant that we shared certain cultural and social values. We also approached the issue of terrorism from a similar angle and had interesting discussions about counter-insurgency. The courage with which he pursued the peace process was remarkable and,

I think, much of the impetus for peace came from his own experience of war and conflict.

Where links with Britain were concerned, Anwar Sadat's interview promised to be the most delicate. Sadat had been imprisoned by the British during the war for collaborating with the Germans and had written some bitter comments in a book published shortly after the war. More importantly, Egypt under Nasser and Sadat had moved close to the Soviet Union and it was only relatively recently that Sadat had signalled a cooling of this relationship by expelling Russian 'experts' from Egypt in 1972. I soon discovered that Sadat's political and economic decision to court Western powers was backed up by some remarkable personal ties with Britain.

Sadat took me to his houseboat on the Nile to meet his wife and family, two pretty daughters of university age and a younger girl and son still at school. They had all been educated at the English school in Cairo and Mrs Sadat – whom the President still called 'Jean' in preference to her Arabic name – was elegant and amusing. It emerged that she was born in Sheffield, where her Egyptian father had been a student at the university and had married an English woman. She clearly still had affection for Yorkshire and had recently returned to Sheffield to visit her aunt and cousin. To the President's amused dismay, she took some delight in telling me the story of how Sadat, in the early days of their marriage, got into trouble with his mother-in-law for criticising Sir Winston Churchill.

Mrs Sadat played an active role in public life and was particularly interested in developing the role of women in Egyptian society. Sadat's policy towards Britain was, of course, dictated by wider considerations, not least his recognition of the dangers inherent in an exclusive reliance on the Soviet Union, but it was interesting nonetheless to find an influential piece of Yorkshire in such an unexpected setting.

Sadat took the opportunity to deliver a conciliatory message during the interview. When I pressed him on the use of violence, especially the threat of terrorism against Israeli and worldwide Jewish targets, he made a rather startling revelation. He told me that during the 25th anniversary celebrations for the state of Israel, an unnamed Arab leader had given the order to torpedo the ocean liner *QEII*, which was carrying some 500 American Jewish families to Israel, using an Egyptian submarine. Sadat claimed that he had intervened at three o'clock in the morning and personally ordered the submarine back to Alexandria. This was, at the very least, a remarkable insight into the nature of relations between the Arab states.

As so often in the world of television, one thing led to another and I found myself involved in a wide variety of programmes, often collaborating with the same excellent producer, Malcolm Brown. A *Shakespeare in Perspective* film on the military aspects of *Henry V* was followed by programmes on the Cyprus counter-insurgency campaign and a documentary on Berlin, as well as a film about the Celtic peoples.

The BBC was also the setting for my first – and by no means my last – experience of British libel laws. I was taking part in a live programme with the misleadingly dynamic title, *Late Night Line-up*, the purpose of which was to discuss a documentary on Philby screened earlier the same evening. One of the participants was the Regius Professor of History at Oxford, Hugh Trevor-Roper. He had been in intelligence during the war and had known Philby professionally and socially.

In the heat of the discussion I criticised the professor for passing moral judgements when he had been involved in the 'same squalid and sordid business of spying'. He got the impression that in my view there was little to choose between the two of them, save for the fact that Philby had been substantially the more successful. Understandably, Trevor-Roper took exception to being bracketed with a traitor and, having elicited no apology from the Director-General, sued both the BBC and me. Some five years after the programme had been broadcast, the BBC paid damages to the professor and issued an apology in court. Fairly recently, Lord Dacre, as he now is, came to me in the Lords and suggested that we bury the hatchet – and not, he added for clarification, in my head. Although I was not aware of any lingering animosity over the years it was pleasant to tie up another loose end.

I encountered more disapproval – from the critics, I am happy to say, rather than the viewers – for taking part in a programme on Marxism in Britain, for which a large number of people across the political spectrum were interviewed. It was unfashionable, particularly in the world of the media, to suggest that any kind of Marxist agenda was being pursued with any seriousness in British society. Those who suggested such a growth in Marxist and far-left activity were branded as 'McCarthyites' or scaremongers. The extreme difficulties experienced by the Labour Party in uprooting the Militant Tendency and other organisations during the 1980s suggests that the infiltration taking place in the 1970s was more effective than many liked to admit.

In contrast to the comparative luxury of the profiles series, this particular programme involved several weeks of unparalled tedium – in and out of newspaper offices, Communist Party headquarters and the Palace of Westminster; setting up cameras on canal banks, street corners and at the foot of Karl Marx's massively uninspired monument in Highgate Cemetery. No one who has ever had anything to do with location work will need reminding of the sequence of events: set up the camera and the sound recording equipment; rehearse; wait for the lighting man, who is stuck in traffic in Potters Bar; wait a little longer till it stops raining; start filming; stop in mid-sentence because someone seems about to land a helicopter in the cemetery; start again; stop for more rain; tea break for the crew; start again; stop to remove a small child sticking his tongue out at the camera; start again; the camera runs out of film; start again; the sound man runs out of tape; and so on. The frustration of asking the same question twenty times a day is so dreadful that when all the equipment is running perfectly, the sun is shining and there has not been a jumbo jet overhead for fifteen minutes, there is a tendency to forget what the question was.

Added to this were the plastic scotch eggs in a series of identical public houses, or hotels with headwaiters who treated the camera crew like escaped convicts until they realised that there was a Lord on the premises, whereupon they began to conduct the proceedings almost on their knees. In the case of the documentary on Marxism, however, the real fun started when the press were given a preview of the film. The *Morning Star*, *Tass*, and the splendid Mr Bert Ramelson, Industrial Organiser of the Communist Party (not, one might guess, a full-time job), lambasted me on the grounds that we had actually cut interviews. The fact that they had agreed to take part freely and willingly on the basis that interviews would be cut had momentarily escaped them.

On one occasion, a bright young man of extreme radical views said to me knowingly, 'I suppose you will distort everything I say by clever cutting.' Having endured a particularly tiresome and frustrating day, honesty prevailed over politeness and I told him that if he really believed all that nonsense then he might have had the decency to refuse to be filmed and allow me to go home. Clearly, television journalism was not the unalloyed pleasure that the profiles series had led me to expect.

13

Leaving the Labour Party

As well as being embroiled in the world of television journalism, I spent much of the early 1970s contributing articles to a variety of newspapers. As a former Labour Minister I was asked to write a regular column for *The Guardian*, and for two years I was given free rein to comment on any subject of interest to me. I was also, briefly, Foreign Editor of the *New Statesman*, at the invitation of its Editor, Richard Crossman.

Crossman was one of those people often described as an intellectual bully, which is usually a relatively polite way of calling someone simply a bully with intellectual pretensions. Although this would be an unfair criticism of Crossman, he was certainly a complicated and abrasive personality. Isaiah Berlin, who was a Fellow of New College with him in the 1930s, once described him as 'a left-wing Nazi' who wanted power, hated liberalism, mildness, kindness or amiability.

Crossman could be an engagingly disputatious character but his forceful intellect did not really welcome debate on subjects about which he had already made up his mind – most subjects one could think of, in fact. I learnt this early on in my time at the *New Statesman*, when Dick suggested that, as Foreign Editor, I should commission a series of articles covering 'the whole spectrum of the European argument'. I went away and succeeded in eliciting some good pieces on Europe, beginning with an impressive expression of Euro-enthusiasm from Shirley Williams. I sent the whole series to Dick and was a little surprised to hear him proclaim that 'These are no good at all ... they're all pro-Europe.' I pointed out that this was not quite the case and that they reflected the broad spectrum of the argument, in line with his original request. 'No,' he replied, 'I meant the whole spectrum of the argument *against* Europe!'

I contributed a string of articles myself to the magazine, on various foreign affairs issues, but it has to be said that the *New Statesman* was not a natural home for me politically or, as it turned out, sartorially: one of the staff was once heard to remark that 'there's a standard of scruffiness at the *NS* which Alun doesn't seem to understand.'

I was also at this time becoming more involved in events in Wales, at first a personal decision rather than a political one. Ironically, the decision to join a Welsh regiment some forty years earlier had ensured that I had seen very little of Wales in those years. By the time army life and government office were behind me, my parents had died and my family links with Wales were weaker. It is hard to say exactly how conscious was this desire to return to my roots; but perhaps anyone who has spent most of his adult life travelling and living outside the country of his birth begins to feel a desire to rediscover those roots and to return home. For me, the most important step in this process was to learn the Welsh language.

I had, of course, survived for half a century without knowing more than the words of 'Land of My Fathers' and 'Sospan Fach'. Yet my involvement in an organisation called the St. David's Trust had impressed on me the centrality of the Welsh language in preserving Welsh culture. The St David's Trust was a body dedicated to providing Wales with a Welsh National Theatre. It was eventually strangled by the weeds which grow so vigorously in the undergrowth of Welsh local politics, but in the course of my involvement with it, I came into contact with a number of Welsh-speaking Welshmen, most memorably Clifford Evans, an actor with a considerable television reputation. His engaging personality and his fierce attachment to his native language had a profound effect upon me. This was more than the realisation that any individual Welshman who does not speak his own language is cut off from many of the treasures of his culture. I began to believe that in an increasingly homogenised and technologically advanced global culture, losing the Welsh language could mean losing the very identity of the Welsh.

My own crash course in Welsh took place at the University College of Wales in Aberystwyth. I was starting from scratch – even my slight Welsh accent had been ironed out over the years: passively, by my absence from Wales, and actively by the army. The rationale of the regiment – despite its fierce Welsh patriotism – was that accent was linked to class distinction and that such distinctions had no place in the army. It was an admirable justification for getting everyone to speak standard English, though how sincerely held I am not sure.

I delivered my first speech in Welsh at the 1974 National Eisteddfod, on behalf of the 'learners'. The tradition of the Eisteddfod decrees that no language but Welsh may be spoken on the *maes* (field), and this applies equally to learners. Thanks to some excellent tuition, mostly through repetition, I gave a fairly confident speech in what I believe was a respectable accent. The drawback was that, as I made my way back across the *maes*, I was hailed by enthusiastic well-wishers congratulating me on my speech. At least I assume they were congratulating me, although their language was about as familiar to me as Japanese; I responded by smiling and nodding so much that an observer might have assumed that the experience of learning Welsh had affected my sanity. I soon took the opportunity to convert this phonetic repetition of the language into real conversational Welsh.

My interest in the cultural life of Wales led to an appointment which was among the most rewarding of my life. In 1979 I was invited to become President of the Llangollen International Eisteddfod, a position which I held with great pride and huge enjoyment for over a decade. The origin of this remarkable marriage of artistic rivalry and international accord was a meeting, in Llangollen at the end of World War Two, of a small group of idealists with the aim, one might almost have said the impossible dream, of making some small contribution to world peace. From a small meeting of musicians of fourteen countries in 1947, the Eisteddfod had grown into one of the largest festivals of folk music in Europe, with up to 200 choirs and dancers from scores of countries.

At a time when international sport was becoming a mixture of show business combined with some of the worst expressions of nationalism, music remained what it had always been – a potent solvent of national prejudice and an effective means of building bridges across geographical frontiers and ideological divides. The inscription engraved on the Eisteddfod trophy encapsulated the spirit of Llangollen: *'Byd gwyn fydd byd a gano. Gwaraidd fydd ei gerddi fo'* (Blessed is a world that sings. Gentle are its songs).

It would be hard to do justice to the atmosphere in the town during the Eisteddfod. The ten thousand or so international visitors form a kind of cultural United Nations, free from the depressing cynicism of its political counterpart, an Olympic games without the commercialism or corruption. It is a place where the Soweto Teachers' Choir from South Africa can compete with the Moravian Teachers' Choir from Czechoslovakia and, perhaps almost as important, mingle with them socially at an event that is still, incredibly, the work of a voluntary organisation. The Llangollen Eisteddfod also boasts that it provided the platform for the debut of Luciano Pavarotti, albeit as a boy soprano in his father's choir.

The simple words on the cover of the Eisteddfod syllabus seem to come from another world – 'Participation in these competitions is open to competitors of all nationalities' – and the fight to maintain Llangollen's position as a place of political neutrality has often been bitter. For some inexplicable reason, the anti-apartheid movement chose the Eisteddfod – an event dedicated to equality – as one of its targets because South African choirs, along with those from all kinds of dubious totalitarian régimes, had been allowed to take part. Although I successfully sued a Euro MP for trying to tarnish me with a pro-apartheid brush, after several years the committee was eventually forced, in 1987, to reject South African applicants, simply because they feared the disruption of the festival and could no longer guarantee peace. It was a sad victory for the kind of bullying narrowness which Llangollen had been founded to counter.

I retired after ten years at Llangollen with a lasting affection for the place, the people, and the extraordinary event. I was particularly honoured to find that the organisers had commissioned Robert Thomas, a Welsh sculptor for whom I had a great admiration, to do my portrait in bronze for the Eisteddfod pavilion.

Cultural concerns were not, however, the only context for my involvement in Welsh public life: political developments had made Welsh nationality a constitutional issue. The Kilbrandon Report, which examined and recommended constitutional changes that are only now being realised, focused attention on the issue of devolution. In the context of British entry into the EEC the place of Wales in the United Kingdom and in Europe was a key issue. The response of the Labour Party seemed to me to be totally inadequate and reflected its pathetic retreat over European entry. To my surprise I found myself in greater sympathy with Plaid Cymru than with the party of which I was nominally a member.

I was, however, a cultural rather than a political nationalist. I have always been deeply uncomfortable with political nationalism. Perhaps anyone of my generation is likely to be: nationalism within Europe did not have a good track record in the twentieth century. Moreover, in the context of Wales, economic separatism seemed fanciful. I have also had reservations about devolution, principally because I worry that regional administrative bodies have a tendency to develop cronyism, particularly if the electorate is less than wholeheartedly behind the devolved assembly.

Having said this, since devolution has been approved I have taken the view that it must be made to work. I was more than happy to collaborate with the Welsh Office in seeing the new legislation through Parliament. In passing, it is perhaps worth recording my admiration for the way in which the Welsh Office carried out this task. It seemed to me that they saw clearly the problems inherent in a devolved assembly and went a long way towards addressing them.

I realised even in the 1970s that a strong interest in Welsh culture would result in pressure to become politically nationalist. There was – and perhaps still is – a tendency among some native Welsh speakers to see those who were rediscovering their culture as somehow suspect, as if there must be some hidden gain to be had from it or some dark political agenda. I certainly experienced this while making a television programme on the Celtic peoples and I had to make my own position on nationalism quite clear.

This was not, however, the only source of political unease for me. Indeed, with the approach of the 1974 election I was forced to consider my increasing political discomfort with more urgency. It would be wrong to say, as politicians who leave a political party so often do, that the party had changed and I had not. The truth was that my own political development had been away from any common ground with socialism, while the Labour Party's development had been a substantial shift to the left. The party's policy over Europe had been a defining moment, but the growing stranglehold of the unions and their increasing use of industrial power for purely political ends was also deeply disturbing. It was only a matter of time before we parted company decisively.

I eventually resigned the whip on 22nd September, at the beginning of the 1974 election campaign. I wrote to Harold Wilson saying that I would like to see a government that would put aside doctrinaire party lines and bring in a package that would have broad popular support. I told him that I was concerned at the growing influence of the left wing of the Labour movement and the 'virtual dominance of larger unions over a wide area of policy making and Common Market policy'. I no longer had confidence in the prospect of a Labour government.

Even after my resignation I retained a very considerable affection and admiration for Harold Wilson. He had a truly impressive grasp of international and domestic politics and was not, as some of our political leaders have tended to be, orientated to one at the expense of the other. Leaving aside his political abilities, which were considerable, he had an immense quality of loyalty. Once he had given you his trust, he would let you get on with the job, and you could be sure that even if things became difficult, Harold would not let you down. The reverse side of that coin was that he was never a good political butcher – he hated getting rid of people. This was, I suppose, a particularly bad thing for the party at that point in its history; but I find it hard to hold this against Wilson – his sense of loyalty outweighed that shortcoming. We remained on good terms after my departure: we met from time to time in the Lords and we lived only a few hundred yards from each other in Westminster.

In passing, it is perhaps worth commenting on the circumstances of his own resignation two years later, in 1976. A few days before it was announced, Lady Falkender, or Marcia Williams, as she then was, asked to see me in the House of Lords. She told me of Harold's decision and said that he had asked her to visit one or two people to forewarn them. She believed – and it was surely her theory rather than Harold's – that he intended to resign and then return at a later date, de Gaulle-like, to save the nation. She did not actually use the expression 'Scilly-les-deux-Eglises', but it hung in the air between us throughout our conversation.

It was a puzzling visit and an even more puzzling theory. My own impression was more straightforward. I believe that Harold became physically and mentally exhausted and ran out of political steam. This was an almost inevitable consequence of his personality, for he was a tireless political manipulator – his mind was never at rest and he was always obsessively energetic. More sensational conspiracy theories to explain Harold's resignation strike me as nonsense. Harold could be a sharp operator and was capable of as much political deviousness as any Prime Minister, but he was no security risk.

One of the most puzzling aspects of the reaction to my own resignation was the outraged resentment by some of my former colleagues at the timing of my decision. To announce my resignation at the beginning of an election campaign was somehow unsporting or devious, a 'stab in the back', as if I had not quite grasped the rules of the intricate game of politics. The reality was that the timing was as deliberate as it was consistent with my beliefs: it was a stab in the front and anything but devious. The fact was that I believed the interests of the country would be served best by the electoral defeat of the Labour Party – followed ideally by its disintegration and the emergence of a new political alignment in which the social democrats of the party could find an effective and honourable role. A re-alignment of sorts did eventually take place, although the death throes of the old Labour Party were a long time coming.

For me to have kept conveniently quiet would have meant tacitly endorsing a party whose policies I believed would take us further than ever before from our European allies, while constructing a chillingly different society at home. It seemed to me essential that centrists and social democrats in the party should end their alliance with extremists and force them into the open: the notion that moderate democrats could work from within to mitigate the worst excesses of the hard left was simply the triumph of hope over experience.

I approached Roy Jenkins privately in the hope of persuading him to break away and lead a social democratic political movement. I was sure that Roy would make an excellent Prime Minister and I still tend to believe that, if he had taken the lead earlier, he would have been successful at the head of a party along the lines of the German SPD. Roy was not sympathetic to the idea; he felt that it was too early and, I suspect, found the prospect of foregoing the real satisfaction of government office too great a risk. He did not seize the historical moment and by the time the Gang of Four made their move it was too late to attract the broad centre of politics. History, and in particular the Conservative Party, had moved on.

The general reaction to my resignation was more dramatic than I had expected. I received a large mailbag applauding or criticising my decision and it was sociologically interesting to note an apparent correlation between the level of abuse and the level of literacy. Many correspondents questioned my parentage or, more tellingly, condemned me for 'betraying my class', an accusation calculated to convince me if nothing else could that I had made the right decision in opting out of their destructive class war.

More reasoned reactions came from other politicians and from former colleagues, many of whom shared my misgivings. In fact there was a steady trickle of 'defections' from the Labour Party in the mid-1970s, notably Lord George-Brown, who left in 1976 on the same issue of personal freedom and the effect of closed-shop provisions. Although George had been out of the top rank of the party for some years, he had been at the centre of the Labour government of the 1960s and had enjoyed, in Harold Wilson's own estimation, far wider popular support in the Labour movement than the Prime Minister and the rest of the Cabinet put together. He had been thirty or forty votes away from election as leader of his party. That such a man should decide to take what must have been an agonising decision to leave his party, after very active membership for over forty years, was truly significant.

Resignation made the election campaign a livelier affair for me than it might otherwise have been. I found myself entering into the political struggle in a way that had been unnecessary while I was allied to a particular party. I genuinely believed that no party had a monopoly of wisdom and that, faced with the crisis of inflation, a centre party with broad popular support was needed. I eventually endorsed the Liberal manifesto as the nearest approximation to a social democratic approach which could break the supremacy of the two major parties.

This did not, however, signal a desire to join the Liberals and to exchange one whip for another, despite an enthusiastic letter from Jeremy Thorpe, promising a warm welcome and a suitable post. I decided instead to pursue a non-partisan interest in politics from the cross-benches, making contributions where they could be of use. To begin with I saw the role of the cross-bencher as that of the resolutely independent individualist: I did not even attend the cross-bench meetings in the early years. But

I have come to see that some co-ordination of cross-bench activity and influence can be extremely useful, and, I think, constitutionally beneficial in the face of large party blocks.

The cross-benchers, or Independent Peers as they should be properly described, have a particularly important role to play in the reform of the Lords, precisely because they do not stand to gain any party political advantage from one reform or another. I have, like many of my colleagues, very mixed feelings about the government's approach to the House of Lords, which has some unpleasant overtones of the politics of envy. While I accept that the principle of hereditary membership of Parliament is outdated, I have heard some extremely impressive contributions to debate from individual hereditary peers over the past thirty-five years. It seems churlish and a little perverse to bar those existing hereditary peers who have made a distinguished contribution to public life purely on the grounds that their membership has been inherited. A more civilised and thoughtful approach would have been to abolish the right of hereditary peers to sit and vote in the House of Lords, as the Labour Party's election manifesto promised, but to allow *existing* hereditary peers to remain in the House for the rest of their lives, without passing on membership of the Upper House to their heirs.

At the same time I have been very nervous about the decision to abolish the rights of hereditary peers without having any notion of what will follow. Indeed, I have been unclear myself about what sort of second chamber we should have: I am against a second elected chamber, simply duplicating or even rivalling the House of Commons, and I balk at the idea of an assembly entirely dependent on party and Prime Ministerial patronage. I would favour nomination of life peers by some sort of independent body, but I accept that the constitution of this body would be complex and, no doubt, controversial. These are matters of such importance and of such complexity that it was right that they should have been addressed by a Royal Commission.

My resignation from the Labour Party also allowed me the

leisure to fulfil a promise I had made to George Weidenfeld as long ago as 1968. George had asked me to write on some aspect of military history and I had planned to begin a new life of Marlborough, a project which I had been considering for some time. I was confident that this leisurely and comparatively undemanding task would fit in well with a busy and often unpredictable life. George then suggested over lunch one day that I might consider a biography of Field Marshal Montgomery.

Although at first doubtful about the idea, I began to find the prospect intriguing. I had been in the army for most of the last half of Montgomery's fifty years as a professional soldier, but had never served under his command or even in the same theatre of operations. This gave me a certain objectivity, but I was keenly aware that the Field Marshal tended to inspire extreme reactions in those who served under or near him. To some, especially to the soldiers of the Western Desert, he was an infallible charismatic hero; to others he was a first-class leader and dedicated professional; to others still he was, as Winston Churchill acidly described him, 'a little man on the make' – a vain, opinionated and overrated showman.

What was beyond argument was that he was a household name and, more to the point, a national legend. To attempt to write a balanced account of his life, to be published while he was still alive, was likely to be a perilous and thankless undertaking. However, when I first approached the subject himself in the House of Lords he appeared to be surprisingly enthusiastic about the project. Early in 1968 he sent me a typically stiff letter, handwritten as always, setting out the conditions for his co-operation and concluding that, if I found these to my liking, I could visit him as often as I liked.

My first visit to the Mill at Isington, Montgomery's home in Hampshire, was an illuminating experience. The house was redolent of the physical and psychological odours of the officers' mess. A powerful sense of order and discipline was reinforced by highly beeswaxed floors and piles of books arranged in strict order of size. On subsequent visits the Field Marshal would often meet me at the gate into the grounds – especially if I was late, when he would be standing with his wristwatch at the ready and would greet me with a genially menacing report on exactly how late I was. Lunch was pleasant and I was allowed one dry sherry before the meal (unless I was late) and a bottle of light ale with it. Montgomery, as usual, drank only water.

After lunch we moved to his first-floor study where, resisting a natural inclination to stand to attention, I would sit opposite the Field Marshal while he consulted papers and delivered devastating judgements on his contemporaries. His favourite advice, endlessly repeated, was: 'If you are going to write about me, you must find out what makes me tick – that's the hub of the whole thing – what makes me tick.' The Field Marshal's absolute refusal to allow any access to his papers or diaries meant that any intention of making the book a definitive biography or work of military history had to be modified; I decided instead to take him at his word and try to discover 'what made him tick'. In this I was helped not only by interviews with his colleagues but by the hundreds of letters from veterans elicited by a letter to *The Times* asking for anecdotal material.

After a while the meetings came to an end, for a number of reasons. A mistake in my diary caused me to miss a visit and provoked a cold letter saying he would be too busy to see me regularly in future. Although I felt this reaction to be disproportionately severe at the time, it was perhaps understandable. An old man who has been a national hero has the right to expect that his hospitality should not be treated lightly.

A more significant reason for our estrangement, however, was the Field Marshal's realisation that I might be taking him at his word and finding out what *really* made him tick. When I spoke to those acquaintances whose admiration for him fell some way short of hero-worship, his enthusiasm began to wane, and I found that hitherto communicative colleagues would explain, with some embarrassment, that 'it would upset the Field Marshal' if they continued to talk to me. Finally, he was beginning to grow really old, and it was this that made writing a portrait of a contemporary such a delicate undertaking.

Even by the standards of the publishing world, *Montgomery of Alamein* had a long gestation; in fact I had deliberately delayed publication towards the end because Lord Montgomery was seriously ill and I was anxious that the book's appearance should not come close to his death. Unfortunately, the timing could hardly have been worse, since the Field Marshal died some six weeks before the official publication date, with the books already in the shops and serialisation in the *Sunday Telegraph* fixed.

Reaction to the book in some quarters was, as the tabloids would (and probably did) say, 'sensational'. The prime cause of the more hysterical complaints was a single sentence (in a book of 150,000 words), which reported, quite factually, that there had been 'suggestions of a homosexual element' in Montgomery's relationship with one of his liaison officers. Not to have reported the degree of speculation that existed on this subject would have been dishonest; indeed, like most biographers, I had suppressed a good deal of material and distilled it to this fairly innocuous, neutral statement.

The Montgomery fan club, already aggrieved by the less than flattering assessment of their hero's personality, went into overdrive. An anonymous writer in the *Sunday Express* declared one week that I was 'not fit to lead a Salvation Army band down Dorking High Street' and the following week that I was 'not fit to lead a pack of pimps down Piccadilly'. These judgements, however accurate, were based on scanty intelligence and a complete ignorance of the book itself.

Not for the first – or last – time in my life I received a large number of letters addressed with ballpoint pens on buff envelopes, most of them illiterate and abusive. From the veterans' letters it became clear that the Desert Army was second to none in obscenity, but it has to be said that they were by no means all critical: one veteran wrote with refreshing simplicity, 'Dear Sir, You were altogether too kind to that little tick Montgomery.'

Even more senior military men sometimes seemed to have read the newspapers in preference to the book itself. At a memorial service in St George's, Windsor, I encountered Sir Gerald Templar – the 'Tiger of Malaya' – whom I had known, albeit at a respectful distance, as my Commander in the Far East. I tipped my hat reverently to him, whereupon he came over to me and said, 'So you're the chap who says Monty was a bugger!'

It was something of a relief to find that my general assessment of Montgomery was shared by many of the more serious and balanced reviewers. Of the historians, A. J. P. Taylor and Correlli Barnett hardly dissented from my portrait of the man; Michael Howard, remarking that 'it is hard to write a good biography when one so patently dislikes one's subject', thought that my treatment of the Field Marshal had been unnecessarily astringent.

It goes without saying – and it is no reflection on their integrity – that my publishers were more than delighted with all the fuss and the foreign reviews and translation deals which followed. But the experience taught me a number of lessons: I resolved never again to write a biography of a living person, and always to review the books I was sent regardless of my feelings for the author. It was also an interesting lesson in marketing that the inclusion of the word 'homosexual' could boost sales and blood pressure in equal measure.

Given the reaction to the Montgomery portrait, it was with some relief that I turned to less controversial subjects. I edited a reassessment of Waterloo, a series on *The Great Commanders*, a world atlas of military history and various other books – anything in fact, rather than enter the minefield of writing about another contemporary personality. The idea for many of these publications took shape amidst the dense aromatic clouds from the submarine-sized Havana cigars favoured by George Weidenfeld, who had been a friend since the 1960s. George was – and still is – a man of remarkable intellectual energy. In the course of a conversation he is likely to spin off as many ideas in five minutes as most other people could encompass in a day.

As a publisher he had the invaluable gift of being able to encourage self-delusion on the part of the writer, by which the prospective author came to believe that he really was capable of the massive work of scholarship that George was proposing; only when the smoke settled did the absolute lack of the necessary time and qualifications become clear. George's remarkable parties at his flat on the Chelsea Embankment were another highlight of those years. To carry on a conversation with Isaiah Berlin on one side and Gregory Peck on the other is a clear recipe for schizophrenia; and it was not entirely impossible to find oneself seated at dinner next to someone with whom one was conducting an implacable vendetta or even a libel action. In short, George brought a richness to the process of writing and publishing that no rival could hope to emulate.

14

The Fall of the Shah of Iran

If the steps from the army to journalism and from journalism to politics had involved moving into worlds of which I was comparatively innocent, the same was doubly true of the next step – into the world of business. My weariness and disenchantment with political life made it clear to me that, for the first time, I would have to make a living outside the security (if not the financial comfort) of the army or government service. It was equally clear to me from the outset that I was not really interested in the minutiae of commerce and that business for its own sake inspired very little excitement.

Moreover, my first experience of business was nearly my last. Certainly it involved one of the worst decisions of my life. I was invited to join a company called Spey Finance, which appeared to be a very enterprising and innovative project, an early example of venture capital. The company crashed in 1974 and my involvement turned out to be an early and salutary lesson in what can go wrong and in the equivocal methods of some in the business world. With hindsight my approach seems to have been at best innocent and at worst incredibly naïve, but a life in the army, *The Times*, and the Foreign Office, for all their complexities, had not prepared me for some of the standards which were prevalent in the business world. Indeed it was largely through the persistently raised eyebrows of friends in the City that I came to realise that I, and others, had made a mistake. I also learnt how easy it is to have one's reputation tarnished by association – to that extent I had a lucky escape.

My colleagues on the *New Statesman* did at least derive some satisfaction from the collapse of the company: having already commented adversely on my habit of wearing dark suits, they now turned to humorous references to 'Graf Spey'. But the experience at Spey tended to confirm what I already suspected, that I could make a more useful and more personally satisfying contribution by becoming involved in strategic planning for international business.

It is easy now to speak glibly of the 'certainties' of the Cold War, but in reality the 1970s presented more than enough global uncertainties. The end of the conflict in Vietnam left Indo-China in turmoil and provided greater scope for the expansion of Soviet influence. The Middle East existed in a state of permanent crisis and the East-West conflict continued to be acted out in sub-Saharan Africa. Meanwhile British ambivalence towards Europe ensured quite unnecessary uncertainty in that arena throughout the mid-1970s. As a board member of IBM(UK) and Lazard Bros, I was asked to engage in a certain amount of soothsaying on likely developments in foreign affairs and their possible impact on business interests. It was a particularly interesting time to be at IBM, as the microchip revolution ushered in the personal computer.

It is hard now to believe that computers were still regarded as 'new' and the idea of a personal computer meant little to most people. We were still at the stage when everyone spoke in reverential terms about the power of computers, but few could actually explain what they did. When I arrived at IBM, there was a popular story, no doubt apocryphal, doing the rounds: it described a school to which IBM had donated six computers. When senior executives of this company visited the school to see the fruits of their generosity – and acquire some favourable publicity – they were shown into the classroom where the computers were kept. Using a blackboard to illustrate his sums, the teacher was pointing at the machines and asking, 'If I have six computers and I take away four, how many computers have I got left?' Whatever happened in the field of education, it was clear that the speed of change would demand greater flexibility than ever before in business strategy; it would also inevitably lead, at home, to confrontations with the unions.

Some years later I also established my own consultancy by taking over the Abington Corporation from John Lehman, a good friend who later became Navy Secretary in the Reagan administration. This was really a matter of convenience as it gave me the advantages of a corporate identity; the work of analysis and advice on the implications for business of international developments remained constant.

These were more than merely philosophical speculations. Substantial amounts of money and, therefore, many thousands of jobs rested on political developments in far-flung corners of the world. In 1976 I embarked on an extensive tour of Asia and the Far East on behalf of British Airways, to discuss with political leaders the future of the region. The fall of Saigon had forced BA to adopt new flight paths south of Danang which had a very significant impact on fuel costs. Not surprisingly they were anxious to take all political considerations into account in planning future routes and negotiating traffic rights.

My conclusions cannot have been a great comfort to their planners: the general picture of the area which emerged was one of kaleidoscopic change and a state of almost chronic perplexity and indecision among the governments of the area. The only safe bet, as the Prime Minister of Singapore, Lee Kuan Yew said, was that 'there will be considerable competition for influence among the major powers over this region.' At the time of my visit, this competition was gathering momentum as the superpowers eyed the great arc of nations around the Indian Ocean, turning their greediest gaze towards the centres of world oil production.

The price of oil and the behaviour of the OPEC countries dominated the world economy in the mid-1970s and concentrated the minds of politicians on the strategic significance of oil-producing states. It was in this context that I became interested in the affairs of Iran – the world's fourth largest producer – and its extraordinary potentate, Mohamed Reza Shah Pahlavi. In writing about the Shah and his country I found myself, for the first time, up against a remarkable tide of political fashion, a fashion almost universally and uniformly imposed by the media, and characterised by extreme moral self-right-eousness. In the decade that followed I met this again and again in debate on subjects as diverse as unilateral nuclear disarmament and the political future of South Africa. Now that the Soviet empire has crumbled and the situation in Iran has moved on, it might be instructive to look back – with a little of the distance allowed by history – at my encounters with the Shah.

The first of these took place in 1975, as part of the preparation for the BBC profile of the Shah. I went with the film crew to St Moritz and ended up skiing with the Shah, which led to an hilarious occasion on which a businessman introduced me at a City function as 'the Shah's skiing companion'. Companion is hardly the word because the Shah – in contrast to his wife – was a forbidding character. There was never any perceptible warmth amounting to the preliminaries of friendship, even after a number of meetings over the years, and the Shah's conversation was punctuated by long periods of silence (quite a challenge to television editors).

Seated rather stiffly in a reception room of his heavily guarded villa in St Moritz, the Shah came across as an almost puritanical figure. This impression was reinforced by his attitude to the British, whom he regarded as a parent might a wayward and work-shy adolescent. When I suggested that he seemed to think we in the West were indeed lazy, he replied, 'I don't think, I *see* ... People work less and try to earn more ... you write too much and you work not enough.'

Behind this headmasterly rebuke lay a complex and deep-rooted ambivalence towards Britain. The Shah had witnessed the invasion of his country in 1941 by the unusual coalition of Churchill and Stalin; the humiliation of his father, who had abdicated in favour of his twenty-one-year-old Crown Prince, had made a deep and lasting impression. More significantly, he was bitter about what he regarded as the outrageous exploit-ation of his country for half a century by the Anglo-Iranian Oil Company, until he nationalised the industry in 1951.

Nevertheless the Shah retained a real affection for Britain and had a keen interest in British history. He was also implacably opposed to communism, although he often recalled the contrast between the courtesy paid to him by Stalin at the 1943 Teheran Conference and the indifference of Roosevelt and Churchill. His overriding ambition was to make Iran strong enough to resist the manipulation of any great power, but the immediate threat was from the Soviet Union, with whom Iran shared a 1100-mile border. More to the point, another 800-mile border separated Iran from Iraq, which was, in the 1970s, engaged in a military build-up supplied by the Soviet Union. The Shah had also suffered from small but active cells of communist dissidents in his own country.

When I questioned the Shah about what appeared to be well-documented evidence of political repression and brutal interrogation by Savak, the Iranian secret security police, his reaction was resolute and unconciliatory: the freedom of the individual stopped where the safety of the nation began. It was an uncompromising philosophy autocratically enunciated.

I might have been left with only this impression of steely detachment if I had not travelled to Iran itself to film other parts of the programme. We arrived in time to witness the extraordinary spectacle of the Persian New Year 1354 – the Year of the Rabbit. Amidst the dazzling trappings of an imperial court and the ancient honorifics of 'King of Kings', 'Light of the Aryans', and 'Centre of the Universe', the Shah addressed his people and then proceeded to the New Year Salaam at the Gholestan Palace. Here leaders of Iranian public and religious life and ordinary citizens came to make their obeisance, much as the kings of the ancient Persian empire must have made their pilgrimage to the King of Kings many centuries before.

More importantly, from the film-maker's point of view, two things became clear during our visit to Iran. First, despite the sometimes arcane court protocol, and notwithstanding the autocratic exercise of power, there was a genuine popular affection for the Shah. Second, and more significantly for ordinary Iranians, the Shah had undoubtedly presided over a remarkable programme of modernisation in his country – the pursuit of a dream which, arguably, led to his eventual downfall and exile.

Through the 'White Revolution' of 1962, the Shah had implemented a massive and ambitious programme, covering land reform, productivity incentives, rights for women, electoral law reform, national health and literacy projects, education reform, and rural and urban regeneration. By the time I came to meet the Shah, he had gone a considerable way to creating a modern society, as the 300 new cars which joined the choking streets of Teheran each day testified.

He had also, in 1975, made two decisions calculated to infuriate Western liberal sensibilities. First, he had agreed to end military support for the Kurds in their fight against Iraq, in return for a treaty securing the Iran-Iraq border and the Shatt-el-Arab waterway. He had not, in fact, abandoned the Kurds and had offered full Iranian citizenship to any Kurdish refugees wishing to settle in Iran. Moreover, as he pointed out to me, the West was not in a strong position to complain: 'Who else,' he said, 'has ever done *anything* for the Kurds?'

He had also taken the decision to amalgamate political parties into one 'National Resurgence Party', effectively turning Iran into a one-party state. If this was intended to quell dissent in his own country it failed, and it provoked further criticism abroad; the Shah had become a fashionable bogey for Western campaigners, and all strategic considerations – not to mention the possible fate awaiting ordinary Iranians if the opposition were to replace the Shah – could be conveniently overlooked.

Ironically, reviews of the BBC profile of the Shah were among the best for any programme in the series. Critics were intrigued and at times mesmerised by the man, by his extraordinary sense of power and by his manifestly genuine belief in the 'mystical bond' between himself and his people. His presence was undeniably powerful and – to his courtiers – almost petrifying.

I continued to take an interest in Iran as opposition to the Shah grew during the mid-1970s. I watched as legitimate political grievances and aspirations of Iranians were exploited by a series of groups in a bizarre coalition: religious fundamentalist mullahs, who saw the country's modernisation as a threat to

Islamic life, joined up with the Iranian communist party (the Tudeh), backed by the KGB and supported by broadcasts from the Soviet Union, Libya and elsewhere. I watched with mounting horror as the West and, in particular, the media, fell in behind this campaign of destabilisation and smeared anyone who dared to question the wisdom of expediting the Shah's downfall.

The consequences of that downfall for the East-West balance of power and for the ordinary people of Iran were conveniently ignored in the rush to enshrine the Shah in the new demonology of the left. Such was the ferocity of the contempt for anyone seen as questioning this fashionable view, that it was even suggested that I and others had received financial reward from the Shah in return for questioning the perceived wisdom. This particular smear subsequently cost several publications a great deal of money in libel payments, as my only remuneration from the Shah had been a signed portrait at the end of filming for the BBC.

One of my fiercest critics, Fred Halliday of the Transnational Institute, having castigated me for describing the mullahs as 'fanatical', admitted in *The Times* that 'there certainly are retrograde aspects of the protest movement.' In the light of the bloody history of Iran since 1979, it is hard to know whether that statement should inspire tears or hysterical laughter. As I never tired of pointing out, the Shah's régime created a police apparatus which became a law unto itself. Although the Shah's isolation was such that I suspect he was unaware of much that was done in his name, he could not entirely escape responsibility for the brutal methods of Savak.

But what replaced that régime was brutality of another order. It is difficult to decide which has been the worst consequence of the victory of the Shah's opponents, so willingly helped along by the cream of Western radicalism: perhaps the fanatical violence, detention without trial, and extra-judicial killings of Ayatollah Khomeini's early years in power; or the senseless war of attrition in which the mullahs sent millions of young Iranian men to die fighting Iraq in a macabre re-run of World War One; or the massive sponsorship of international terrorism that has blighted the lives of so many people all over the world during the last two decades; or the persecution of minorities, notably those of the Baha'i and Christian faiths; or, perhaps, the proclamation of a *fatwah*, or official death threat, against a British citizen. The list is impressive.

Perhaps some consolation could be taken from the fact that the alternative fears which I expressed at the time were not realised: the communist groups in Iran lost out to the religious fanatics, avoiding a further escalation of the East-West conflict. This, however, is surely scant consolation.

The truth is that from the Shah's absolute power there flowed logically a number of consequences which – without support and correction from countries who could have been friendly – were eventually to prove fatal. The first was his almost total isolation from the realities of political life, as a result of which the first stirrings of political unrest were kept from him. The second corollary of centralised power was corruption, which began to be endemic in Iran as modernisation gathered pace. Finally, the most deadly consequence was the creation of a police apparatus which began to operate above the law.

Of course, there also followed from absolute power a tendency not to listen to bad news. I discovered this myself in attempts to spell out to the Shah the crisis facing him in his last months.

Mohamed Reza Pahlavi was a complex, remote and sometimes arrogant man. In spite of his autocratic manner he was strangely vulnerable to what he came to regard as the ingratitude of his people. He had a strong streak of mysticism and told me of three occasions in his childhood when he had mystical experiences. He was genuinely committed to the progress and prosperity of his people and, whatever cruelties were perpetrated in his name – and there were many – few would now seriously contest the proposition that when he fell he was succeeded by a régime more barbarous, cynical and inhumane than anything experienced in Iran in the short life of the Pahlavi dynasty.

The Shah's profound bitterness at what he saw as his betrayal by the West – pushing him to reform too quickly and then encouraging his opponents to topple him – shines through his sad autobiography. He knew that the Carter administration had decided his fate; he believed that the mysterious visit of General 'Dutch' Huyser in January 1979 had ensured that his own armed forces would not support him. He was also bitter at his treatment by the British government, who refused him exile in this country. Only President Sadat of Egypt remained loyal, seeing all too clearly what a Khomeini régime actually meant.

If the Shah was bitter he was also puzzled, for he saw more clearly than anyone that if no internal accommodation could be found (he was open to the possibility of some form of constitutional monarchy – a possibility I discussed at some length with him and with the Empress), then a proud nation of vital strategic and economic importance would pass out of the Western sphere of influence for the foreseeable future. It may be that history will judge him more kindly than it does the policy-makers of the West in those final years of the 1970s.

Long after the Shah's fall I had letters from Iranian exiles – even today I receive a few. The Shah's heir came to see me in the early 1980s to discuss his political future in Iran. I had to tell him that I agreed with the Foreign Office assessment that there was no political role for him in the foreseeable future: that era had passed.

With their favourite hate-figure deposed and a régime installed in Teheran whose antics veered between surreal incompetence and sheer barbarity, the champions of the politically fashionable moved on to find new victims. In fact what was happening in those years was a process admirably described a decade later by Bernard Levin as a 'political Doppler shift'. In short, Levin argued that the standard of political acceptability had moved persistently leftwards. The effect of this on sensible debate was dramatic, because the Doppler shift brought with it a phenomenal moral self-righteousness. Thus, certain political positions were absolute and to question them implied at best eccentricity on the part of the challenger and at worst villainy.

The example Levin used was the insidious way in which

several newspapers sought to dismiss me from the realms of the politically acceptable by a number of assertions which were obviously deemed to be enough to brand me as depraved. I was described as sympathetic to an organisation which had criticised the African National Congress; I had chaired a charity which was 'an opponent of the sports boycott of South Africa'; I had signed a newspaper article 'supporting the visit to Britain of Jonas Savimbi'. So far had the whole spectrum been dragged leftwards by the Doppler shift that these descriptions were enough to damn me.

It was simply not possible to point out that the ANC had been responsible for a number of particularly horrific murders and that its leader, Nelson Mandela, had been denied 'political prisoner' status by Amnesty International precisely because he had supported violence; that a sports boycott, while salving some consciences in the West, was not necessarily the best way of encouraging real racial integration in sports within South Africa; that Third World leaders who attacked left-wing régimes also had a right to freedom of speech.

In the context of Soviet expansion in Africa, I had supported Jonas Savimbi's campaign against the Marxist government of Angola and its Cuban backers. Savimbi was a rotund individual for whom the word 'jolly' might have been invented, notwithstanding the fact that the war he was waging at home was anything but jolly. He laughed constantly and loved food, drink and company.

His visits to England were not official – indeed they were diplomatically improper – but they were politically important. The Foreign Office, squaring the circle as ever, asked me to entertain Savimbi 'unofficially' for one of the evenings of a particular visit. For some reason it occurred to me that he might enjoy dinner at the Garrick Club and an invitation was duly despatched and accepted.

I expected him to arrive with an assistant, but on the night in question he appeared – smiling as ever – escorted by eight bodyguards dressed in combat fatigues and bristling with weaponry. Having manoeuvred their considerable bulk and scarcely concealed firearms through the front doors of the Garrick, sweeping before them any curious officials, they followed us through to the Card Room for what was certainly the most bizarre dinner I have ever had at the club. During the main course I was discreetly called away by the Chairman of the Garrick, the unfailingly urbane 'Nunc' Willcox, who tactfully reminded me that this was a gentleman's club and not a military training area.

I began to visit South Africa itself in the mid-1970s and to write on the situation in the region. After one particular visit a series of articles provoked extreme reactions from both sides. First, I was castigated by the left for suggesting that we should be helping the South African government to reform rather than pushing them into violent confrontation with their black population: it seemed that nothing short of bloody revolution would be acceptable to some campaigners. When, two weeks later, I wrote describing the appalling conditions of the residents of the black township of Soweto and called for a change in the leadership of the National Party, I received similar abuse from the extreme right: 'nigger lover' was one of the more printable epithets addressed to me. Clearly I would have to get used to the fact that the path of moderation was going to be lonely and inhospitable.

Above all, my fiercest critics could not bring themselves to place the question of South Africa within the global strategic context of the East-West military confrontation. They could only argue on the basis that South Africa was an isolated 'human rights' case of no importance in the Cold War conflict. Looking back from the perspective of a post-Cold War and post-apartheid world, this manifestation of the Doppler shift can be seen for what it was: a relentless and dangerous – if often unwitting – convergence of radical Western opinion with Soviet foreign policy. For a glance at the strategic map of Africa in the late 1970s showed an alarming spread of Soviet influence in Africa as Marxist governments and 'front line' states queued up to accept Soviet arms and the ubiquitous Cuban 'advisers'.

My interest in South Africa and, equally, in the strategic

importance of the oil routes around the Cape, persisted into the 1980s. If I had set out to court maximum controversy with the radical elements of the anti-apartheid movement, I could hardly have done so more effectively than by agreeing to take on the presidency of the Freedom in Sport organisation in 1982. The central question under discussion at the time was whether it was possible to encourage change in South Africa by maintaining normal relations with what was by any standards an abnormal régime, or whether it was necessary to break off those relations and isolate the South African government.

It appeared to me that the first course was preferable for two reasons. First, the global context – the Cold War – meant that the West could not afford to isolate South Africa and risk losing it, and the oil routes around the Cape, to Soviet expansion. Second, although the policy of isolation might lead to change within South Africa, that change was far more likely to be bloody and ultimately disastrous for the future development of the country and the region.

Along with the golfer Tommie Campbell (who, I was told, held the world record for driving a golf ball the furthest distance), the former British Lions rugby player Jeff Butterfield and others, I had the temerity to suggest that British citizens should not be denied the right to pursue their sporting interests wherever they wished. It seemed to me that the blacklisting and denigration of sportsmen and women with 'South African connections' – those who had dared to defy the dictates of political fashion by playing in that country – was an unwelcome lurch towards political witch-hunting.

Moreover, South African sporting authorities were making real efforts to achieve racial integration, often in the face of opposition from extreme elements in their own country, and boycotts by the West did nothing to help them. I had visited projects run by the cricketing authorities in South Africa and had been impressed by what appeared to be a genuine desire for racial integration in sport. I found it deeply depressing that the South African team should be barred from the paraplegic games at Stoke Mandeville or that the South African athlete

Zola Budd should be relentlessly hounded. How could this be in the interests of sport or of international understanding? Had I not been inured to the hypocrisy of much of the campaign against sporting contact, I might have been surprised that those who complained so vociferously about the boycott of the Moscow Olympics (in protest at the invasion of Afghanistan), suddenly fell silent when the object of the boycott became South Africa.

Beside my involvement with this great international pariah, my interest in areas such as China and South America – which I visited frequently and wrote about at length in the 1970s – was relatively uncontroversial. Even analysis of the never-ending turmoil of the Middle East failed to provoke quite the same degree of vitriol as discussion of South Africa. Yet in this area too, anyone who quietly questioned the role of the Soviet Union, or looked at its ambitions in the region, could be safely portrayed as scare-mongering.

There was, in those years, a stubborn resistance to the idea of placing any local conflict in its global setting: each conflict was seen as entirely a result of internal forces and legitimate local grievances. That this was also the textbook view in the Kremlin seemed to cause little concern. But it would be wrong to suggest that there were no voices, apart from the admirable Bernard Levin – a great companion as a journalist and a writer of focused brilliance – resisting the Doppler shift and trying to drag the political standard back to the centre.

At a time when it would have been easy to imagine that one was taking a political position akin to suggesting that the world was flat, it was encouraging to receive a note from Isaiah Berlin, one of the towering intellects of our time, declaring that 'I am altogether your follower – on reds under and in the beds and in all that you believe and say.' He went on to discuss some articles on the Middle East which I had recently published, particularly relating to Soviet policy.

At the risk of seeming ungrateful for some welcome and truly distinguished support, it might be worth repeating that I had never, even jokingly, used the phrase 'reds under the beds', nor did it characterise my position accurately. I never suggested a vast, well-oiled conspiracy of communist infiltration on a fifth column model. Certainly active measures taken by the Soviet Union were to emerge from the shadows during the 1980s, but far more worrying in the 1970s was the political pusillanimity, the lack of intellectual rigour in the face of the fashionable. On this I was in the happy position of being at one with Isaiah Berlin.

15

Unilateralism and Terrorism

After an association with *The Times* spanning some twenty years, I wrote my last regular column for the paper in 1981. Apart from an industrial dispute which had kept the paper off the streets, and six years in government, which had done the same for me, I had, throughout that period, contributed articles on foreign and defence policy. If there was one unifying theme to this disparate body of writing, it was, I suppose, an abiding concern for the preservation of individual liberty – the same concern that had dominated my experience as a soldier and my thinking on the use of military force.

To others it sometimes seemed that my real concern in the 1970s and '80s was a disproportionate preoccupation with the 'Soviet threat'. In response I can only say that the two issues – freedom and Soviet ambitions – were not unconnected. I should explain that I was not principally concerned with the possibility of crude military expansion, although it seemed unwise to discount the possibility: I had lived long enough to find it difficult to reconcile the image of a pacific, defensive Soviet Union with the harsh reality of Berlin in 1953, Hungary in 1956, Czechoslovakia in 1968, and Afghanistan in 1979. Indeed, it seemed quite likely that the 1980s would begin with a new addition to this list: Poland in 1981.

However, at the risk of disappointing those who enjoyed caricaturing my position, I must insist that I was not kept awake at night by the spectre of Red hordes sweeping down to the Channel ports; the nightmare was of a more subtle kind. The Soviet Union was for me an ever present and forbidding reminder of the moral and intellectual bankruptcy of the totalitarian left. The lasting tragedy of the Second World War, which appeared to negate so many of the sacrifices made by ordinary soldiers and civilians, was the sentence passed on the countries of Eastern Europe as they succumbed to the claustrophobic and depressing philosophy of Marxism.

Perhaps it might also be said that, in assessing Soviet intentions, I suffered from two further disadvantages which prevented me from holding an over-optimistic view. First, my experience as a Russian speaker in military intelligence had left me with the uncomfortable habit of reading and listening to the speeches and strategic pronouncements of Soviet leaders. When I heard the relentlessly consistent proselytising of military and civil leaders, explicitly stating their expansionist aims in foreign policy, I felt it prudent to consider the possibility that they might actually mean what they were saying. Moreover, when a group of governments holding these views, who rejected the basic principles of human dignity in their own societies, equipped themselves with one of the most powerful military machines in history, acute anxiety did not seem to be an over-reaction.

A further insurance against any complacency in this respect, was the experience of negotiating with the Soviet Union in government and, in particular, at the arms control talks in Geneva. What eventually became little more than a sterile diplomatic ritual of saying good morning in various languages convinced me that the Soviet approach to arms control was deeply cynical. It became increasingly clear that the Russians intended to stall indefinitely, while taking advantage of the openness of democratic societies to wage a 'hearts and minds' campaign in the West.

The alarm caused by the Soviet annexation of Afghanistan, combined with the dithering leadership of the Carter administration and an ever-escalating arms race between the superpowers, promised to make the 1980s a uniquely dangerous decade. Although the arrival of Ronald Reagan at the White House and Margaret Thatcher in Downing Street brought a new firmness to Western defence policy, the public debate over nuclear disarmament was becoming increasingly one-sided.

Appropriately enough, as we approached 1984, the nuclear debate had taken on some of the characteristics of Orwellian 'Newspeak'. The Campaign for Nuclear Disarmament, and other groups pushing for a unilateral abandonment of nuclear weapons, had effectively hijacked the word 'peace'. In a classic example of the political Doppler shift in action, CND had succeeded in giving the impression that anyone who was not part of their 'peace movement' must be an enthusiastic proponent of global nuclear conflagration. This seemed to me to be breathtakingly arrogant, suggesting that those who took a different view about the Soviet threat and how best to counter it were no better than warmongers.

I was asked by members of the new Conservative government to take some part in redressing the balance by speaking and writing in the national nuclear debate which gripped the country in the early 1980s. One of the less subtle smears launched by an angry 'peace' movement was that I was paid by the government to do this; in fact, the importance of the argument was such that I needed no encouragement, financial or otherwise.

At that time, opposition to the CND and other groups was unfocused and rarely rose above a whisper: the silent majority was understandably reluctant to face the emotive passion of the radical activists. For the CND argument had the popular advantage of being based almost entirely on emotion – harnessing the justifiable fear of nuclear weapons and an equally understandable despair at the concept of Mutual Assured Destruction (MAD) which underpinned deterrence. The most urgent task was, therefore, to set out calmly the rational arguments for peace through security and to show that fear of nuclear war need not – and indeed should not on any account – lead to the fallacy of the unilateralist position.

For some years I took part in discussions and debates in schools and universities and wrote extensively in the media on the illusion of unilateral disarmament. To do so was to place oneself against the fashionable tide, particularly in universities, where a CND badge seemed to be an essential item of student clothing. Although arguing at university level was essential, it has to be said that it was not always an inspiring experience: debates were often characterised by hectoring displays of emotion and a worrying lack of intellectual application.

Yet it was possible to make progress in stemming the tide of organisations like CND; there were others prepared to speak out or to take time researching the unilateralist opposition, a task pursued with great diligence and considerable success by Dr Julian Lewis, an enthusiastic campaigning politician who has since become a Member of Parliament. I remained convinced that the bulk of the population supported a strategy of disarmament negotiation from a position of strength and security; the total rejection of the Labour Party's disastrous adoption of unilateralism only confirmed this.

Those of us who recognised the internal corruption and external aggression inherent in the Marxist-Leninist system of government believed that the best strategy was to hold the line against the Warsaw Pact until communism collapsed from within. None of us, of course, expected that to happen quite as quickly as it did, but the success of unilateralism in the West would surely have delayed that process considerably – perhaps even indefinitely. In the end it was the economic and military strength of the West, not the 'peace' movements, which made the position of Kremlin hardliners untenable.

It was perfectly understandable that the general public should be largely uninterested in the details of the disarmament debate, from the complexities of SALT I and II and the START talks, to the specific capabilities of Cruise, Pershing and the neutron bomb. What mattered was that they should see the overall global context of the East-West confrontation. General and complete disarmament was – and still is – at best a theoretical possibility. Most people understood the cliché that these weapons could not be 'disinvented' and, that being the case, were best kept in safer hands.

The realistic objective was to stop the spiral of nuclear development, to safeguard against proliferation, and to make balanced cuts in the conventional forces of both sides. But even these objectives depended on a level of pacific intent which was not easily identifiable in the Soviet régime. The CND, of course, tended to portray the East-West relationship as a mirror image or moral equivalence, a viewpoint which was staggeringly naïve but much favoured by those in the Labour Party who based their foreign policy on wish-fulfilment rather than experience. As so often with political fashions, vigorous attempts were also made to foist it on a whole generation of schoolchildren and students.

In the course of these debates I encountered many supporters of unilateral disarmament, from concerned students to the leaders of the CND. The vast majority were, no doubt, well-intentioned and motivated by real fears about the future. Others were political activists who, like E. P. Thompson, openly proclaimed that the CND was an integral part of a general effort to advance socialism. One did not have to look far to find links with the British Communist Party and others whose aims in supporting the so-called 'single issue' campaign were undeniably driven by political cynicism.

One of the most prominent members of the CND was a Roman Catholic priest, Mgr Bruce Kent (he subsequently left the priesthood), whom I had faced across numerous debating chambers. While he was fully entitled to express his undoubtedly genuine political beliefs, it seemed to me that he was using his position within the church to promote the CND, which may have led some to conclude that the church sanctioned his views. This was a particularly worrying aspect of the CND 'newspeak', in the sense that supporters liked to give the impression that no serious Christian could, in good conscience, hold a position different from theirs.

I approached the Cardinal Archbishop of Westminster, Basil Hume, to discuss this and went to see him at Archbishop's House, which happened to be a stone's throw from my own home. It was not, of course, the first time that the Cardinal had listened to concerns about the Monsignor, both from within and without his own church. Although he was sympathetic to the problem, he felt that he could not be seen in any way to put pressure on Bruce Kent, since the position he held in the CND was not a public or political office (which Catholic priests are not allowed to hold).

Having dealt very briefly with this issue, there followed a most interesting discussion of the doctrine of 'conditional intent'. It was the first serious conversation I had held with a churchman on this subject and I found that we were in complete agreement on the moral basis for nuclear deterrence. In short, the conditional intent argument runs that, although the threat to use nuclear weapons might be itself immoral, holding such weapons with the threat that they will only be used in certain extreme conditions (a potentially devastating attack on human life) is morally justifiable. The Cardinal set out this argument with great effect in a subsequent *Times* article. It was important for Catholics – and indeed for other Christians – that the Catholic Bishops' Conference was able to demonstrate that Mgr Kent's moral vision was not obligatory.

There were, however, more worrying aspects of the 'peace movement'. As early as 1950, Clement Attlee, then Prime Minister, had refused to grant visas to delegates of the World Peace Council on the grounds that it was a Soviet front organisation; indeed, until 1973 it had been on the Labour Party's list of proscribed organisations. Undeterred, the WPC had flourished under the benevolent direction of the International Department of the Central Committee of the Communist Party. By the mid-1980s it lay at the centre of an interlocking network of fourteen major international Soviet fronts, seventy-two lesser ones and more than 140 national 'peace' committees.

Even some of the CND's supporters admitted that these committees have scarcely, throughout their thirty-year existence, fluttered an eyelash against any action of Soviet militarism. Instead they contented themselves with ritual denunciations of the United States, doubtless following Lenin's famous definition of peace: 'As an ultimate objective, peace simply means Communist world control.' Perhaps they used the same Novosti book that I acquired during the early 1980s, entitled *Political Terms: a Short Guide*; the use of language in this seminal work is well worth revisiting: 'Arms race' is defined as 'arms manufacture on an ever-increasing scale carried out by aggressive circles of imperialist states'.

Of course the suggestion that the CND itself was 'Moscow-inspired' or Soviet-funded came only from its more paranoid opponents. In fact it was a useful straw man, carefully constructed to allow unilateralists to knock it down with cries of 'smear!' and 'McCarthyism!' The reality was far more prosaic: the movement in Britain was a political organisation of the left, with a hierarchy comprising many members of the extremist left, and like all such organisations it was exploited to its full potential by the Soviet Union.

The simple and ironic reality was that the 'peace movement' operated within the very privileges of a free society which I, and others, felt to be at stake. As its supporters admitted, the unilateralist position led quite logically to a final conclusion summarised by the slogan 'Better Red than Dead'. This position had a certain attraction to those who had an understandable horror of nuclear war. But perhaps it is worth saying, in passing, that those of us who had lived through a 'conventional' war did not welcome that as an alternative, particularly since the development of non-nuclear weapons of mass destruction. Indeed, it was for this reason that Leonard Cheshire, who had seen the full horror of the atomic bomb dropped on Hiroshima and who was a devout Roman Catholic, nevertheless supported the necessity of deterrence and doubted whether total nuclear disarmament was truly desirable if that meant a return to 'conventional' warfare.

More importantly, the 'Better Red than Dead' thesis had two serious shortcomings. First, it set up a false antithesis between nuclear annihilation and surrender, neither of which was inevitable, provided the West made it clear that the price of aggression would be just too high for anyone to contemplate. Second, it viewed nuclear war with appropriate horror but seemed to regard Soviet occupation with some degree of equanimity. In the climate of the early 1980s it seemed almost impolite to point to the realities of communist police states, to the concentration camps and 'psychiatric hospitals', and the grim conformity of repression. One thing was sure – any Russian citizen minded to protest on the streets of Moscow for the unilateral disarmament of the Red Army's nuclear capability would not have stayed on the streets for long. When the history of the 'peace' movements comes to be written, an appropriate footnote should take account of the flood of information from the East German Stasi files and from former KGB agents, now confirming beyond any doubt the delight with which the Kremlin saw the CND prosper.

Into this heated debate, in March 1983, President Reagan tossed what could, in any other circumstances, be described as a bombshell. He announced that he was 'directing a comprehensive and intensive effort to define long-term research and development programs to begin to achieve our ultimate goal of eliminating the threat posed by strategic nuclear missiles ... This would pave the way for arms control measures to eliminate the weapons themselves.' This rather bland statement heralded a new concept in nuclear strategy: a system of defensive weaponry – including space-based weapons – which would provide a protective shield against ballistic missile attack. The Strategic Defense Initiative (SDI), promptly named 'Star Wars' by media pundits either awe-struck or sceptical, would involve a wide range of research projects on the very boundaries of high technology.

Contrary to dark suggestions that SDI emanated from the 'military-industrial complex' of the United States, the idea was in fact Ronald Reagan's. This is not to say that no one had thought of the possibility before or engaged in any related research. But the President had, with an engaging openness, asked his Chiefs of Staff if it might be possible to use the latest space technology to develop defensive weapons to 'take out' missiles as they left their silos. Might it be possible to construct a kind of protective umbrella over the West? To his surprise the military men had not laughed at the idea and had agreed that, at the very least, such a possibility should be researched.

Reagan himself painted a typically dramatic picture for the American people, using some cogent and attractive imagery. He saw a vision of a world where 'free people could live secure in the knowledge that their security did not rest upon the threat of instant retaliation to deter a Soviet attack.' Would it not, he asked, 'be better to save lives than to avenge them'? This was an enticing prospect for anyone who had seriously confronted the possibility of nuclear warfare: a system that could make nuclear weapons obsolete.

I experienced Ronald Reagan's enthusiasm myself at a meeting with him in the Oval Office shortly after his announcement. He was a delightful character and after a few minutes it was easy enough to see the traces of his former career and the roots of his remarkable success as a communicator and a politician. He was quite genuinely excited at the prospect of a world which could live without the fear of Mutual Assured Destruction. My own view was more circumspect, not least because of the practical problems involved, but I certainly agreed that the idea was an exciting one. Thereafter I followed the developments of SDI closely through regular contact with President Reagan's Scientific Advisor, George A. Keyworth.

The SDI was not, however, greeted with universal enthusiasm. The President of the USSR saw the initiative as an act of aggression, carefully omitting to mention that his own government had started research on similar weapons as long ago as the 1960s. Even when Mr Reagan held out the prospect of sharing the defensive system with the Russians, Moscow remained unimpressed. In a bizarre display of intellectual gymnastics, the CND condemned SDI because it might undermine the principle of Mutual Assured Destruction on which deterrence was based – a doctrine which they had fiercely opposed for years.

In addition, there were more reasoned objections from serious scientists and military strategists. There were doubts about the scientific feasibility of the project and concerns that it raised an illusion of invulnerability as an escape from the harsh realities of the nuclear age. The sheer cost of the programme was an obstacle to some, while others recoiled from the idea of an arms race in space, although, in truth, space had already been exploited for military purposes. Unfortunately, many of these sensible doubts were accompanied by the latent anti-Americanism that was never far below the surface in certain bands of the European political spectrum.

It seemed to me not only that SDI had received a bad press but that many of the objections to it arose from a refusal to leave behind outmoded habits of strategic thought. I attempted to give the other side of the story in a series of articles on SDI and a book, *Star Wars – Suicide or Survival?* There seemed to be a real possibility that the East-West conflict could move away from a dependence on the idea of mutual vulnerability towards an assurance of mutual security, within which it would make sense to reduce drastically the number of offensive weapons held by both sides. At the very least, the idea was worth researching and, in the context of the arms race of the mid-1980s, was worth the money. Although the urgency for such a project passed with changes in the Soviet Union, the possibility of nuclear proliferation, particularly the possible involvement of international terrorists and terrorist-sponsoring states, means that we may one day need to revisit President Reagan's defensive vision.

If the nuclear debate was the dominant issue of foreign relations in the 1980s, then terrorism came a close second. In some ways it was more disturbing, not least because it threatened to sap the morale of Western societies from within. Carlos Mirejeva, the Brazilian theorist of terrorism, once said that terrorism had two aims in a political system – to make life unbearable for ordinary people and to create a climate of collapse in which a society would lose the will to defend itself. My own experience in counter-insurgency and anti-terrorist operations in Malaya and Cyprus had led me to write extensively on terrorism in Northern Ireland and the Middle East during the 1970s, years in which the number of terrorist incidents grew alarmingly.

The Middle East offers a distilled example of the destructive and negative power of terrorism on every level, a power which, quite apart from causing terrible physical suffering, tends to embitter constitutional politicians, pushing them to the extremes of their position and entrenching them. In Jerusalem

I became involved in the work of the Jonathan Institute for the study of terrorism, established as a memorial to Jonathan Netanyahu who was killed in the Israeli commando raid on Entebbe. I came to know Benjamin Netanyahu well and it has always seemed to me that the death of his brother has left a mark which explains much of his attitude to the present peace process in the Middle East. His government's intransigence and reluctance to follow the Rabin strategy – which seemed to me to be a genuinely hopeful sign for the region – springs in part from his own family's experience of terrorism. As so often, terrorism hardens opposition rather than shifting it.

In the early 1980s I had taken part in numerous international conferences and seminars on the terrorist threat, and in 1985 I was invited to become Chairman of the newly-formed Institute for the Study of Terrorism. Under the direction of Jillian Becker, the Institute assembled an impressive library of research material. In its short life it provided a valuable flow of information to the media and others, and it did much to raise the standard of debate in this country about international terrorism.

That debate had previously been hampered by a reluctance to see international terrorism as in any way 'organised'. Terrorism could conveniently be portrayed as an expression of legitimate local grievances, taking place in a landscape of moral neutrality where 'one man's freedom fighter is another man's terrorist'. The first response to the rise in international terror needed to be a firm statement of the amoral basis of terrorism as a strategy that routinely rejected the political process and the exercise of popular political freedom; a strategy that promoted totalitarianism and, at least in those years, targeted democratic countries almost exclusively.

What became clear, and has been definitively revealed since the collapse of the Soviet empire, was the extent to which terrorism was a truly international phenomenon with international paymasters. Again, it was unfashionable at the time to point to the Soviet Union and the Eastern bloc countries as the sponsors of terror. Much of the evidence has now been published and does not need to be repeated here. But even at the time a wealth of intelligence material provided documented examples of assistance in training or weapons given by the Eastern bloc to groups like the Red Army Faction (successor to the Bader-Meinhof group), the IRA and, of course, the PLO.

Indeed, the sponsorship of terrorism through client states in the Middle East was the favourite channel by which the Kremlin sought to wage a low intensity war against the West in furtherance of its objectives. Terrorism is here to stay, but the disintegration of the Soviet Union has at least denied it some of the coherence and generous funding with which it was able to inflinct misery on ordinary people for more than two decades.

In the post-Cold War environment, terrorism is now described by strategists – not entirely helpfully – as an 'asymmetric' threat. Leaving aside the jargon, it seems that terrorism will continue to be a favoured method of warfare, used by small groups, organised criminals, and sponsoring states, to strike at governments and their peoples. If this 'asymmetric threat' comes to replace inter-state warfare, then logic requires some kind of forceful response to that threat. The notion that 'there can be no military solution to terrorism' has gained ground to the point where it is almost seen as self-evident. But the truth is that there often *is* a military solution and governments will increasingly need the political resolve to use it. This is not to say that solutions can be purely or exclusively military, but the use of force should be seen as a weapon in the preparation for and evolution of a political settlement: to dispense with the military solution is simply to surrender to the use of armed force by a terrorist minority.

16

Building the Trident Submarines

The dramatic changes to the Soviet system brought about by the accession of Mikhail Gorbachev in 1985 demanded in turn a radical reappraisal of Western defence strategy. These considerations took on a practical urgency for the British defence industry; the question of how to adapt to a reduction in East-West tensions and, ultimately, the end of the Cold War became the focus of my interest as I joined the board of VSEL, the shipyard responsible for the new generation of Trident nuclear submarines. The prime responsibility of my Chairmanship was to steer the company and its huge workforce through the uncertainties of the late '80s and early '90s, towards a viable business position in the post-Cold War order.

Not that the arrival of Gorbachev seemed to me to justify the unbridled optimism of some observers. Certainly, he had transformed the face of Soviet diplomacy. He had a genuinely attractive personality and showed a willingness to exchange ideas that contrasted with the slogans and sterile dialectics of his predecessors. If even Mrs Thatcher, who was not easily susceptible to the exercise of personal charm, could describe him as 'a man with whom it is possible to do business', then there were grounds for hope.

On the other hand, the twin pillars on which Gorbachev's political strategy was based – *glasnost* and *perestroika* – universally declared by the Western media to be 'good things', were less attractive when analysed in detail. *Perestroika*, which might best be translated as reconstruction, implied a radical transformation of Soviet society, designed to revive the stagnating economy. It was, however, made clear that this reconstruction was to take place within the strict limits laid down by the party, and its primary goal was 'to revive the Leninist concept of socialist construction both in theory and practice'.

Glasnost (which can be translated literally as 'publicity', but which in this context was meant to denote 'openness' or 'transparency') appeared to be an equally desirable term at first glance which, needless to say, was all it got from the 'peace' movements. It suggested that the obsessive secrecy and manipulation of the Soviet police state was about to give way to something like the freedom of information which – with all its imperfections – was characteristic of most Western democratic societies. It was, of course, nothing of the kind. Gorbachev himself set out the rules of the game: 'criticism,' he said, 'must always be conducted in the spirit of the party.'

At the same time it would be wrong to suggest that Gorbachev's initiatives were designed simply to deceive the West. His purpose was far more immediate and less complicated, for he had inherited a disaster area in 1985. The Soviet agricultural and industrial infrastructures were hopelessly inefficient and nearing collapse; the state bureaucracy was ever more cumbersome and incurably corrupt. Moreover a massive defence budget – at least 14% of GDP – made it impossible to provide enough food, clothing and consumer goods for an increasingly demoralised people.

Mr Gorbachev's determination to remove the stranglehold of bureaucracy, especially in the regions, and his drive to raise standards of living by increasing efficiency and productivity, were undeniably praiseworthy. But unless they could be irreversibly linked to real progress in human rights and individual freedom in Soviet-controlled countries they were of little value. In fact, a prosperous Soviet Union pursuing a Marxist-Leninist foreign policy would be still more alarming. The reality was that Gorbachev, for all his impressive achievements, was a child of the Komsomol and a protégé of the KGB; even in the late 1980s it was not impossible to foresee that his inability to break free from the constraints of the party apparatus would eventually bring him down, as it did in 1991.

Despite Mr Gorbachev's highly effective courtship of the West and the extensive agreements on disarmament initiated at his summits with President Reagan, the more sinister side of the Soviet foreign policy apparatus had been grinding on, unhindered by this political climate in the pursuance of its expansionist aims. I had the opportunity to research this in some detail when I was called upon as an expert witness in a libel trial involving *The Economist* and a Greek newspaper called *Ethnos*. The case is interesting in as much as it gives a concrete example of the Soviet 'disinformation' machine at work in the 'free' press of the West.

Ethnos had first appeared on the streets of Athens in September 1981, shortly before the Greek general election. It was colourful, lively and modern, well-produced on some of Greece's most up-to-date machinery. Like the English tabloids it seemed sometimes to owe more to the genre of comics than to serious journalism, but on the wave of Andreas Papandreou's election victory, which it had enthusiastically promoted, *Ethnos* became the country's biggest-selling daily, with a circulation of more than 150,000.

As such, it had to be taken seriously, and it was not long before commentators began to notice that, amongst the lively sex and sports coverage, there was a somewhat incongruous approach to foreign affairs. The tone of this coverage was strangely evangelical, invariably anti-American and never critical of any Soviet policy or activity. The world according to *Ethnos* was a strange and fantastic place: one could be forgiven for believing that the CIA, fresh from inventing AIDS in a Pentagon laboratory, had gone on to assassinate Mrs Gandhi and perpetrate just about every international disaster worth mentioning. Meanwhile, Soviet forces were in Afghanistan for the protection of the territorial integrity of the USSR and Lech Wałesa had been detained by Polish authorities because of financial irregularities in his Solidarity union. In the Disneyland of *Ethnos* foreign affairs, the Chernobyl nuclear disaster was the perfect opportunity to attack American propaganda and to list minor accidents at US power stations over the years.

Laughable though this might appear, it was nevertheless important to look at the motivation behind this editorial policy and to acknowledge that someone was directing it. The proprietor, Mr Bobolas, had previously been the co-publisher of the Greek version of the *Great Soviet Encyclopaedia*, a turgid literary monument to Leonid Brezhnev, which did not make the Greek bestseller lists. More significantly, *Ethnos* itself also began to lose steam and its circulation was reported as falling significantly within a year of its launch.

It was at this stage that *The Economist*'s confidential subscription-based newsletter, *Foreign Report*, pointed to the proprietor's Soviet links and suggested that the USSR might be footing the bill for losses. Mr Bobolas indignantly sued for libel because the allegation of subsidy suggested that *Ethnos* was not part of a free press but rather 'the mouthpiece of a communist and totalitarian state's propaganda machine'. *The Economist* never tried to defend the allegation of subsidy, but it maintained that *Ethnos* was indeed a mouthpiece of Soviet propaganda.

In fact, it was claimed that the editorial group in charge of the paper at its launch formed a close-knit communist cadre absolutely committed to the Moscow line. With heavy irony, *The Economist*'s lawyers quoted the definition of journalism given in the *Great Soviet Encyclopedia*: 'one of the forms through which mass propaganda and agitation are conducted … The Marxist-Leninist theory of journalism proceeds upon the premise that a truly objective picture of reality can be provided only by a journalism that adheres to the communist party point of view. In socialist countries journalism is truly free.'

To those of us called as defence witnesses in the trial, none of this Soviet manipulation was exactly news. *Ethnos* was a classic case of the Russian strategy of 'disinformation' in practice, under which the Soviets used unwitting news media to put their case across and which was defined by the KGB as 'directed at misleading the enemy concerning basic questions of state policy'. A senior KGB officer, who had defected in 1980, described the propaganda apparatus and the policy of making contact with Western journalists. Strategic disinformation was run by the International Department of the Communist Party and the First Directorate of the KGB, which handled covert propaganda and 'agents of influence'.

My own report outlined the scale of the 'disinformation' machine, on which the Soviet Union was estimated to be spending some $4 billion a year. I went on to point out that Greece in 1981–2 was a particularly attractive target for Soviet propaganda; Greek hostility to Turkey, which *Ethnos* seemed to encourage, and Greek anti-Americanism made this NATO's weakest point. Intelligence testimonies which have come to light since the fall of the Soviet empire have confirmed the extent of Soviet disinformation, but at the time it was not always easy to persuade the public and, of course, the media themselves that they might be the unwitting instruments of a highly sophisticated propaganda machine. In the event, the jury were unable to agree at the trial and the parties settled to avoid an expensive re-trial. To onlookers the result appeared inconclusive with both parties maintaining the justice of their position.

The trial marked another watershed for me. The end of the Gorbachev era and the rise of a then energetic Boris Yeltsin marked the end of the Cold War. It might be thought that this would be a source of regret, or at least nostalgia, for someone regularly dubbed a Cold War warrior. In fact it was a source of great relief. Of course, some argue that the Cold War could reassert itself if economic instability leads to a revival of the Communist Party, and Russia retains a daunting nuclear capability. But the prospect is highly unlikely.

More to the point, the very possibility of an unstable government controlling these weapons has led me to stand my Cold War attitudes on their head. It seems to me to be essential to offer Russia every possibly economic and military assistance to preserve her stability and relieve the understandable discontent of her vast population. It will also be important to avoid any unnecessary provocation which would encourage the uglier forms of Russian nationalism and the remnants of the Communist Party.

To that end, NATO must proceed with extreme caution in expanding to include states formerly within the Soviet empire. While I wholeheartedly welcome the addition of, for example, Poland to the membership of NATO, nothing should be done to give the impression that the West intends to 'take over' the Warsaw Pact through the extension of military influence. Even at the height of the Cold War, NATO maintained its moral stance as a defensive alliance.

It may, of course, one day be possible to envisage a NATO which includes Russia and all the former Soviet states. This would, however, be an entirely different type of organisation, more along the lines of a global peace-keeping alliance than a defensive pact. But this remains at the level of pure speculation: given the disarray of the former communist states, the potential for nuclear proliferation and escalation in South Asia and the threat of terrorism, NATO, and in particular the United States, will remain the guarantor of our security for the foreseeable future.

The end of the Cold War was also closely tied to my business preoccupation during the early 1980s: the task of re-structuring VSEL and putting it in a better position to face an uncertain future in national defence strategy. The company, which had started life with a variety of names until bought by Vickers Brothers at the end of the last century, had a proud history. The Vickers shipyard at Barrow-in-Furness had built its first frigate for the Royal Navy in 1877 and, over the years, some of the great names in surface ships – HMSs *Ajax*, *Invincible*, *Hermes*, and *Sheffield* – had been launched from Barrow.

Vickers had been involved in submarine construction from the very beginning, selling two 'Nordenfelt' submarines to Russia and Turkey in 1886. Having produced the Royal Navy's first 'Holland' submarines at the turn of the century, Barrow was again chosen to build the first nuclear-powered submarine for the navy, HMS *Dreadnought*, which was built in 1960. The 'Holland' vessels had been produced under licence from the US company Electric Boat, and it was the same company, by then a division of General Electric, that collaborated closely with us in the production of Trident nuclear submarines in the late 1980s and early 1990s.

When I joined the board of the company, British ship-building seemed to be in terminal decline and Barrow, which had already been through a difficult few years, faced an uncertain future. The nationalisation of ship-building in 1977 had two effects on Barrow: first it withdrew the yard from the Vickers group of companies and, more significantly, it brought a halt to surface ship construction so that Barrow came to be seen purely as a submarine yard. In the early 1980s the Thatcher government took the decision to privatise British Shipbuilders and clearly saw the warship yards as the most viable concerns. To add to subsequent problems, the decision was taken to make Cammell Laird at Birkenhead a subsidiary of the Barrow yard before privatisation.

When, in March 1986, the government accepted the bid of the employee group, VSEL Consortium plc, over a rival offer from Trafalgar House, the new company found itself in the happy position of having a massive block of employee shareholders; equally, it found itself out of the habit of surface ship production, with little obvious direction for diversification, and extreme uncertainty over submarine orders in the light of the changing international situation.

The key to VSEL's success in the immediate future lay in securing orders for the four Trident nuclear submarines which the Conservative government had announced as the replacement for Polaris. I had expressed misgivings about Trident at the time of the parliamentary debate – it had seemed to me that its massive cost would only be secured by cuts in defence elsewhere – but I accepted the final decision to go ahead with the project. The first submarine, HMS *Vanguard*, was ordered in April 1986 and the second, HMS *Victorious*, in October of the following year. This provided VSEL with some short-term security, along with other work in progress, such as production of Trafalgar class nuclear-powered 'hunter-killer' submarines, one of which – HMS *Talent* – was launched in April 1988. It was, however, absolutely clear that the company needed to be streamlined with a view to developing a business strategy for the medium to long term, when the Trident orders were finished.

The culture of a heavy engineering company, perhaps especially when it has been nationalised in the recent past, is not one that welcomes rapid change. There was no doubting the professionalism and achievement of the workforce at Barrow, but the headquarters had a faintly decayed feel, as if time had not moved on much since the 1950s. I soon discovered that the company's computer system was in a similar state and urgently needed upgrading.

I had come to VSEL via a circuitous route. Lord Montgomery, the son of the Field Marshal, who was a consultant to the company, had invited me to meet the Chief Executive, Dr Rodney Leach, with a view to joining the board as a non-executive director, a post I was more than happy to accept. However, within a short time of my appointment I was approached by a delegation of senior executives who asked me if I would be prepared to take on the Chairmanship of VSEL. Since the company already had a Chairman, Sir David Nicolson, who had guided VSEL through privatisation, I made it clear that I was not willing to be involved in any sort of coup.

At a difficult board meeting I told Sir David that I was prepared to become Chairman, if and only if, he resigned. He decided that he could no longer continue without the backing of his executives and decided to go. Having accepted the Chairmanship, I then found myself running the company as acting Chief Executive, when Rodney Leach had a heart attack and subsequently left the company.

The most urgent task was to restructure the board of directors and to appoint a new Chief Executive who could steer VSEL through some difficult times ahead. Noel Davies, who had worked for the company some years earlier and had a thorough understanding both of its past and of what it needed to prosper in the future, returned to Barrow in 1989. He did a remarkable job in winning the confidence of the workforce, while introducing sweeping changes and a new business strategy.

The first step in this was to streamline the board so as to focus its efforts on strategic planning, while freeing others to concentrate on the core subsidiary at Barrow. Like all boardroom changes, this naturally had its fall-outs. Two directors, one of whom had incurred the wrath of the workforce during a recent thirteen-week strike, left the company in protest. But the change was generally seen as a success and VSEL began to attract interest in the City as a potential target for takeover.

The new board's first responsibility was to draw up a medium to long term strategy for VSEL. This process did not, of course, take place in a vacuum: 'Options for Change', the government's defence review in 1990, attempted to align defence strategy and spending to the new world order as the end of the Cold War became a reality.

With some justification 'Options for Change' acquired the nickname of 'Options for Cuts'. It was hard to disguise the fact that the process had effectively been hijacked by the Treasury, perhaps while the Ministry of Defence was distracted by the Gulf War. The review appeared to open up a wide disparity between military resources and commitments, and even the much-vaunted Rapid Reaction Corps seemed to be overstretched even before it was fully formed. But of all the armed forces, the navy seemed to have fared worst in the proposed changes.

For VSEL 'Options for Change' had profound consequences. Although Tom King, the Secretary of State for Defence, had restated the government's commitment to the Trident programme, at least in principle, the Royal Navy's total submarine force was cut from twenty-seven to sixteen. In particular, the diesel electric submarine programme was cancelled. The navy's requirement was reduced to four, which they already had. Since this was to be the cornerstone of Cammel Laird's projected activity, the completion of the last diesel electric submarine at Birkenhead in 1993 effectively meant the end of work at that yard. We could not find a buyer and failed to persuade either the government or the European Union to redesignate Birkenhead as a commercial ship-building yard, which would have given it access to intervention funding. It is fair to say that we at VSEL resented being cast as the villain in Cammell Laird's closure. It seemed to us that the government could have done more, given the political will, and we could not easily see why Cammell Laird should attract less sympathy than Swan Hunter.

Of more immediate impact on VSEL was the cancellation of plans to develop a new nuclear-powered attack submarine, the SSN20, which had been expected to follow on neatly in the order books from the completion of the fourth Trident. Instead, it was decided that an updated version of the Trafalgar class (SSN19) should be developed.

Anyone who has visited Barrow-in-Furness will know that the town depends on the shipyard more comprehensively than perhaps any other ship-building centre. Barrow is relatively isolated and, before 'Options for Change', around 14,000 of the 60,000 population worked in the yard, with many more in related businesses; by 1994 the workforce was reduced to 6000.

There was a good deal of glib talk about the 'peace dividend' and the savings in defence spending that would allow people like the workers of Barrow to find new jobs in new industries. The reality, as always, was a little different. My own experience in the War Office, as it then was, had taught me that savings made in the armed forces tended to be illusory; any savings likely to become real soon found their way to the Treasury.

Although VSEL set up its own 'Jobshop' and the Department of Trade and Industry established a team to look at the problems of the Barrow area, the money made available was never likely to be adequate to the scale of the task. Moreover, a workforce and infrastructure which has been producing military vessels for over a century cannot easily start to manufacture washing machines, even in the unlikely event that other washing machine manufacturers kindly leave a gap in the market. The reality is that the culture and workforce of a major defence contractor are not easily transferable. The standard of debate about the peace dividend owed more to wishful thinking than to any deep knowledge: I well remember one colleague enthusiastically recommending the construction of oil rig platforms by VSEL on the grounds that the platform feet 'looked a bit like submarines'.

This problem of defence diversification was brought home to me during a debate in the House of Lords, during which one peer expressed his dismay at redundancies announced by Vickers at their tank factory in Leeds. I pointed out to him after the debate that a decline in arms sales – for which he had been pressing for many years – had inevitable consequences. If we sell fewer tanks then we will need fewer people making them. It does not follow that we should go on producing more weapons regardless of the need for them. But those who campaign against the production of arms on moral grounds have a moral duty to extend their thinking and their campaigning to the consequences of any success they might have. This is not merely a debating point. Campaigns against the production of arms should not stop with the salving of the campaigners' consciences, they should extend their interests to include the economic and social consequences.

It was clear that, faced with a fundamental shift in defence policy, VSEL was largely on its own. We therefore set about a strategic response to the new situation. In 1991 we drew up three key objectives for the company in the short and medium term. First, we had to win the order for the fourth Trident submarine. There was increasing pressure on the government to drop this, despite the fact that servicing requirements made three submarines a less than credible force.

Needless to say, the CND, frustrated by the demise of the great unilateralist illusion, were busy demonstrating in Barrow, particularly at the naming ceremony for the first completed Trident submarine, HMS *Vanguard*, carried out by the Princess of Wales in April 1992. This was an unforgettable experience. The sheer size of a Trident submarine, even the small proportion visible above the surface in dock, is an awesome sight and reinforces the impression of immense destructive power.

After some frantic shoring-up of confidence, we finally

secured the order for the fourth submarine, HMS *Vengeance*, a few months later and turned to our second objective. This was to allow VSEL to re-enter the surface ship-building market. The competition here was extremely fierce but, in May 1993, we succeeded in the bid to build a Landing Platform Helicopter carrier (LPH), to be built in conjunction with Kvaerner Govan. This was a turning point for VSEL and opened up far wider possibilities for future construction of surface ships.

Next, and most ambitiously, we determined to begin a gradual process of diversification, in the hope of achieving 25% non-defence income in the medium term. Despite successful moves into engineering for the oil industry and environmental projects, the target remained a long way off and our attempts to reach it were further frustrated by the recession of the early 1990s. We had been more successful in promoting other non-naval defence projects. A major order from the British Army in 1989 for 179 self-propelled howitzers was a significant boost for the Armaments Division of VSEL.

A final, if unspoken, part of the strategic plan was to look for a partner in the British defence industry. 'Options for Change' had made it abundantly clear that VSEL's survival could be assured only as part of a strong group. By 1995, VSEL was an attractive proposition for any bidder, with streamlined management and workforce and a healthy order book. It was somewhat gratifying to see GEC and British Aerospace in competition over who was going to buy VSEL; although GEC was ultimately successful, it was clear that either way VSEL was going to be the winner.

The takeover seemed an appropriate moment for me to step down, after nearly a decade at VSEL, and I returned to the more leisurely consideration of defence matters as Chairman (later President) of the All Party Defence Group in the House of Lords. This body had been established in the hope of harnessing the very considerable experience and expertise on defence matters available in the House. It continues to provide opportunities for interested peers to keep themselves up to date with developments in strategic thinking and with rapid changes in military technology.

I was also able to devote some more time to writing. In the late 1980s I was commissioned to write a book on the future of British defence policy, which eventually appeared as *Defence of the Realm*. Looking back, this was a particularly difficult moment for such a task. Within a few years the Cold War would be more or less at an end and the Soviet Union would have disintegrated. In short, it was not a good time to be predicting the future. But the exercise seemed worth undertaking, if only because, closer to home, there was virtually no common ground among the country's political parties on defence policy.

I began by analysing the nature of the threat to the survival of free democratic societies. I drew extensively on Soviet sources to outline the view from the Kremlin, describing Soviet 'Active Measures' and disinformation strategies. Prominent amongst the threats was the growth of state-sponsored terrorism.

I went on to look at the global context against which these threats had to be assessed, describing the pressure points in the structure of international relations and underlining the limitations of a post-imperial power in the management of global crises. I concluded by looking at Britain's role and responsibilities in this rapidly changing strategic environment.

Ten years on, the priority in the landscape is radically changed, but the threats are ever-present. The rise of nationalism in Europe and the instability of the former Soviet Union are real causes for concern; the arms race in South Asia continues to be alarming. But faced with these threats, the analysis of the response is not so different from that proposed in the late 1980s. The very unpredictability of the current situation is such that the United States remains the only credible guarantor of global security. It must therefore remain our prime objective to uphold the integrity of the Western alliance. Any closeness in Europe – however welcome that may be – must not be at the expense of the transatlantic link.

17

Television and Radio

Throughout the 1980s I had maintained a strong interest in journalism and the media. Even after finishing my regular column in *The Times* I still contributed occasionally, and I began a weekly column in the *Daily Express*. In the light of the sheer scale of disinformation campaigns at the height of the Cold War, I was also becoming preoccupied with – and at times troubled by – the principles and practice of journalism in a free society.

Where the Eastern bloc was concerned, the issues were, inevitably, shown in stark relief. The premise on which organisations like the CND conducted their campaigns was that there was some sort of symmetry between the societies of East and West. The reality – as I continued to point out, to the irritation of my detractors – was that there was no free press in the East.

I once had a Russian tutor in Paris who conducted all lessons in his own language and had the irritating habit of making obscure puns in Russian. One of these remains indelibly etched in my mind, perhaps because he repeated it relentlessly every morning as we sat at a pavement café, drinking lemon tea out of tumblers and reading the latest news from Moscow. At the time the two main official Soviet newspapers were *Pravda*, meaning 'Truth', and *Izvestia*, meaning 'News'. Having read through the two papers, he would deliver an audible nasal premonition, take a sip of tea and announce, in his ineradicably pre-revolutionary Russian: 'In *Truth* there is no news, and in *News* there is no truth.' He would then utter a mirthless and peculiarly Russian laugh, consisting of the monosyllable 'ha' repeated exactly three times on precisely the same note.

My inclination to be sceptical about my teacher's political judgement was dispelled by reading the output of these two organs over the years. Throughout the Cold War they gave assessments of the relative strength of Soviet and American forces that were grossly distorted. The articles were usually well written and persuasively argued and, crucially, they were the only facts which Russian newspaper readers were ever allowed to see.

The Kremlin spent millions of dollars jamming Western broadcasts, in violation of treaty commitments, and this itself pointed to the value of those services. By contrast, Western governments did not jam the English language service of Radio Moscow. Those who wished to listen to a lugubrious lady reading out the latest glorious achievements of the workers at the Moscow No. 1 Tractor Factory – where production always seemed to be reaching new heights – were free to do so.

My own involvement with Radio Free Europe and Radio Liberty, as a member of the West European Advisory Committee, convinced me of the importance of trying to beat the Soviet jamming tactics. Both stations tried to provide an alternative 'home service' for those behind the Iron Curtain and they achieved a status in those countries hard to comprehend in the media-saturated West. Polish government spokesmen pointed to Radio Free Europe as the lifeblood of the Solidarity movement, and Soviet dissidents like Natan Sharansky testified that Radio Liberty had kept their hopes alive through periods of intense repression. Ironically, both stations, despite being unashamed instruments of Western foreign policy, observed the strictest standards of balance and objectivity in news reporting, which was certainly the key to their popularity.

In company with Lord Bethell and others, I also helped to raise money for the fledgling Radio Free Kabul in 1983. Run by a coalition of Afghan independence groups, the station broadcast not only to the citizens of occupied Afghanistan, but also to the Soviet military. Vladimir Bukovsky and other Soviet dissidents appealed directly to the demoralised and miserable Russian soldiers who had arrived some four years before to pursue the ageing Brezhnev's expansionist dreams. The ferocity of Russian retaliation against the radio station suggests that the broadcasts were having some success.

My concern with broadcasting at home was a little different. Those who believe everything they read – still more, those who believe everything they write – in the newspapers, may be surprised to learn that I never suggested that the BBC and ITV were under the direct editorial control of the KGB in the 1980s. The problem was, in fact, a far deeper crisis of confidence in journalism and its place in a democratic society. The newspapers in general were peripheral to this problem because they were unashamedly partisan: one did not expect to find a glowing endorsement of monetarism in *The Guardian* or a plug for Mgr Bruce Kent in the *Daily Telegraph*. But the television broadcasters, with unparalleled power and unequalled access into people's homes, were in a different position.

Until the growing profusion of channels makes this issue of balance largely irrelevant, the two dominant television news channels – BBC and ITV – have a responsibility to provide a balanced and accurate reporting of current affairs. It appeared to me that in the 1970s and 1980s, they had begun to interpret this in terms of a kind of adversarial journalism, by which they preserved an often stultifying and ultimately false neutrality. Broadcasters seemed to regard it as their duty to be hostile to institutions and any other expression of the established order of society. Perhaps because the political opposition was so weak and ineffectual, the broadcasters were positioning themselves as a *de facto* opposition to the government.

A number of events helped to convince me of this. In 1984 the editor of BBC Radio News and Current Affairs invited me to take part in a confidential internal research project as an aid to forming editorial policy. This involved looking in detail at a vast amount of coverage of a particular 'day of action' organised in response to the government's decision to ban trade unions at GCHQ. A number of people were invited for lengthy taped discussions after looking at the material. It was my own clear impression that the unions were given a substantially better platform for their views than the government.

I was also asked to write a foreword to a report produced by the Media Monitoring Group, an organisation quickly rubbished as 'right wing'. In fact, as I said in my foreword, the report would give no ammunition to those seeking to condemn the BBC or ITV out of hand; it revealed that some of the most careful and objective reporting and some of the worst examples of unbalanced propaganda can occur on the same network or even within the same series. What the report did seem to show was a strong strand of anti-American, anti-police, pro-unilateralist dogma running through much of television's current affairs output. By prompting a debate in the Lords on a particularly offensive anti-American drama, called *Airbase*, I did manage to draw a sheepish admission from the Chairman of the BBC that the programme was 'of little merit' and 'one of those failures that are inevitable'.

By attempting to reach a position of moral neutrality, broadcasters found themselves in a position where they would routinely describe the IRA as 'interrogating' soldiers and 'executing' informers; what these words meant to the vast body of society was 'torturing' and 'murdering'. Journalists would high-handedly speak of 'innocent' victims of terrorism, as if a young soldier blown to pieces in the course of trying to keep the peace on behalf of other citizens was somehow a 'guilty' party.

It seemed to me essential that journalists should realise that they were not disembodied voices above the political influences of society; the free press had to establish its moral position as between a society which existed and those who threatened to destroy that society by violence. The Cold War was a war for the survival of a free society as much as the Second World War; the broadcasters had to accept the heavy responsibility that if their activities weakened democratic society to the point of undermining it, then their concern for editorial independence could become a matter of purely academic interest.

I appreciated, as I said to broadcasters in person when I was appointed to their regulatory body, that this placed them in an acutely delicate position. Every government wishes to tame or control the media. For the media to give in to that control would be as dangerous for a democratic society as the threat from outside; the answer was to find the right balance between the freedoms of the media and its responsibilities. It was this balance that was so seriously askew in the 1980s.

In passing, it must also be said that much of the unsatisfactory television coverage was the result of a lowering of professional and ethical standards rather than the grinding of political axes. The relentless drive to entertain meant that television news was dictated by pictures; when Norman Tebbit complained that some particularly good trade figures had been left out of a television news bulletin, the answer seemed to be that they did not make good viewing, no matter how important they were to the country. In other words, if dull but crucial economic statistics could somehow involve a popular celebrity or member of the royal family, preferably cuddling a suitably cute animal, they would get top billing. This tyranny of pictures and the desire to entertain remain a problem which television has not solved. Perhaps we simply need to reconcile ourselves to the fact that hard news reporting is not an area in which the medium of television excels.

Ironically, governments of different complexions have found similar problems with television. The tendency of news editors to choose to lead the news with an international crisis, often in an arbitrary way, sometimes seems to put national foreign policy at the mercy of journalists. The power of television is such that a reporter can stand in a war zone or crisis region and demand, through pictures, that the government intervenes. The fact that the consequence of this is that many British soldiers may lose their lives settling an internal conflict in which we have little right to intervene is not considered in the immediate urgency and drama of the news flash. One thing is for certain: news editors will not have to pay the price or take the consequences of the decisions they make.

In this respect I have some sympathy with Clare Short's

broadside against the media's coverage of famine and crisis in Africa. It is often ill-informed and grossly simplistic, as any assessment of a complex situation by a man or woman who has recently flown into a country with a camera crew is bound to be. The fact that there are powerful images of suffering to be shown does not alter this complexity.

In case this sounds hard-hearted, it does not follow that we should never intervene or that we should fail to respond to humanitarian crisis. Nor is it to deny that the media can play an important role in stirring conscience and motivating charitable donation. But the media need to spend more time reflecting on their own role and responsibilities and, above all, considering the consequences of their actions and their undeniable power.

The 1980s saw the beginning of a remarkable revolution in broadcasting which is still far from complete. The government of the day responded to the arrival of satellite television and the likely profusion of channels with a Broadcasting Bill in 1990; this envisaged the creation of a new Independent Television Commission to replace the Independent Broadcasting Authority, and the Home Secretary asked me to act as Deputy Chairman of the IBA, with a view to succeeding Sir George Russell in the long term as Chairman of the new ITC.

In the short term, the intention was that my experience of Whitehall and Westminster would be a good complement to George Russell as Chairman. Contrary to later reports, I was not appointed by the Prime Minister as 'a close personal friend': we were close politically rather than personally. Although it is prudent to take anything written in Woodrow Wyatt's *Journals* with large helpings of salt, it may well be true that Woodrow suggested my name to the Prime Minister. The appointment was unashamedly political in the broadest sense: Margaret Thatcher clearly felt that the world of television was getting out of hand. Indeed, her exact words were, 'I want you to get a grip on this lot.'

Thames Television's highly selective attack on the activities of the SAS, *Death on the Rock*, in which IRA violence was all but ignored, was a recent example. I had made it clear, as had many others, that I shared Mrs Thatcher's disgust at this programme. However, in accepting the invitation to join the IBA, I had reckoned without the bitterness of the media establishment – those who, since the 1960s, had been the self-appointed guardians of everything to do with broadcasting. My appointment as Deputy Chairman of the IBA provoked the usual storm in the left-wing press. *The Guardian* headlined me as an 'arch enemy of CND', as if that alone put me beyond the pale of civilised society (no doubt it did to *Guardian* readers). The *New Statesman*, that bastion of impartiality, cast doubt on my own ability to be unbiased with a long and distorted profile, which appeared under the screaming sobriquet of 'television's new McCarthy'. Most of this was to be expected, but attacks in *The Observer* were of a different order altogether; so too was what struck me as a vendetta mounted under the protection of parliamentary privilege by the Liberal Democrat leader, Mr Paddy Ashdown.

The Observer published an article shortly after the announcement of my new post. It attempted to link me with every conceivable group of which it did not approve, noting with obvious disgust that I had been President of the Committee for a Free World, an organisation 'formed in 1981 to oppose Marxists in Latin America', an activity which these journalists clearly regarded as morally equivalent to eating babies.

Of greater concern was the fact that the article sought to link both myself and Sir James Goldsmith to a private security consultancy, linked this consultancy to surveillance of protesters at the Sizewell nuclear power plant inquiry in the mid-1980s, and then appeared to link all of us to the murder of a Miss Hilda Murrell, an elderly rose-grower and environmentalist. I was used to being caricatured as a right-wing ogre, but the suggestion that I was travelling round the country murdering elderly ladies was a smear too far. The journalists in question had failed to mention the fact that an inquiry into the handling of the Murrell murder case had stated categorically that there was no link between this crime and surveillance or intelligence operations of any sort; clearly these were hacks who preferred not to have their 'investigative' minds clouded by such facts. I sued *The Observer* and won an apology, costs, and handsome damages.

The Observer seemed to have climbed on a bandwagon which Mr Ashdown set rolling at Prime Minister's Question Time earlier in the week. He had asked Mrs Thatcher if she had been aware that I was on the board of a private security firm 'with extremely grubby connections in the past'. At the height of her formidable powers, Mrs Thatcher could – and no doubt regularly did – consume Liberal Democrats for breakfast; in pausing to swat this particular irritant, she noted that Mr Ashdown was surely 'the first leader of his party to pursue a vendetta in that way'. I wrote to the Speaker of the House of Commons, Bernard Weatherill, expressing some dismay that members of one chamber could use parliamentary privilege to make personal attacks on members of the Upper House. I had a sympathetic but quite properly neutral letter in reply; in private Jack Weatherill was more forthright in his disapproval of the attack.

I had never sought to hide the fact that among the many companies on whose boards I sat, all listed in *Who's Who*, was a consultancy called Peter Hamilton (Security Consultants) Ltd. I had acted as a non-executive director in the mid-1980s. I was, in common with my fellow directors, Major-General Sir Philip Ward and Sir Dallas Bernard, quite satisfied with the professional standards and conduct of this company and saw no conflict of interests.

Hamilton had indeed undertaken minor work under instruction from a firm of City solicitors to track some stolen documents relating to nuclear power; this had involved obtaining a list of objectors to Sizewell, which in any case was published for all to see. It was particularly disgraceful that Hamilton employees were hounded and harassed after the death of Hilda Murrell, in some cases being implicitly accused. They had, as police enquiries showed, absolutely no interest in Hilda Murrell and nothing whatsoever to do with her death. But obsessive conspiracy theorists were never likely to be satisfied with the police conclusion on the Murrell case.

Writing to Mr Ashdown, I pointed out that he was perfectly entitled to oppose my appointment on political grounds as vigorously and publicly as he wished – others had already done so. But to cast slurs on a business and personal reputation built up over some fifty years, and to do so under the privilege of Parliament, where the protection of libel laws could not reach, was hardly the action of a genuine 'democrat' (I believe his party was called the Social Liberal Democrats at the time, although the party's name tended to be as fluid as its policies). An early day motion followed, principally sponsored by what appeared to be Mr Ashdown's entire party in the Commons – a veritable landslide of six MPs.

Mr Ashdown never repeated his innuendo outside the Commons and I later learnt that much of the material aimed at me had come from a questionable former employee of another security company; this did little to raise my opinion of the standard of research deemed satisfactory by some in the Lower House. As is so often the case in the Commons, after this raucous excitement politicians lost interest in the affair, rather as a child loses interest in a new toy, and I was allowed to get on with the job in hand.

It did not take too long to convince the ITV network companies that I was not quite the unthinking Thatcherite enforcer portrayed by the left. In any case, it was not long before I moved away from television to responsibility for radio. This was my own choice in response to a clear conflict of interests whereby Shandwick, the public relations firm of which I was a non-executive director, was acting for two television companies. It has always seemed clear to me that anyone who is active across a broad spectrum of public life is bound to encounter such conflicts; the key is surely to react openly, straightforwardly, and quickly – within hours, if possible. I resigned from the IBA because I did not want Shandwick to sacrifice important contracts; equally, I withdrew from other corporate interests, for example, Hamilton Ingram, because I considered my commitment to my regulatory post took precedence.

On leaving the IBA I was asked to transfer to the chairmanship of the proposed regulatory body for radio, since my responsibilities had already taken in radio. The relentless logic of the civil service decreed that, with the disappearance of the Independent Broadcasting Authority, the new regulatory body should be called the Independent Radio Authority. Having weathered one media storm over my appointment to the IBA, I did not relish the thought of headlines proclaiming 'Chalfont to be IRA Chairman'. The new body would simply be called the Radio Authority.

The Broadcasting Act itself was a complex piece of legislation, with some 176 clauses and twelve schedules. Despite the forecasts of the prophets of doom that the bill would mean 'the end of the best broadcasting service in the world', the government had drawn up a sensible piece of legislation. The aim was to take account of the rapid development of information and communications technology, while at the same time avoiding the worst excesses of unbridled deregulation.

As far as television was concerned, the bill seemed to me to have a number of shortcomings. The possible emphasis on finance rather than quality in awarding franchises – in other words giving them to the highest bidder – was not likely to serve the best interests of viewers, at least without some power of intervention by the regulatory bodies. Secondly, the profusion of bodies, such as the Broadcasting Standards Council and the Broadcasting Complaints Commission, seemed destined to cause confusion for viewers, broadcasters, and regulators. Finally, the vexed issue of balance arose and became the subject of heated political debate, without any very useful conclusions.

My principal concern, however, was with the provisions for the Radio Authority. The government had given us three aims as a regulating body: to widen the choice available to listeners, to protect those listeners, and to enable broadcasters to maximise their audience and resources. As a group we determined on a policy of regulating with a 'light touch'; although we had wide powers under the Act to fine companies or revoke licences, we did not expect to have to use these sanctions often.

There is no question that radio has undergone something of a renaissance – at least in quantity, availability and size of audience – in the 1990s. The Authority has granted scores of licences to local stations, as well as decided between candidates for the new national frequencies that became available soon after we were established. Both the government and the Authority were anxious that the dramatic increase in the number of stations should not lead to a decline in overall quality. Safeguards were introduced, including a guarantee that at least one national station should exist which was not wholly devoted to pop music. This entailed a lengthy and largely sterile discussion of what exactly constituted pop music and how it could be defined in legal terms, a more demanding task than it might sound. In the end, Classic FM has made a great success of this slot.

It is fair to say that the worst fears of the Broadcasting Bill's critics have not been fulfilled. The airwaves have not been entirely swamped with rubbish and small stations have been able to prosper. This was in great part due to the dedication and professionalism of the small staff who ran the Radio Authority. Peter Baldwin, a retired army general, was a remarkably effective Chief Executive, with very able assistance from a team which included Ranjit Sondhi, who overcame a considerable disability in his sight and later went on to join the BBC Board of Governors and to become a Commander of the Order of the British Empire. The advent of digital radio will no doubt tax the Authority's skills still further in the next few years.

Looking back at the changes in the media and journalism over the past forty years, I wish I could be as enthusiastic about the standards and quality as I am about the technological advances. I am well aware that it is easy enough to fall into the 'things ain't what they used to be' mentality; but I suspect that even the most objective of observers would not honestly claim that the quality of journalism – printed and broadcast – has actually improved. There are a number of reasons for this, many of them related to our education system and a period in the recent development of our society which regarded the pursuit of excellence as, at best, embarrassing.

There is also a more mundane explanation. The speed, ease and relative cheapness of printing newspapers has led to a proliferation of column space which simply cannot be met by quality. There has been a direct and inverse relationship between quantity and quality – a glance at the ludicrous piles of pulp material posing as Sunday newspapers is enough to confirm this.

Digital television seems to offer prospects of the same development for broadcast journalism. In reality the virtual duopoly of the BBC and ITV has been preparing viewers for this future by a gradual process, well described by that appropriately ghastly linguistic impostor, 'dumbing down'. There may be some consolation in the thought that, amid the hundreds of channels of repeats, cheap chat shows and mindlessly rolling news, there may be room for channels specialising in a more carefully crafted approach. What is a genuine cause for sadness is that the BBC will probably be forced to abandon any pretence of being a national or public service network; it seems inevitable that it will finally and irrevocably relinquish the Reithian ideal of the pursuit and promotion of excellence, and instead devote itself to the lowest common denominator in the pursuit of ratings.

18

The King and the Sultan

The conclusion of the great confrontation between East and West did not, predictably enough, leave international relations in a state of utopian harmony. International terrorism and the threat of nuclear proliferation remain ever present dangers. The failure to find peace in the Middle East has pushed the West into an uncomfortable confrontation with what is simplistically referred to as the 'Islamic world'. In fact, the tendency of Western strategists to lump together disparate political entities under the heading of Islam, and then to view that with suspicion and a fair degree of prejudice, is itself a major part of the problem. The Western approach to the Middle East has often seemed to reflect Warren Austin's famous remark that 'The Jews and Arabs should sit down and settle their differences like good Christians.'

It has been apparent to me for some time that those who wish to avoid global confrontation in the future should devote themselves to understanding the great political, national, intellectual, and ethical traditions so casually identified by Westerners under the title of the religion they share. My own interest in Islam was awakened by visits to the Middle East and to Iran in the 1970s, and I have had the opportunity to deepen my understanding through associations with two other Islamic countries during the 1980s and 1990s, the kingdoms of Morocco and Brunei.

My first meeting with King Hassan II of Morocco had taken place many years before, in December 1963, while I was defence correspondent of *The Times*. My visit had been arranged by a public relations consultancy, a useful experience on which to

228

reflect when I later became involved in public relations myself. The problem was that the trip, while fascinating and personally absorbing, was all but useless in professional terms. It produced nothing of immediate news value and little that came within my sphere – I was unable to see anything of the Moroccan armed forces or of the disputed frontier area. The King himself, obviously and understandably wary of journalists, was inclined to dismiss the military problem as being a matter of secondary importance. It was clear to me that the Moroccan government had not been well served by the quality or appropriateness of its public relations advice.

However, I maintained an interest in the affairs of the kingdom over the years, not least because of its strategic and political importance in the Cold War battleground of the Near East. When, in 1977, King Hassan decided to institute a unique new body – the Academy of the Kingdom of Morocco – I was genuinely delighted and honoured to be invited to become a member.

The royal decree establishing the Academy declared that its purpose was 'to promote the development of research and reflection in the principal fields of intellectual activity'. The body consists of thirty Moroccans distinguished in the law, in literature and in science, and thirty foreign 'associates'. At its inauguration this exclusive group included Henry Kissinger, Edgar Faure, the former Prime Minister of France, Konstantin Tsatsos of Greece and Maurice Druon, resplendent in the laurels of the Académie Française. Indeed, the Academy of Morocco owed some of its inspiration to the Académie Française, and its creation was the result of the imaginative exercise of individual royal patronage. I was consistently impressed by the personal interest taken by King Hassan in the proceedings, which take place twice a year under the expert direction of the Academy's Permanent Secretary, Abdellatif Berbich.

The Academy sessions move between the ancient cities of Morocco, with occasional forays overseas. I had even hoped to bring a session to England, but it seemed unseemly to jump the queue of countries hoping to host the Academy. One of our most enjoyable sessions was in Paris at the invitation of the Académie Française in June 1987. I was invited to deliver a fraternal address, in French, on behalf of the Moroccan Academy. Addressing Cardinal Richelieu's great foundation in the language of its own 'Immortals' was a memorable experience, and an even more formidable assignment than addressing the National Eisteddfod in Welsh.

The interests of the group are remarkably catholic – from a Turkish professor working on a monumental *catalogue raisonée* of Arabic literature, to Leopold Senghor, the poet, philosopher and President of Senegal, equally convincingly analysing the geopolitics of his region or translating Dylan Thomas into French. The Russian representative is Professor Anatoly Gromyko, the son of my old Cold War sparring partner, Andrei. It has been pleasant to exchange Cold War anecdotes now that we are both released from the glowering threat of East-West confrontation.

Neil Armstrong from the United States and Maurice Druon have become particularly close friends through long and leisurely discussions of diverse subjects. Although the Academy has considered many topics at its sessions over the years – from global crisis management to the desert locust problem – its most important function is, perhaps, to underline and possibly even help to repair the cultural failure of communication between the Judaeo-Christian traditions of the West and Islam.

For this reason it was particularly appropriate that the King chose the ancient city of Fez as the venue for the first session of the Academy in 1980. In this city, a river runs through the site of the Islamic university, arguably the oldest university in the world. This river used to separate the Andalusian community from the Kerouine – a symbolic meeting place of cultures, religions and civilisations, Atlantic and Mediterranean, Christian and Muslim, African, Arab and European.

King Hassan himself had some carefully formulated views on the place of Morocco in world affairs. He recognised the potential for bridge-building between the Arab world, Europe and the continent of Africa. While perfectly aware of the intentions of Soviet foreign policy during the Cold War, the King was not about to write off the demand of Palestinians for a homeland and the aspirations of the developing world. In 1984 he concluded a treaty with Colonel Gaddafy which caused some alarm in Western diplomatic circles; but it was clear from the outset that this was a marriage of convenience, the principal effect of which would be the end of Libyan support for Polisario rebels in the Western Sahara. King Hassan was not likely to align his country with the wilder excesses of Libyan foreign policy. Like many Arab leaders, he was frustrated by the Eurocentric obsession which leads people to believe that the values of Western society and the ethics of the Judaeo-Christian tradition are normal and that those of Islam and the rest of the world are somehow exotic and incomprehensible.

The Academy's first session was followed shortly afterwards by a State Visit to Morocco by the Queen. Having seen the slightly hysterical coverage of this event in the British press, which seemed to interpret every change in the programme as a deliberate snub to the Queen, the King was genuinely surprised. It was clear that his concern had been to make the Queen's visit as interesting and pleasant as possible. Although he ruled in the unambiguously autocratic tradition of the Arab sultan, Hassan was in fact a man of elaborate courtesy and impressive dignity. He talked easily and listened quietly, and displayed none of the petulance sometimes associated with absolute rulers.

As a result of my involvement with the King, through his Academy, I came to act as an emissary for the British government on a number of occasions over the years. Occasionally these visits were intended to repair some of the damage done by the very failure of communication which the Academy, albeit in a more leisurely and rarefied setting, tries to address.

In December 1982 I happened to be in Rabat for a session of the Academy when a crisis developed in Arab-British relations. The Arab League summit in September had decided to send a mission to the five permanent members of the UN Security Council to outline an eight-point Arab peace plan for the Middle East. The status of the delegation was such that it was to be led by King Hassan himself, with delegates from six Arab nations and the 'Foreign Minister' of the PLO, Farouk Qaddoumi. The British government then made it clear that neither the Prime Minister nor any Cabinet minister could receive a PLO official unless the PLO renounced violence. This, in turn, prompted the cancellation of the visit by the delegation and an angry broadcast on Radio Morocco by King Hassan.

The King also took the opportunity to relay his anger to me, asking me to transmit to Downing Street his sense of frustration at what he plainly regarded as a high-handed snub to the entire Arab League. I passed this on to the Prime Minister, and she then asked me to go straight back to Morocco to try to repair the damage by explaining the basis for British objections to the use of violence, meanwhile assuring the King that no affront to the Arab League had been intended.

I returned a few days later with Stephen Egerton, Under-Secretary at the Foreign Office responsible for North African and Middle Eastern Affairs. After a good deal of discussion and explanation, the King was persuaded to take the delegation to London, as planned. A suitably diplomatic compromise was reached, whereby the full delegation would be received by the Foreign Secretary, Francis Pym, and by Douglas Hurd, the Minister of State; the PLO official would, however, absent himself when the delegation met the Prime Minister.

I was also asked to approach the King to discuss the details of his State Visit to Britain, planned for July 1987. Margaret Thatcher had decided that, given the diplomatic fall-out from the difficulties encountered during the Queen's visit to Morocco, someone should make sure that the same thing did not happen in reverse during the King's visit. In plain words, this meant asking King Hassan to be punctual at all occasions. The Foreign Office, who know a hot potato when they see one, asked me to pass this one on to the King.

Asking an absolute ruler who is not best known for his time-keeping to be punctual is a delicate undertaking. At an audience in March we went through the usual preliminaries to such a State Visit, trying to note any particular requests the King might have for the optional parts of the visit and securing his patronage for a prestigious Anglo-Moroccan project to be announced while he was in London. Finally, after a good deal of throat-clearing and some suitably self-deprecating references to the English obsession with punctuality, the point obviously registered. The King gave one of his rare smiles and made no reference to time-keeping himself; but he was not late for any of his engagements.

The State Visit was deemed to be a success and, in amongst the diplomatic pleasantries, the King made a strong plea for Morocco to be considered for membership of the European Union, a development that would do much to bridge the gap and increase the level of understanding between the West and Islamic countries.

This is perhaps an appropriate place to record my own fears about the lack of understanding that currently exists in this area. This is particularly true in the United States where, even amongst politicians and public leaders, the fear of Islam seems to be growing. This fear was articulated most strongly by Professor Samuel Huntington of Harvard University as early as 1993. His influential article in *Foreign Affairs* argued that, with the decline of the nation-state as the basic unit of international relations, future conflicts would find expression in clashes between 'civilisations' or cultures.

Interpreted more crudely than Huntington perhaps intended, his thesis has been used as a justification for seeing a monolithic 'Islam' as the next great enemy, a successor to the old communist threat. Each time 'Islamic terrorism' strikes at the West, and America in particular, there is a perceptible call to arms in what appears to be a new version of the crusades. This seems to me not only grossly inaccurate but highly dangerous for the future of international peace and security. Anyone who takes the trouble to acquaint himself with the reality of an individual state which professes Islam as its dominant faith, will know that there exists as much political and social complexity, and as broad a spectrum of opinion, as in most Western societies.

Of course Islam has political significance and can, in certain circumstances, become a binding political force between nations (just as it can also be a divisive force between Muslim states). Certainly this political element is stronger than in the Confucian cultures of the East – the only other real contender for a clash with the West in the Huntington thesis. But there is no monolithic Islamic foreign policy with an agenda for the subjugation of America and Europe. Ironically, the belligerence with which some in the West demonise Islam actually helps to bind Islamic states into a common stance towards the West which is more hostile than it needs to be.

Before making any attempt to propose remedies for this situation which might head off confrontation before it arises, it is worth considering the background to the growing conflict. The reality in the Arab world – which is what many mean when they speak of the Islamic world – is that the Muslim citizens of those countries have not enjoyed a happy history of relations with their Christian neighbours in Europe.

It is easy enough to blame the crusades, or the Muslim incursions into Europe to which the crusades were a largely inept response. But more recently Muslims in the Arab states have been ruled by Westerners, and their post-colonial governments have often been inefficient and corrupt. Descendants of an unparalleled tradition of learning and self-confident civilisation have had little to feel proud of. The context of the Cold War made Western support for some of the more unsavoury régimes the lesser of two evils; it also helped to paralyse the Middle East peace process. We cannot expect all those involved to forget these Western policies, however necessary they were at the time. It will take time and goodwill for this collective resentment of the West to wear off.

Even the blessing of oil wealth has been mixed. It has been perceived, with some justification, at least during the Cold War, as the sole interest of the West. Meanwhile it has failed to reach many ordinary citizens of Arab countries and has fuelled their frustration and anger rather than their prosperity and development. Against this background it is not surprising that the popular response should be a return to the Koran, a religious revival and a rediscovery of Islamic culture. But this does not amount to 'fundamentalism'. I am constantly aware that Muslim friends find the careless use of this word by so many commentators deeply offensive. The implication is that fundamentalism equals extremism, at best, and terrorism and violence at worst. Yet there is no inevitable link between a deep practice of faith and violence. Committed fundamentalist Christians would rightly object to being seen as violent extremists.

Of course there have been ugly expressions of intolerance by groups of self-appointed would-be theocrats, notably in Algeria. But even Iran, that cauldron of theocratic revolution, has begun to accept that peaceful co-existence with the West is not just possible but actually desirable: the experience of government softens even the most zealous radicals. Even the worst excesses of committed extremists cannot alter the fact that co-existence between 'Islam' and the West is possible.

Re-establishing trust between the two will not be an easy or quick process. But perhaps it should begin in two distinct areas. First in a greater understanding and genuine acknowledgement of the richness of Islamic civilisation, so often patronised by the relatively recently developed Western world. In this the Prince of Wales has played an important part and his example should encourage other leaders and politicians to establish much closer personal ties with their counterparts in Islamic countries.

The second and perhaps less obvious area for developing relations is in the rediscovery of the ground shared by the great monotheistic faiths. The demonising of Islam has obscured the fact that, notwithstanding the obvious differences of belief, Christians and Muslims share many basic values, from an emphasis on personal responsibility, through the nature of good and evil, to the environment and medical ethics. Of course it may be argued that the Western half of this equation no longer holds, that we are post-Christian. I have my doubts as to how far we have really abandoned the deep-rooted Judaeo-Christian values which have shaped our society but, if we have, Islam perhaps has something even more valuable to offer.

Muslims hold before us an example of a system of shared values based on an awareness of a spiritual life which is inseparable from the day-to-day material life of the human race. A similar view prevailed in the West until the Enlightenment. But the age of scientific certainties which followed – and which found its political expression in the theory of Marxism – failed to fill the gap.

We now find ourselves, at the end of the twentieth century, endlessly debating where we should look for our moral guidance. Successive political movements, of which New Labour is by no means the first, have tried to re-invent a moral order by which society can steer a political and economic course. If dialogue with Islam can remind the West of where it came from and give us a stronger sense of our own moral history, then we will have much to be grateful for and perhaps Muslims will cease to see us as either amoral or immoral. This should not be such a far-fetched concept: it was, after all, Islamic civilisation which helped to propel the West out of the mediaeval era and into the cultural, economic, and religious explosion of the Renaissance.

My second experience of the inner workings of an Islamic monarchy began in 1988 when Shandwick plc – the public relations company of which I was a non-executive director – undertook a project on behalf of the government of Brunei. Working in Brunei was also the clearest possible evidence of the sheer diversity of social, political and cultural experience within the Islamic nations.

I had visited Brunei once before, in 1964, during the campaign against Indonesian-backed communist terrorists in Borneo. As a defence correspondent I had spent a highly enjoyable few days with the SAS and the Argylls in the jungle around Limbang and had gone on to stay with Major-General Walter Walker at Muara Lodge, his headquarters in Brunei. The 'Konfrontasi' campaign was certainly one of the most effective uses of British military force since World War Two; it is a measure of the influence of *The Times* in those days that my call for more helicopters to be made available infuriated the Ministry of Defence, although it delighted commanders on the ground in Singapore and Borneo.

When I returned to Brunei in 1988 my knowledge of the country was therefore largely restricted to military affairs and the strategic position of the country. I knew that a battalion of Gurkhas was based in the south of Brunei to protect the oil fields and I was aware that the SAS and other special forces had been using a jungle training school in the interior for many years. It soon became clear that even this sketchy impression was significantly more than many knew of Brunei; an opinion poll revealed that over 90% of those questioned had never heard of it. Among those who had, most placed the country in the Gulf, presumably on the basis that it was Islamic and oil-rich.

The Brunei government's purpose in retaining Shandwick was directly related to this widespread ignorance in the West. Brunei had become fully independent a few years earlier and the time had come to raise its profile. The Sultan also wished to make constitutional changes, including dropping the technical state of emergency which had existed since the 1960s, and he wished to do this in the context of a wider understanding of his country. Finally, the government hoped to balance some of the unfavourable publicity which had been generated at the time of independence.

On that occasion, the government had innocently invited hordes of Western journalists to inspect the new palace and seat of government. With a depressing inevitability, the reporters had gasped their way round, counting the number of gold taps in the bathrooms and other essential facts about the country. They had then regaled their readers with this tittle-tattle without bothering to give any serious account of the people, heritage, history, or modern economy of Brunei.

Anyone who has seen how newspapers work will know that this material had passed into cuttings files and, since many journalists equate in-depth research with flicking through such a file, it had been endlessly recycled. Any extra material tended to be taken from the gossip columns, where an obsessive interest in the Sultan's spending habits predominated. Shandwick there-fore embarked on an ambitious programme to publicise the country, producing information and inviting journalists and politicians to visit more than just the palace.

It was also clear that the picture of the Sultan as a profligate oriental potentate needed to be supplemented with a dose of reality, reflecting at least something of his day-to-day work in government and his place in regional and international affairs. Persuading him to give an interview, on and off camera, and to address some of the more sensational reports about him in the West was not an easy task – he was understandably wary after one bout with the media. He did, however, agree to speak to me, both in preparation for a television profile and as part of the research for a written portrait of the ruler and his country.

It cannot be said that my expectations were high at our first meeting, given his profile in the Western press. I was therefore a little surprised, and relieved, to find that the Sultan was quiet, reserved, almost diffident, but with a keen sense of humour. We spoke at length about his country, and his enthusiasm in explaining new developments was patently genuine. Only when he was asked to turn to what he regarded as a Western obsession with his private life did he seem a little weary and perplexed.

Sympathy is not always the primary emotion in attitudes towards people of great wealth and power, but when one surveys the ghastly crew of international financiers, fixers and parasites who attempt to ingratiate themselves in a wealthy royal court, it is difficult not to feel sorry for the object of these attentions. It was clear that the Sultan, particularly in his younger days, had attracted more than his fair share of fortune-seekers – from Asian gurus to Western lawyers – and was now keen to move on.

At the time of my first visit to Brunei, press speculation about the Sultan's role in the acquisition of the House of Fraser by the Fayed brothers had reached a climax. The Sultan was adamant that he had never given the Fayeds power of attorney over the relevant amounts, but this did not satisfy those who were determined to involve him. Most determined of all was R. W. 'Tiny' Rowland. His single-minded campaign to wrest Harrods from his rival became quite comical towards the end; whatever justice there may have been in his cause became submerged beneath a tide of vitriol.

Railing against the establishment, from Ted Heath to Margaret Thatcher, was something that Rowland did with style and at great expense. The Chairman of Lonrho, Edward du Cann, called on me during this bizarre campaign with a view to my meeting with Rowland in some sort of intermediary role. But it was immediately clear from a letter which Rowland despatched to the Prime Minister that there was little room for mediation. Having spiced the letter with insulting remarks about both Margaret Thatcher and the Sultan, Rowland proceeded to give a fantastically distorted history lesson on Brunei.

When I wrote pointing out the shortcomings in this version of history, which were apparent to me both from my own coverage of the revolt as a defence correspondent and from reading the official history, I received a classic reply from Rowland himself. It would be more accurate to say that most of London received the reply, because Rowland habitually 'published' his tirades, on paper of admirable quality in a glossy binding, before distributing them to the press. His epistle to me was called 'Ignorance is bliss – a letter from Lord Chalfont', and already has the feel of a collector's item. It is certainly a masterpiece of the Rowland genre, accusing me personally of just about everything that he considered negative in the history of Brunei.

No one involved in public relations would deny that the business involves presenting what is best in a person or country; this does not seem to be an entirely unreasonable or unworthy aim, particularly when others are systematically engaged in presenting only the worst. What public relations does not mean is trying to present the bad as somehow good, when seen from the right angle. That would be as futile as it would be dishonest. In the case of Brunei, for example, one cannot – and should not – pretend that the existence of political prisoners is anything but bad. But that does not preclude the presentation of positive developments in the country.

My final task in Brunei was to complete a book on the Sultan, which aimed to balance some of the treatment that he had received in the West and to offer the public a more rounded picture of the man than could be gleaned from a list of his latest purchases. It cannot be said that the book is a biography – the necessary time and access were not possible during my visits to Brunei. It is simply a portrait in which I tried to put on record some of the less sensational and more genuinely fascinating aspects of a truly remarkable country, whose citizens experience the paradoxes and tensions inherent in their position as the unusually wealthy subjects of an ancient Malay Islamic monarchy.

There is no question that Brunei has made remarkable progress in development over the past two decades. But diversifying an economy which still benefits from substantial oil and gas revenues is a difficult task: it is fair to say that the true incentive for free enterprise will only come when those resources begin to run out. The Sultan, in common with many other absolute rulers, will also continue to experience problems of perception until he is able to make the public finances transparent to the point where the division between royal and national wealth is readily recognisable to all. Shandwick began to help Brunei in this process, and coverage of the Queen's recent State Visit, when some journalists showed a refreshing tendency to speak about the country itself as well as its sovereign, suggests that the work was not entirely in vain.

My involvement with Shandwick has more than a purely business significance for me. The company had brought me back to the jungles of South-East Asia which I had first visited as a soldier during the Malayan Emergency and, later, as a defence correspondent. But in fact my association with Shandwick goes back further still, to my earliest years in Wales.

In the early 1970s – I cannot remember the exact date – I was at the Oval Cricket Ground pursuing an interest arguably more pressing than international business or politics, when I heard a strikingly familiar voice behind me. I turned round to see a man on whom I had not laid eyes for nearly forty years.

He had been the vicar of our church in Llantarnam, the Rev. Selwyn Gummer, and had been a good friend, indeed something of a spiritual mentor in those days before my departure for the war in Burma. Rediscovering this friendship was one of the most significant elements of returning home to Wales in the 1970s, a process I have already described. We took up where the war had interrupted us and, if it is not a cliché to say so, Mona and I became part of the extended family.

All Selwyn's children have had remarkable careers and at the time of our meeting at the Oval, Peter Gummer (now Lord Chadlington) was setting up a public relations company and invited me to join the board. The company name, Shandwick Ltd, was in fact a tribute to his father's entrepreneurial spirit: Selwyn had established a small business of this name through which he published and distributed copies of his sermons to other clergymen who were, to put it kindly, either less expert or less industrious in the area of homiletics. The Gummer children were enlisted as a production line, stuffing envelopes with copies of the latest sermon.

From these slightly bizarre and unusually spiritual origins, Shandwick grew under Peter's direction to become a publicly listed company and, by the end of the 1980s, the biggest public relations firm in the world. My role as Chairman of the International Advisory Board involved visiting the rapidly growing network of international offices, bridging the gap between far-flung subsidiaries and what could otherwise be perceived as a distant parent company in London. I was also able to satisfy a certain curiosity in some quarters about what a Peer of the Realm actually looks like. At home, the board had to manage the group's expansion and weather some difficult times, particularly during the recession of the early 1990s. My own involvement with Shandwick ceased in 1994, when I stepped down after two decades on the board, but the family connections have always given me a particular pleasure in seeing the company prosper and have made my role there more a pleasure than a duty. At the same time we have watched Peter Chadlington's children growing up with as much pride and pleasure as if they were our own grandchildren. Indeed, we sometimes think they are.

My retirement from Shandwick and, in the space of two years, from VSEL and the Radio Authority, did not quite signal the end of my involvement in business. I still sit on the boards of a number of companies. But I am more than happy to have relinquished the day-to-day running of major industrial and public organisations. In doing so, I have also stepped out of the main arena of public and political controversy. Readers who have persevered to this point may have gained the impression that I have not always been reluctant to enter into such controversies; it would be fair to say that I enjoyed public debate and argument and, it must be admitted, sometimes made provocative remarks just to stir things up.

Now, a little peace and quiet seem to be in order, with time to reflect on what stays most in my heart and mind from all the days that have passed since I climbed the gentle slopes of the Mynydd Maen and held my mother's hand under the lilac tree.

Epilogue

Nostalgia, someone once said, is not what it used to be. It is all too easy to slip into the 'good old days' mode, to deplore the harshness and materialism of modern life compared with the gracious civility of earlier days. It is, of course, true that standards of dress, courtesy and manners, especially those of young people, have deteriorated alarmingly. The pace of life has quickened, and everything seems noisier, dirtier and more dangerous than it used to be. Against this must be set the advances in science and technology which have revolutionised medicine, travel and communications; and the changes which have taken place in attitudes towards racial and ethnic minorities and the role of women in society. To yearn for a lost Elysium is a futile occupation.

It is, however, possible to reflect on some of the ways in which life has changed in the years since I grew up in South Wales, without succumbing to the demoralising conviction that 'Earth's joys grow dim, its glories pass away, / Change and decay in all around I see.'

Yet there *are* certain glories which are passing away. There is a growing tendency in the contemporary meritocracy to discount or even to dismiss the value of tradition and of the ceremonial which often goes with it. The State Opening of Parliament, the Royal Tournament and many other occasions associated with a degree of pomp and ceremony are being devalued or dropped altogether because they are no longer 'relevant' or 'in tune with our contemporary culture'. At a stroke, the government has ended the right of hereditary peers to sit and vote in the House of Lords, thus ending, in the interests of ideological correctness, 700 years of constitutional history.

Together with this distaste for formality or tradition has gone a decline in public manners. This is perhaps most notable in sport. The phenomenon of football hooliganism is too familiar to need much elaboration; but the culture of the jungle has spread to other sports. Tennis, cricket and golf, for long associated with sportsmanship and good manners, have become occasions for exhibitionist and often abusive behaviour by those participating – an infectious disease which very quickly spreads amongst those watching as well. These are depressing enough phenomena but there are weightier matters to contemplate.

One of the concerns which has been at the heart of most of what I have said and done and written in my adult life is that of the liberty of the individual human being. I have opposed, as far as I was able, any political system or philosophy which attacks or erodes the right of an individual to act freely according to his own conscience, provided always that in doing so he does not inhibit the freedom of others to do likewise. There have been many ways in which this liberty has been, and is being, endangered – not always consciously or malevolently.

One of these is the moral and ethical issue of what is called genetic engineering. There is, understandably, a great deal of concern about this new technology. Whereas conventional medicine treats existing individuals, genetic engineering, when it is fully developed, will be able to make changes which can be passed on to succeeding generations and may even alter specific individuals *in advance* by treatment of the embryo. The implications of this for human dignity, and even individual freedom, are enormous, and the public debate about it is only just beginning, although the development has been progressive and inevitable since Crick and Watson began their investigations into the DNA structure in the 1950s.

Information technology, too, has brought significant changes to society. The country is full of 'notebook' computers, pagers and mobile telephones. The internet, which started life as the information superhighway, brings a vast accumulation of information, entertainment and pornography to anyone with access to a computer. Meanwhile, the more conventional sources of information, newspapers, radio and television, all seem to be suffering from that depressing syndrome known in the current jargon as 'dumbing-down'. There are obvious implications for the freedom of the individual in the kind of brainwashing and indoctrination associated with huge and monolithic media of information.

In the wider world, too, there have been dangers and menaces. We have not yet succeeded in dealing with the threat of terrorism, both international and domestic. This is the modern method of making war against democratic societies. Much of our failure to defeat this menace can be attributed to the routine repetition of that familiar *mantra* – 'there is no military solution to this problem.'

Terrorism *can* be defeated by military means. Terrorists are at war with society and it is right that their violence should be met with the violence of established society. Indeed, it can be argued that terrorism has to be defeated militarily before there can be any lasting political solution to the problem which has given rise to it. This is an argument as valid in Northern Ireland as it is anywhere else in the world.

Terrorism is, of course, not the only problem threatening freedom and order. We have confronted and defeated two major tyrannies in the last sixty years – first that of National Socialism and subsequently that of Marxist communism, both with their appalling implications for individual dignity and freedom. The defeat of communism and the end of the Cold War have not, however, left us in a permanently free or secure world. There are dangers from the spread of what are called weapons of mass destruction – nuclear, chemical and biological weapons – and the missiles needed to deliver them to distant targets. No one, incidentally, seems yet to have fully appreciated the role which genetic engineering is likely to play in the development of biological weapons.

In the politico-strategic realignment of forces which has taken place since the end of the Cold War, there has been one especially disturbing development – the progressive erosion of the concept of the nation state. For most of my life, the sovereign nation has been the building block of the international structure and established order. Alliances and collective political organisations have consisted of independent countries, responsible for their own internal affairs and for the freedom of their citizens. Some of these countries have operated political systems which, by the standards of most others, have been oppressive and destructive of individual liberty; but, until recently they have been left to change these systems internally, sometimes under pressure from economic and other sanctions.

Now all that seems to have changed. National frontiers are no longer sacred. Interventionism is the order of the day, and countries are prevailed upon by force to change internal situations which do not meet with the approval of 'the international community'. One of the results of this is that British soldiers have been asked to risk their lives on the territory of what used to be regarded as sovereign nation states, often in indirect support of separatist movements which have used violence and terrorism to achieve their political ends. All this is in the interests of the modern concept of universal human rights, a theory which, although seductive, does not always ensure the freedom of the individual. At a slightly less apocalyptic level, the whole ethos of the sovereign nation state is at issue in the move to create a politically integrated European Union.

It is certainly not possible to declare with any confidence that individual freedom is any less under threat than it has ever been. There are, and probably always will be, those whose political aims can only be achieved by exercising total power over their fellow men. They are not all easily identifiable dictators or madmen. Some of them have the outward appearance of reasonable men with reasonable ideas.

The world has, in my lifetime, become a strange and sometimes bewildering place; but it has its compensations. A walk up Cader Idris or Scafell Pike on a spring day; memories of the Grand Canyon, Angkor Wat and the pink city of Jaipur; the music of Mozart and Beethoven; the songs of Edith Piaf; the poetry of Victor Hugo and Dylan Thomas (not to be compared, but to be savoured for their distinctive appeal to the heart and mind); the paintings of Caravaggio and Claude Monet; the novels of Trollope, Proust and Anthony Powell, the modern standard-bearer of elegant prose and penetrating social insight; an Islay malt whisky or a glass of Dom Perignon at the end of a more than usually trying day; or some 1970 Forts de Latour with a rack of Welsh lamb; an evening at the Garrick Club or the Royal Opera House; all these help one to survive some of the less attractive manifestations of contemporary life, and to identify them might go some way towards satisfying Nancy Mitford's autobiographical imperative – 'one must unmask oneself.'

Of course, the major battles for freedom and dignity remain to be fought in each generation. The liberty of the individual and the values of a free and civilised society are permanently at risk. But there comes a point at which the daily skirmishes which are inseparable from the continuing struggle begin to seem like side-shows to the more important mysteries, and at that point it seems fitting that I should withdraw – at least far enough to allow time for reflection and to offer occasional advice to those still in the thick of things and, of course, to await, calmly, if not with total equanimity, that inevitable moment when time will take me by the shadow of my hand.

Index